Walking in Indian Moccasins

F. Laurie Barron

Walking in Indian Moccasins:
The Native Policies of
Tommy Douglas and the CCF

UBCPress / Vancouver

Printed in Canada on acid-free paper ∞

ISBN 0-7748-0609-5

Canadian Cataloguing in Publication Data

Barron, F.L.
  Walking in Indian moccasins

  Includes bibliographical references and index.
  ISBN 0-7748-0609-5

  1. Native peoples – Saskatchewan – Government relations.*
2. Saskatchewan – Politics and government – 1944-1964.* I. Title.
E78.S2B37 1997   323.1'197'07124   C97-910349-5

This book has been published with the help of grants from the Humanities and Social Sciences Federation of Canada, using funds provided by the Social Sciences and Humanities Research Council of Canada; the Heritage Cultures and Languages Program, Multiculturalism and Citizenship Canada, Department of Canadian Heritage; and the University of Saskatchewan.

UBC Press also gratefully acknowledges the ongoing support to its publishing program from the Canada Council for the Arts, the British Columbia Arts Council, and the Department of Canadian Heritage of the Government of Canada.

Set in Stone by Brenda and Neil West, BN Typographics West
Printed and bound in Canada by Friesens
Copy-editor: Andy Carroll
Proofreader: Randy Schmidt
Indexer: Margalo Whyte

UBC Press
University of British Columbia
6344 Memorial Road
Vancouver, BC V6T 1Z2
(604) 822-5959
Fax: 1-800-668-0821
E-mail: orders@ubcpress.ubc.ca
http://www.ubcpress.ubc.ca

This book is dedicated to my longtime partner, Herta Kukujuk Barron, whose unwavering support of my work has been a constant source of strength.

Contents

Illustrations

Preface

This study is addressed to the era immediately following the Second World War. At the time, few people in Saskatchewan, or anywhere else for that matter, knew much about the Aboriginal community. For most, the Native was a somewhat faceless and enigmatic character described largely in negative and stereotypical terms. Only seldom did anyone fully appreciate the distinctions that defined groupings within Native society, and, initially at least, this ignorance was as true of the CCF government of Tommy Douglas as it had been of previous provincial administrations. Part of the problem concerning Aboriginal terminology – then and now – is that superimposed on both the shared and distinctive features of the various components of the Native community were artificial and legalistic definitions, ascribed by distant federal officials more interested in administering Indian Affairs programs than in recognizing the cultural realities of Native life. As a result, local politicians, bureaucrats, and the general public rarely understood the legal and social niceties associated with the terms 'Indian' or 'Métis' and often confused them. Hence, in the interest of clarifying terminology found in this book, it is necessary to provide some definitions.

The term 'white' has been adopted in reference to everyone other than Native people. In itself, it is not a precise word in that it fails to acknowledge peoples of various ethnic backgrounds and skin colours; nevertheless, it has been employed here out of deference to the currency the term has achieved in popular usage and as a matter of convenience. It can be equated with the expression 'non-Native' and is used interchangeably with the phrase 'Euro-Canadian,' which is equally imprecise. As unsatisfactory as the term 'white' may be, it should be recognized that virtually all existing terminology attempting to portray the wider society accurately is problematic.

As the title of this book implies, 'Native' is the term generally used to describe the subject of the study. It is true that some Native people today reject this label because of its pejorative connotations, associated with colonization; but it is also true that it is still a preferred term, persistently used by Native and non-Natives alike and retained in present-day Native Studies departments and elsewhere. As an all-inclusive term, it encompasses the various components that make up Aboriginal society and, for the purposes of this study, includes Indians, non-status Indians, and Métis. In usage, it can be equated and interchanged with the word 'Aboriginal,' which, as the term used in Canada's constitution, has gained popularity since patriation in 1982. Even then, however, it should be noted that some people reject Aboriginal as an appropriate label because it can be confused with the term 'Aborigines,' referring to the Native peoples of Australia.

Since 1951, an 'Indian' has been defined as a person whose name appears on an official registry in Ottawa. In itself, the term has nothing to do with the degree of Aboriginal blood, nor with ethnicity; on the contrary, it is a legal designation investing a person with special Aboriginal status in the eyes of the federal government. Such a person might be descended directly from the First Peoples who initially had inhabited Canada or be a white female (or her offspring) who, at one time, had achieved Indian status through intermarriage. As such, an Indian whose name appears on the registry is a 'status' or 'registered' Indian, while one whose name has been dropped from the registry (or is descended from such a person), because of marrying-out or for some other reason, is referred to as a 'non-status' Indian. The former is subject to the provisions of the federal Indian Act and is ministered to by the Department of Indian Affairs (DIA); the latter has no official standing in the eyes of the federal government and does not fall under the jurisdiction of the DIA. It should also be noted that, since the early 1980s, the word Indian has been slowly losing ground in favour of two other preferred terms, 'First Nation' or 'First People.' Both underscore the distinctiveness of Indians as historically sanctioned national communities, and the former in particular has been adopted by Indian political organizations, in part to emphasize the right to self-determination.

To further complicate the definition, a 'treaty' Indian is a status Indian whose forefathers, as indigenous inhabitants agreeing to share the soil, had signed a treaty with the federal government conveying in perpetuity rights and responsibilities to the signatories' descendants. In Saskatchewan, as elsewhere in the West, the treaties were numbered in reference to the geographic area covered by the agreements, rather than being assigned descriptive titles; hence, a Treaty 4 Indian is one whose ancestors had signed a treaty dealing with lands in the southern portion of Saskatchewan, while a Treaty 6 Indian is one whose forefathers had concluded a treaty in reference to lands in central Saskatchewan and

Alberta. By comparison, a 'non-treaty' Indian is someone whose forefathers did not enter into a formal treaty arrangement. A case in point is the Sioux who moved from the United States into Manitoba and Saskatchewan in the latter part of the nineteenth century; because they were not indigenous to the Canadian West, they had no land rights to surrender and therefore were not admitted to treaty, although they were still status Indians.

'Métis' is the final term that needs clarification. The word comes from the Latin root *miscere*, meaning to mix, and speaks to the fact that the Métis are of mixed Indian and white descent. Historically, governments acknowledged the Aboriginal status of the Métis but, out of self-interest, were reluctant to extend special rights to them other than by granting them relatively small chunks of land meant to extinguish whatever land rights might be implied by their Aboriginal status. As in the case of non-status Indians, the Métis do not fall under federal jurisdiction or the authority of the Indian Act; instead, they come mainly, although today not exclusively, under provincial jurisdiction. Pejorative variations of references to the Métis, found in conversations, newspapers, and documents during the Douglas era, included 'half-breed,' 'breed,' and 'half-caste,' speaking to the supposed mongrel nature of the group. Such terms have sometimes been applied by Métis people to themselves as a matter of self-deprecating humour and ethnic self-definition, but their use by others has commonly been rejected as being racist. Today, the definition of Métis status in Saskatchewan hinges on a person's claim to Métis ancestry and recognition of that claim in the Métis community.

Acknowledgments

Walking in Indian Moccasins is the product of assistance from a number of individuals and institutions, instrumental in either the preparation or publication of the finished manuscript.

The research would not have been possible without the services of many librarians and archivists. Of particular note was the contribution made by the staff of the Saskatchewan Archives Board at the University of Saskatchewan: D'Arcy Hande, Maureen Fox, and Nadine Small were consistently supportive of the project and readily provided the necessary expertise and assistance. Similarly, the research process was greatly facilitated by student assistants Ron Laliberte, Cathy Burton, and Carol Metcalfe. In compiling bibliographic information and ferreting out references, each contributed significantly to the overall result. A special note of thanks is due to Ron Laliberte who, although now a Professor of Native Studies, in his former incarnation as a student provided invaluable assistance in the early stages of the project.

A number of individuals offered editorial and content suggestions in the interest of refining the argument. The anonymous reviewers of the manuscript, appointed by both UBC Press and the Social Science Federation of Canada, provided critiques that were both insightful and constructive. Laurie Meijer Drees, a colleague and friend, likewise made a number of important suggestions.

Herta Kukujuk Barron acted as a sounding board for ideas throughout the preparation of the manuscript and, among other things, quite correctly identified the need for a more refined gender-neutral language. And UBC Press editors Laura Macleod and Camilla Jenkins recommended changes that benefited the final product in numerous ways.

A significant contribution was made by the people who willingly participated in interviews recounting their personal experience and insights about the CCF. This was especially true of those who endured lengthy interrogations on the campus of the University of Saskatchewan for the benefit of students in my senior research course: they included Stan Cuthand, Allan Blakeney, Leona Tootoosis, Napoleon Lafontaine, Gordon Ahenakew, as well as Roberta and Allan Quandt. The views expressed by informants often shaped the content of the manuscript at critical points and provided a richness of detail unavailable in archival sources.

The University of Saskatchewan also played an important role. It not only furnished a supportive context for inquiry and research but also provided specific assistance in the creation and publication of this work. Among the university's many contributions, for which I am grateful, are two sabbaticals, travel and research grants, grants-in-aid of manuscript preparation, as well as a publication subvention.

To all of the above, my sincere thanks!

Introduction

In 1944, the Co-operative Commonwealth Federation (CCF) swept to power in Saskatchewan, thereby establishing what the popular press described as the first socialist government in North America. Those on the far right of the political spectrum professed to see the election results as a menacing disaster for the people of Saskatchewan. They confidently predicted that the socialists would mount a legislative assault on private property and that, if left in power for any time, would destroy the very foundations of civilized society. For many, the CCF was little more than a clever mask for communism and, indeed, some of the statements by committed socialists, both before and during the election, did little to dispel the notion that Soviet-style collective farms were not far off. At the other end of the spectrum, Marxists were quick to hail the election as the beginning of the socialist millennium, a new era in which the entire capitalist system would be condemned for its inherent social and economic injustice. As time would tell, neither view was very accurate. During its twenty-year reign, the CCF government defied predictions and proved to be a grave disappointment to both political extremes.

It was precisely because the CCF was a self-styled socialist party that its election commanded such inordinate attention. While civil servants flocked to the province in anticipation of massive social and economic reforms, journalists of every political stripe eagerly probed for details about the radical experimentation implied, if not promised, by the CCF victory. The rise of the CCF, its political philosophy, its reform agenda – all were carefully scrutinized and made the subject of lengthy editorials. This was especially true of the Saskatchewan print medium, which, dominated by the Liberal-associated Sifton newspaper chain, tended to be ideologically opposed to the CCF. And to further heighten the interest, there was the dynamic and charming CCF premier of the province, Tommy Douglas. In 1944, Douglas was already recognized as a consummate debater,[1] a man whose wit and humour not only devastated opponents but also greatly enlivened the press gallery. He was clearly the most quoted politician in the province and, judging by the series of biographies since written about him, he was one of the most interesting. Perhaps more than anyone else, it was Douglas who personified all that was new and exciting about socialism in Saskatchewan and, for that reason, he personally was the focus of media attention.

The story of the CCF has also commanded attention in academic circles. Political scientists and historians, in particular, have been anxious to explain the apparent anomaly that a socialist government would have been elected in a predominantly rural province dominated by farmers. Did the CCF phenomenon speak to the tendency of socialism to emerge in backward rural economies, as had been the case in Czarist Russia or Mandarin China? Given Marx's understanding that socialism would flourish in the advanced industrial countries of western Europe, why was the CCF not elected in industrialized Ontario? Is it accurate to describe prairie farmers as 'agrarian socialists' when, as a class of small-business people, they seek to benefit from the capitalist system? Was it the farmers' movement that brought the CCF to power, based on indigenous agrarian unrest, or was it the result of leaders and ideas imported to the rural hinterland from urban areas outside the prairie region? These and similar questions have led to a veritable plethora of books and scholarly articles, collectively embracing a range of theoretical perspectives and addressed to almost every aspect of the CCF presence.[2]

Despite the range and diversity of these published sources, most of these works have one thing in common. They have a mindset that focuses solely on the relationship between the CCF and mainstream settler society, paying almost no attention whatsoever to the province's Native community. Occasionally, analyses of provincial voting patterns do include passing references to Natives, but at best they tend to be cursory and sometimes inaccurate, saying almost nothing about the relationship between the CCF and Native society. Indicative is Seymour Lipset's classic study on *Agrarian Socialism*, first published in 1950 and reprinted in paperback in 1971.[3] The text of the more recent edition comprises more than 350 pages, but its entire treatment of the Native issue consists of only a one-sentence oblique reference to a village of Métis, mistakenly described as 'French Indians.'[4] Moreover, the revised edition contains five essays written twenty years later as an update to Lipset's original work. The sole reference to Natives is in a paper by Sanford Silverstein in which 'Native Indians and Eskimos' are included in a table identifying the voting behaviour of 'ethnic groups' constituting a majority in rural municipalities.[5] There is also a brief one-paragraph discussion of Native voting patterns in which Indians and Eskimos are inaccurately identified as being mainly northern residents and 'relatively apolitical.' Silverstein then goes on to cite an informant, 'long familiar with Saskatchewan politics,' to the effect that these same groups tended to favour the CCF during the 1940s and then withdrew that support when the party failed to ameliorate their poverty. Quite apart from the erroneous comment on demographics, the analysis is both unsubstantiated and superficial and completely ignores the existence of the Métis, the people of mixed Indian and white ancestry. Numerically the Métis were almost as important as the Indian population in the province, but culturally and historically they were not the ethnic equivalent of either the Indians or the Inuit. In all, the account is so flawed that it contributes nothing to an understanding of Native politics.

The same neglect is reflected in the popular biographies of the premier. Douglas was personally shocked by the social pathology that wracked Native communities in Saskatchewan and, soon after coming to power, he publicly committed his government to doing something on their behalf. Despite this, biographers have largely ignored the Native policies of the CCF, instead preferring to judge Douglas and his government in light of the policies and programs applied to white society. In 1962, for example, Robert Tyre published *Douglas in Saskatchewan*.[6] The book was the first biography of Douglas, and it was written by a newswriter who, as a local journalist and for a time a public relations man in Douglas's office, was a firsthand observer of the CCF administration. Although Tyre admitted that Douglas was a 'spellbinder' and 'a silver-tongued apostle of Saskatchewan-style Marxism,' he was extremely hostile to socialism and the book itself is little more than a diatribe against the CCF record in office.[7] Nowhere in the 212 pages is there any reference whatsoever to Natives or the Native policies of the Douglas regime. For Tyre, either Indians and Métis did not exist or the policies addressed to their plight were irrelevant.

Equally indicative is the unduly sympathetic biography *Tommy Douglas*, published by Doris Shackleton in 1975.[8] To the author's credit, she quite rightly acknowledges that, of all the problems facing the Douglas government, the most difficult to solve was that associated with the Native people.[9] Moreover, her treatment of Native issues is far more extensive than that contained in any other biography of Douglas, including the more recent *Tommy Douglas: The Road to Jerusalem*, written by Thomas and Ian McLeod.[10] Nevertheless, Shackleton's account consists of only a few pages and is anything but comprehensive. She does make a necessary distinction between Indians and Métis and she pays lip-service to early CCF reforms, including hospitalization services, northern fur and fish marketing, and attempts to organize Native lobbies.[11] But, essentially, the pages devoted to Natives are under-researched and represent little more than a laundry list of disjointed, and sometimes inaccurate, facts.[12] Also, there is little interpretive value and few meaningful judgments about what the CCF actually accomplished during Douglas's premiership.

The overall result is that not much has been said about the Native policies of the CCF. It is true that a few academics have published brief accounts of certain aspects of Native society in relation to the CCF but, for the most part, such accounts are limited in scope and application and usually appear only in academic journals, hidden from public view.[13] This means that the epic story of the CCF in Saskatchewan has largely been about white people. In part, this is a reflection of the fact that, traditionally, Canadian history has been written from a Euro-Canadian perspective in which Native peoples have been systematically ignored. Seldom have writers felt the need to include Natives in their narratives, simply because they have assumed – falsely and ethnocentrically – that the primary function of history is to record the achievements of those who dominated development, the men and women who fashioned Confederation and made the West safe for settlement. In the case of the CCF, writers have made little attempt to differentiate between the components of Native society; instead, they have been content to lump them together as an amorphous and faceless group of people whose abject poverty meant that they related to the CCF mainly as welfare recipients. Moreover, there seemed to be little need to include Indians and Métis in the political analyses of the era because, as the underclassed of society, Natives lacked political and social power of every description. After all, for most of Douglas's premiership, status Indians, with the exception of veterans and their families, were prohibited by law from voting both federally and provincially, while the remainder of Native society was deemed either apolitical or marginal.[14] In effect, past neglect served as a precedent for ignoring the role, and sometimes the very existence, of Native people during the CCF era.

As a consequence, writers have painted a greatly distorted picture of Saskatchewan's evolution, effectively robbing Natives of their rightful place in history. While it is never wise to equate government policy with actual development in the Native community, an appreciation of public policy is nevertheless crucial to understanding the context within which Native society evolved and how that society affected provincial development. The treatment Indian and Métis groups received at the hands of the CCF government had a direct bearing on the long-term evolution of Native society, and to disregard that treatment is to reinforce the kind of public ignorance often associated with racial bigotry and intolerance. Moreover, it was during the CCF reign that Native society surged into public awareness and produced a new generation of leaders and visionaries, many of them Indian veterans. John Tootoosis and Malcolm Norris, for example, were spokespeople who demanded a 'new deal' through which their people could achieve a measure of self-determination, and, in some ways at least, it was precisely because of that demand that the government did introduce reforms. For writers to ignore that fact is not only to write Natives out of history but also to grossly misrepresent the CCF record. It also explains why later – in the seventies and eighties – Native demands for self-government were such a surprise to a historically uninformed public.

At the same time, by turning a blind eye to Native issues, writers have missed an invaluable opportunity to evaluate the performance of a would-be champion of the oppressed. Unlike its predecessors, the CCF government promised to be the instrument of social and economic justice in an otherwise stratified and privileged society. It was a promise, of course, that was fundamental to the avowed socialist philosophy of the party. But quite apart from that, Douglas and others publicly espoused the canons of Social Gospel, based on biblical invocations, to create a godly and moral order on earth.[15] A core idea of Social Gospel was that unfettered competition, which only served to create and reinforce social and economic inequality, should be replaced by cooperation and sharing.[16] It was a philosophy underscored in the official slogan of the CCF government – 'humanity first' – and one that insinuated itself into the public posturing of Douglas and his followers. For that reason, judgments on the performance of the CCF government can hardly exclude the treatment of the Native community, by common consent the most dispossessed and dislocated segment of the population. In the same way that democracy is judged by the treatment of minorities, the championship of social justice can only be measured by the treatment of the most vulnerable and least privileged in society. That writers have failed to apply this criterion – that they have been more concerned about how the CCF related to business and the middle-class farm community – is an indication of the inherent weakness of most accounts of the CCF.

As long as the existing literature is predicated on the false assumption that the history of the CCF is about white people only, the whole story will never be told. In addressing this concern, *Walking in Indian Moccasins* attempts to present a more focused and comprehensive analysis of the CCF's Native policies than can be found in existing sources. This will allow for a more acute understanding of Native development during a formative period in Saskatchewan's history. It will also provide a more adequate basis for judging the CCF's record in office.

The study is confined to the period covered by Douglas's premiership, ending in 1961 when the premier resigned from office in order to assume leadership of the federal New Democratic Party (NDP). The focus on this period is not meant to suggest that Douglas was the CCF or that the CCF after his departure was a spent force. In fact, the fall of the CCF government three years later represented only a narrow victory for Ross Thatcher's Liberals and was certainly not the electoral repudiation some have suggested.[17] The fact remains, nevertheless, that it was during Douglas's reign that the main parameters of the government's Native policies were defined, with little of importance being added during the last few years of the regime. Moreover, the emphasis on Douglas's premiership quite rightly underscores the importance of Douglas himself. As a young MP in Ottawa, he had familiarized himself with Indian issues, in part as a result of his participation in debates concerning Indian Affairs expenditures, and, as early as 1943, he had publicly declared his support for the idea that Indians should be given full citizenship rights, including the right to vote.[18] As premier of Saskatchewan, fresh from electoral victory in 1944, it was he who first proclaimed the government's commitment to addressing the problems of Native society and, more than anyone else, it was he who made that commitment a matter of moral imperative.

The title of this study, *Walking in Indian Moccasins,* comes from a 1960 election document penned by John Sturdy, who at the time was a special assistant to the premier. It was written just after Indians had been given the provincial vote by the CCF and on the eve of Douglas's departure from provincial politics. The phrase was probably borrowed from a Catholic Sioux prayer in reference to the Christian message of brotherly love and forgiveness in the New Testament, but its origin is uncertain because the phrase had been used by various Indian groups as far away as California. Sturdy's comments, accompanied by a rather stereotypical analysis of Indian culture by an Oblate priest, were addressed to an election strategy for CCF candidates whose ridings contained a significant number of Indian voters. It read in part:

> Until we have 'walked in the Indian's moccasins' we have little chance of gaining his confidence or of influencing him in any way. It seems to me that integration of the Indian into the social and economic life of Saskatchewan is the desirable goal and this will become more acceptable to him if we can put across our socialist idea of 'sharing' and 'production for use' and the basic philosophy of our Founder, Jim Woodsworth ...[19]

The reference to Indian moccasins spoke to the need for politicians to understand and empathize with Indian concerns and problems as a basis for winning the Indian over and introducing change. As such, it nicely encapsulated the essence of both the attitude of the CCF and the intended means to Native reform. The wording of the passage is specific to Indians because, unlike the Métis who had long had the franchise, status Indians were voting for the first time; however, in terms of CCF Native policy, the message was applicable to the Métis as well.

As Sturdy suggested, 'integration' was the stated goal of the CCF's Native policies. The Douglas government came to believe that traditional Native culture had been founded on socialist principles and that, for that reason, Native society would be intrinsically receptive to socialist experimentation. Integration, as the ultimate goal of that experimentation, implied that Native people would be participants in mainstream society, fully enjoying all the social services and individual political rights others took for granted, all the while enjoying their own cultural integrity and collective rights as Aboriginals. As the policy unfolded over two decades of CCF rule, the intent of the integration policy seems to have been honoured where Indians were concerned, but far less so in the case of the Métis who, as it turned out, were targeted by government for total assimilation.

The avowed aim of walking in Indian moccasins implied a degree of sympathy for Native aspirations and culture; in addition, it invited a measure of CCF influence and involvement in Native society that would prove to be both paternalistic and heavy handed. It also spoke to the more crass, political side of CCF motivation – the hope of enlarging its voter support by making inroads into the Native electorate. It was well known that the Métis tended to support the Liberal Party during elections and it is quite possible that many in the CCF saw the possibility of Indian electoral support as a way to offset that fact. Few in the party believed that anything was wrong with winning votes as a by-product of Native reforms, and, like all parties, the CCF equated its own survival in office with the best interests of society generally.

The story of North America's first experiment in so-called socialist government is important because it raises questions about the very nature of Saskatchewan society. In light of the enduring and uninterrupted rule of the CCF, it is impossible to escape the conclusion that government policies were an accurate reflection of what most people in Saskatchewan wanted. Douglas and his party did not rule in a political vacuum, but rather with the consent of the provincial electorate, and what they attempted to do for the Native community – and what they failed to do – were symptomatic of broadly based attitudes. In a very real sense, then, *Walking in Indian Moccasins* is not only about the policies that the CCF applied to Native society; it is also an examination of the social assumptions and predilections that prevailed in Saskatchewan society in the postwar period.

Walking in Indian Moccasins

1
Historical Setting

No understanding of the CCF and its Native policies can be complete without some appreciation of the historical background. By the time Douglas came to power, Native society was in a state of acute crisis, characterized by abject poverty and social disintegration. The explanation of why this was so is intimately connected with the creation and westward expansion of the Canadian nation state after 1867. With some justification, the settlement of the prairie West has been described as a noble, even heroic, enterprise by people of vision and drive. What has not always been acknowledged is that it was also an ignoble process, operating under the guise of 'national interests' and 'progress' but predicated on the displacement, if not destruction, of the Native community. It was in recognition of that fact that, on the eve of the Second World War, the Saskatchewan government grudgingly conceded that there was a Native problem; and it is within the context of that larger historic process – chronicling both Native displacement and early government initiatives – that CCF reforms must be seen.

Confederation itself had been created by politicians and business people who believed that Canada's economic salvation was to be found in the acquisition and development of a western frontier. Consequently, in 1869, the dominion government concluded an agreement with the British government and the Hudson's Bay Company whereby the latter surrendered its charter rights over the Prairies and agreed to transfer jurisdiction over the area to the dominion. The central idea was that these lands could be settled by a European peasant stock, developed as a farm hinterland, and used as a springboard to national prosperity. An identical kind of process had taken place in the United States decades earlier and, to John A. Macdonald and the other fathers of Confederation, the need to imitate the American formula for prosperity was self-evident.[1] It was only through such prosperity, they believed, that Canada could acquire the necessary economic strength to survive independent of the American giant to the south.[2]

Absolutely crucial to this plan was the fact that Indian and Métis peoples, the original inhabitants of the soil, would have to be disabused of their land rights and moved out of the path of development. To that end, the Canadian government appointed government officials – scrip commissioners for the Métis and treaty commissioners for the Indians – who were authorized to negotiate with the Natives for the surrender of their Aboriginal land rights in the West. Contrary to popular conception, the Métis and Indians themselves were not averse to such negotiations because they fully realized that, with the disappearance of the buffalo and the impending disruption of traditional pursuits, they would have to adapt to the new order; moreover, they were anxious to secure land grants as a patrimony for future generations, as well as concessions from the government that would facilitate their transition to a new way of life.[3] But, as recent studies indicate, the government's role in settling Native claims was less than honourable and somewhat akin to a land grab.[4]

Initially, Macdonald acknowledged that the people of mixed white and Indian ancestry had certain rights to the land by virtue of the Aboriginal status of at least one of their parents, usually the mother; but he soon regretted that recognition because, in his mind, it necessarily complicated and prolonged the land settlement process.[5] As a result, he did little to allay the concerns of the Métis who, lacking deeds to the properties on which they had squatted for generations, feared the loss of their land holdings. In the Saskatchewan region, government officials made no effort to reassure the Métis, or to curb the illegal activities of land speculators, colonization companies, or settlers. As late as 1885, the Métis of the Batoche-St. Louis area, despite their urgent pleas, were unable to obtain government surveys of their lands as a precondition to official registration of their holdings.[6] Nor was there any sign of the promised scrip commission.

Indians received a different treatment because their Aboriginal status was more self-evident; moreover, in transferring the Hudson's Bay Company lands to the dominion in 1870, the Imperial government had, as a condition of the transfer, insisted that the Canadian government acknowledge Aboriginal title to the lands in question.[7] Consequently, Indians in southern and central Saskatchewan – the area earmarked for immediate settlement – were invited to participate in treaty negotiations. But here again, national interest seems to have been more important than justice or fair play. Treaty commissioners were not above using high-handed or irregular methods to get Indian compliance, nor did they make much effort to acquaint the Indians – who were illiterate – with the legal niceties of the agreements. It is true that Indian signatories were not the wide-eyed innocents that some have maintained; it is equally true, however, that the Indians were not fully informed about the meaning and implications of the treaties. Only a few understood the extent to which the treaties called for a complete surrender of independence, and even fewer understood that the land surrender provisions of the treaties called for the complete extinguishment of Aboriginal rights to the land.[8] Also hidden was the fact that many of the treaty benefits accruing to Indians were discretionary and dependent on government goodwill.

No sooner had the Indian leaders affixed their 'X' to the agreements than the government's duplicity became painfully evident. Central to the treaties was the provision that small tracts of land would be set aside for the use and benefit of the Indians. The intent was that the scattered bands roaming the southern and central portions of Saskatchewan would be moved onto these reserves as soon as possible – a process that was completed by about 1883. During the treaty negotiations, government commissioners had promised that the reserve would be a 'homeland,' a place where Indians could enjoy their traditional culture and pursuits, undisturbed by incoming white settlement.[9] But it quickly became evident that reserve life was not what had been promised and that the government was systematically reneging on its treaty obligations.

During the early years, starvation was rampant on most reserves, especially during the winter months. To meet the crisis, the government reluctantly introduced food rations, in keeping with the pestilence clause of Treaty 6. But the aid came in the form of a 'work for rations' program, based on the principle of 'less eligibility.'[10] The core idea was that the test of eligibility for relief would be whether the recipient would submit to deplorable work conditions. In the case of the able-bodied Indian, this usually meant cutting cord wood, even though such work was not always available and despite the fact that Indians rarely had the necessary clothing and footwear to withstand winter temperatures. As a relief measure, it was certainly a pale shadow of what Indians had been led to expect and, in effect, it did little more than contain the rising death rate on most reserves. Moreover, far from being a homeland, the reserve soon took on the air of an interment camp, confining Indians against their will. The government simply arrogated to itself the power to refuse Indians the right to leave the reserve without the expressed consent of the Indian agent; those who did so were summarily arrested by the North-West Mounted Police and returned to the reserve for disciplinary action. The measure was entirely illegal and a complete violation of the treaty and human rights of reserve residents.[11]

By the early 1880s, discontent was rife, especially in the Cree communities. Indian leaders realized that the time had come to act. What they attempted to do was to channel the discontent into a pan-Indian movement, one that would unite the various tribes into a single voice demanding a revision of the treaties.[12] There were, of course, those on the fringe who preferred a military confrontation with Canadian authorities but, for the most part, the Indian leadership was committed to a peaceful course of action. Nevertheless, John A. Macdonald and his government saw these developments as a menacing threat to the building of the CPR railway, the vehicle of national economic expansion. Any form of Native solidarity in the West was potentially dangerous, even if it only delayed development. For that reason, the prime minister professed to see in the Indian movement the roots of armed insurrection, analogous to the kind of Indian warfare that had erupted in the American West earlier.[13]

The Indian threat seemed all the more real when, as a movement completely divorced from developments in the Indian community, the Métis at Batoche took up arms in what has been described as the North-West Rebellion. After years of neglect and frustration, the Métis had turned to the leadership of Louis Riel whose militancy promised to get the attention of government. At least one writer has argued – rather unconvincingly – that Macdonald, by purposefully alienating the Métis through the use of an agent provocateur and other means, had manipulated the Métis into insurrection.[14] The intent, he said, was to prod Parliament into financing the completion of the CPR, ostensibly as a means of troop movement to quell the Rebellion, but really as part of his grand design for western development.[15] Whether this was true or not, what is certain is that Macdonald used the Métis insurrection as an excuse to crush, once and for all, all Native resistance.

The government's commitment of men and arms was totally disproportionate to the threat, whether real or imagined, and assumed the guise of a vengeful military subjugation.[16] Quite apart from the actual bloodletting, punctuated by the looting and burning of Indian and Métis homes, Native society was effectively emaciated. Louis Riel and eight Indians were executed for their part in the resistance, while much of the remaining leadership was removed by the imposition of prison terms for those found guilty of treason-felony. Combined with this social decapitation was a complete suppression of all forms of further resistance. Native society was effectively stripped of any semblance of self-determination and integrity and, unable to respond to change in any collective way, it was pushed aside by the flood of development permitted by the completion of the CPR railway. Middleton's victory did more than guarantee agrarian capitalist development in the West: it also unleashed a pattern of social evolution through which Native communities would be marginalized.

In the case of the Métis, dislocation was not immediate. As Diane Payment's study of Batoche indicates, the Métis did not leave the area en masse after 1885 nor did their economy immediately collapse.[17] For a time, they continued to struggle for their land rights and they adopted strategies for participating in the new regional economy. But conflict with the government continued, mainly because of 'conflicting ideologies' regarding land tenure and also because of the inability or reluctance of the Métis to adapt to agriculture.[18] By the time Saskatchewan was created as a province, in 1905, Métis communities generally were being engulfed by an unsympathetic settler society, whose ability to monopolize social and economic power cast disdain upon Native values and their way of life. Symptoms of community crisis were reflected in alcohol abuse, family breakdown, internal political divisions, and a tuberculosis rate that reached epidemic proportions.[19] Some attempted to escape their plight by migrating to the more remote and isolated areas of the province, especially to the North where subsistence activities were still possible. But for many, the only option was to eke out a meager existence in the peripheral rural areas in the southern half of the province, where families often squatted in hovels illegally located on provincial road allowances or near Indian reserves. It was a life of almost total destitution and poverty and, apart from the social and racial condemnation it sometimes aroused, it met with little public sympathy or government action. The Métis have been described as 'Canada's forgotten people,'[20] and nowhere was this more fitting than in Saskatchewan.

In the case of Indians, the impact of military suppression was immediate and far reaching. Without any means to protest their treatment, they were now subjected to the full weight of government authority. Unlike the Métis, who had the same status as other citizens and therefore fell under provincial jurisdiction, the Indian population was deemed by the British North America Act – in effect Canada's constitution – to be exclusively under the jurisdiction and purview of the federal government.[21] In theory, the treaties that had been concluded in the pre-1885 period were to have a bearing on the relationship between Indians and government, but in practice it was an unequal relationship in which the former were relegated to the status of wards of the state. Whatever rights the treaties conferred on Indians were largely nullified by the carefully framed wording of the treaties, which made such rights contingent upon government consent; where this was not so, Indians lacked the political and judicial means to enforce their own interpretation of the treaties. The net result was an overbearing and tyrannical administration of Indian reserves, unchecked by popular opinion or legal restraint.

The specific policy now imposed on western reserves consisted of a series of assimilationist schemes, originally developed in Ontario after 1828.[22] It was generally assumed that the pre-industrial culture of the Indian was irrelevant to modern-day society and that, for practical and humanitarian reasons, Indians should be Christianized, civilized, and schooled in agricultural methods. Essentially, the aim was to remake the Indian in the image of a white rural farmer, and it called for a process of 'detribalization,' through which old habits and values were to be destroyed. The Department of Indian Affairs (DIA) did everything in its power to subvert the authority of traditional chiefs and mounted a concerted assault on Aboriginal religious practice. It also formalized the segregation of Indian society by instituting a series of administrative and legislative measures meant to confine Indians to their reserves, including measures that prevented reserve Indians from competing head-to-head with whites in the local and regional markets.[23] Eventually, it was understood, Indians would leave the reserve and be assimilated into mainstream society, but until that time they were to have a special status, that of dependent wards denied citizenship rights, including the right to vote. The entire scheme was riddled with racist assumptions and plagued with inherent contradictions, not the least of which was the aim of assimilating the Indian population into a society from which it was segregated.

Contrary to design, Indian reserves proved impervious to the machinations of government officials. Recent studies make it quite clear that, far from being the docile and unwitting subjects of government policy, Indians reacted to their treatment with steel determination, resorting to the only weapon at their disposal: passive resistance.[24] To protest the interference of the DIA in the choice of Indian leaders on the reserve, they sometimes refused to send their children to school or to farm. They systematically ignored the requirement that they obtain a pass before leaving the reserve – so much so that the pass system proved unworkable and had to be abandoned.[25] And covertly, under the cover of darkness or in remote sections of the reserve, they continued the traditional healing and spiritual practices that were fundamental to Indian culture. In reality, the reserve functioned as two parallel social systems: the official one defined by the government; and the Indian one, which adhered to long-standing traditions, albeit sometimes modified to fit the changed circumstance. Reserves, in fact, evolved as tight little islands of Indian culture in an otherwise Euro-Canadian society.

The failure of government policy was underscored by the fact that Indians steadfastly refused to enfranchise voluntarily.[26] Enfranchisement was the process whereby Indians legally abandoned their special status, left the reserve, and integrated into Canadian society. It offered them full citizenship rights, including the right to consume alcohol off the reserve and to vote, but these benefits did little to offset the fact that the process also meant that they would surrender all treaty benefits, their income would be taxable, and, in effect, they would be isolated from their friends and culture on the reserve. Enfranchisement really meant they would be required to cease being Indian and, for that reason, it had no appeal.[27]

To government officials, the unwillingness of Indians to assimilate was often misinterpreted as the inability of Indians to adapt. As decades passed, DIA personnel became increasingly frustrated in their attempts to engineer the required changes in Indian society, and this was often expressed at the political level by a growing disinclination by governments to allocate adequate funding. The spending estimates for the Department of Indian Affairs seemed to be on an ever-ascending scale and were often attacked in Parliament on the grounds that the past performance of the department had produced few tangible results. The actual amounts of money spent on Indians had never been lavish or even adequate, but given the low priority normally assigned to Indian affairs and now the pessimism over results, underfunding of reserve programs became a standard feature of Indian life. According to Noel Dyck, it was exactly for that reason that the agricultural program on most reserves in the West proved unsuccessful.[28]

The same factor was also at work in the education system, geared to training Indian boys and girls in agricultural pursuits as a precondition to assimilation into white society. For a time, the industrial school was considered the best means to that end. These were schools located in strategic centres, such as Battleford, Lebret, and Regina. They were administered mainly by the Catholic, as well as the Anglican, Presbyterian, and Methodist, denominations, with the federal government providing financial subsidies based on attendance. Whereas the religious influence was deemed appropriate to the goal of Christianization, equated with civilizing the Indian, the residential nature of the school guaranteed that the children would be removed from the reserve and hence from the corrupting influence of Indian culture. However, starting in 1906 under the Laurier government, industrial schools were increasingly disbanded because they were too costly and were replaced with day-schools and residential schools located on or near reserves.[29] The new school system abandoned assimilation as a goal and aimed only to teach the fundamentals of literacy, lessons in Canadian civics, and skills appropriate to life on a reserve.[30] In addition, it mirrored the all-pervasive pessimism that by the beginning of the century had infiltrated the administration of Indian Affairs. The perception was that Indians would not assimilate, that even graduates were not well received in the larger society, and that ultimately it was unkind and unwise to educate Indians above their expected station in life. The change in school system was tantamount to a declaration that, if Indians refused to assimilate along the lines defined by government, there was little point in financing further attempts to make them competitive in the outside world. It also suggested that Indians, like the Métis, were not expected to rise above their underprivileged and underclassed position in life.

Emergent Awareness of the Native

During the early decades of the twentieth century, successive provincial governments more or less ignored the plight of Native communities. They were able to do so largely because of the initial 'invisibility' of the problem, stemming from the fact that Indian reserves and Métis settlements were often found in the more remote areas, removed from the main centres of development. Equally at play was the fact that standards of social welfare were woefully low. Few in Canada thought that government should act as an all-pervasive instrument of social policy and even fewer believed that it was the legitimate role of government to homogenize class differences. Historically, governmental laissez-faire, both in the market place and in the social realm, had been the veritable handmaiden of unrestricted and often unregulated economic development, and it was deeply ingrained in those who sought to apply large-scale capital to the marketing of agricultural production in the Canadian West. It was also a dogma that effectively masked the resulting social inequalities, and it allowed Canadians to ignore the fact that the poverty and social pathology of the underclassed were beyond the control of those affected.

In Saskatchewan, the enthusiasm for curtailing the role of government was considerably tempered by problems peculiar to the prairie West.[31] The sparseness of population in the province inevitably meant poor health and education facilities, with the result that farmers and others increasingly looked to government for an extension of social services. More than that, government was often seen as the only effective counterpoise to a system of monopoly that victimized the western farmer. The perceived enemy was large-scale financial interests, usually associated with eastern Canada, that not only siphoned off western wealth by manipulating grain markets, but also imposed monopoly prices on westerners for transportation and consumer goods. In response, both large and small farmers increasingly banded together in what has been described as an agrarian populist movement, one founded on an emerging class consciousness in the farm community. By definition, populism proclaimed the importance of collective action by the farmers and called for a free enterprise system of grain marketing in which the farmer would get a fair share of the wealth. The movement was not opposed to capitalism per se; on the contrary, as independent producers – sometimes described as the 'petty bourgeoisie'[32] – western farmers were business people very much committed to a free enterprise system, but one that would benefit the 'little guy.'[33] To prevent the operation of monopolies, government intervention would be necessary, and among the earliest demands of farmers was the call for government regulation of the grain trade and public ownership of the elevators. In the rhetoric of farm politics, government was to be an instrument of public policy and had a definite role to play in both social and economic affairs.[34]

Notwithstanding this political difference, western attitudes toward Natives were not appreciably different from those found elsewhere. Although government intervention was thought to be appropriate under certain circumstances, such intervention was usually class- and interest-specific, confined to agrarian concerns, or at least to the white community. It is a matter of public record that municipalities in Saskatchewan regularly refused membership to indigent Indians and Métis living within their borders because they would be a drain on welfare funds.[35] It is also true that Natives were systematically excluded from provincial schools on the grounds that they were dirty or unhealthy, and therefore a health problem for other students.[36] While it might seem contradictory that Natives should receive such treatment in a province noted for cooperatives and community-based assistance, it should be remembered that many of the values underpinning western settlement were rooted in an ethos of individualism and self-enterprise. Such values were often at odds with the surviving communal traits found in Native society and served as a frame of reference for castigating a people perceived as dependent and lazy. Although western farmers were able to see that the capitalist system could yield corruption and monopolies that worked against their own interests, they were less able to see that it also produced, of its own volition, a residue of underclassed people. For many in Saskatchewan, the ills of Native society were a self-induced, self-perpetuating disorder resulting from outdated values and a disinclination to work hard. For that reason, it was widely believed that massive government assistance, whether at the municipal or provincial levels, could do little to obviate the problem and would only serve to destroy initiative and overburden public spending. This understanding was further reinforced by the belief that, in any event, the Native problem ultimately would solve itself. Statistically, it could be shown that the Native population had been in steady decline and that, if nature were allowed to take her course, the Native fact would simply disappear from the landscape.[37] Thus, the state of Native poverty and dislocation tended to provoke only ignorance and indifference.

Although much of this social understanding remained in effect, and indeed would survive to the present, the intellectual climate in Saskatchewan, as elsewhere, was amenable to change and did reflect new currents of thought. Especially important in breaking down old attitudes were the momentous events associated with the Great Depression and the Second World War. These were cataclysmic developments for the Western world generally, and within all countries they unleashed social and economic ferment. This was no less so in Saskatchewan, where both events had a major impact.

Nowhere were the 'dirty thirties' more keenly felt than in the prairie West. The onslaught of the depression was first signalled by the collapse of foreign markets for primary products, and, among other things, this meant that western wheat was virtually unsaleable at any price. In Saskatchewan, the average annual income plummeted by no less than 72 percent,[38] and this was only one aspect of a complex of factors that conspired to destroy the farm economy. Whereas farm debt soared to new heights, thousands of farmers saw the equity in their land, built up over a thirty-year period, unceasingly eroded. And if this were not enough, the ravages of drought, beginning in 1930, stripped the land of its top soil and prevented even a subsistence form of living in many rural areas.

Once more, the target of seething agrarian protest was the capitalist system – a system seemingly perverted by the machinations of 'big money' and 'vested interests.' In characteristic fashion, farmers turned to radical political experimentation as a way out of their depressed state. Some got caught up in near-evangelical enthusiasm for the right-wing Social Credit Party; others flirted with left-wing socialism and even communism. But no matter what the political persuasion of the individual, the unmistakable impression left by the Depression was that the free enterprise system could be a wanton and destructive force, capable of condemning whole sections of the population to destitution through no fault of their own. For the first time, and despite years of hard work and dedication, some farmers found their standard of living approaching that of the Native community during normal times, and it was a shattering experience.[39] It not only set the stage for growing demands for enhanced social services – which would become the cornerstone of CCF appeal – but also ushered in a new empathy for the underprivileged in society. Certainly, Natives were not the immediate focus of such empathy and in most ways would remain excluded from white communities. Nevertheless, the lessons of the Depression were bound to transcend the narrowly defined interests of the farm community. The 1930s produced a social conscience that, in the abstract at least, condemned poverty in general. At the same time, past tendencies to 'blame the victims' of such poverty no longer seemed as persuasive. If nothing else, the Depression led to a new critique of both the economic and social environment, and within that context the plight of Native society could no longer be ignored or sanitized.

These tendencies were reinforced by the events of the Second World War. Quite apart from military strategy and actual battles, the war effort was a struggle for the minds and hearts of ordinary citizens who were asked to make the human and material sacrifices. The Allied war machine could sustain action on a long-term basis only as long as the civilian populations were effectively mobilized for sustained industrial and agricultural production. To that end, the Allied governments mounted an all-pervasive propaganda campaign, which, in association with greatly enhanced communications systems, attempted to mould public opinion. In Canada, as elsewhere, the war was billed as a struggle against fascism and foreign tyranny and it promised national self-determination and social justice for the oppressed. Such heady idealism was meant to sensitize Canadians to the suffering of people in other parts of the world, but it also had the effect of making them more introspective about what was happening within Canada. This was especially so at the conclusion of the war when veterans returned home to face an uncertain future. At the same time, the necessities of war tended to break down the isolation of Native society. In part this was a function of the fact that, owing to war-time communications networks, Natives were increasingly incorporated into the information flow. Indian reserves, for example, were frequently targets of the numerous recruitment teams that swarmed through the rural areas of Saskatchewan. Equally important, both Métis and Indians enthusiastically volunteered for service at a rate totally disproportional to their overall population.[40] No doubt some saw the Armed Forces as the only alternative to destitution, but most were animated by an unmistakable sense of patriotism. Although the number of Native servicemen was not large, their participation in the war nevertheless was of considerable importance to the overall Native cause. In many cases, they served with great distinction and heroism, and this not only provoked a groundswell of pride in their home communities but also earned the recognition of other Canadians as well. Moreover, because of their overseas experience and service training, Métis and Indian servicemen at the conclusion of the war came to represent a cadre of relatively well educated and articulate spokespersons for Native people generally. It was precisely for this reason that in the immediate postwar period the newly elected CCF government of Saskatchewan found itself confronted with ever more insistent demands in the Native community for government aid. The leadership of Native veterans also contributed to postwar political organization. Whereas the interwar period had witnessed the birth of formal political associations in both the Indian and Métis communities,[41] it was in the aftermath of the Second World War that those earlier efforts were crowned with success, particularly in the case of Indians.

Moreover, overlapping both the Depression and the war was a long-term fluctuation in Native demographics, which also had a revolutionary impact. The decline in the Native population across Canada, noted earlier, proved to be an enduring trend for almost half a century after the North-West Rebellion. Unfortunately, census data do not yield a totally accurate assessment of the Native population simply because Native people, as a response to growing racial discrimination, often failed to acknowledge their Aboriginal status.[42] In addition, the census material reflects some confusion over the categorization of the mixed-blood population. In 1931, for example, the Métis people of Canada were included in the 'Indian' category, but in the 1941 census they were identified in a footnote as the majority component of the 'other' category.[43] Nevertheless, these shortcomings notwithstanding, and assuming that the Métis were also included in the population figures of the Indian and Eskimo prior to 1931, existing census data do illustrate the decline in the Canadian Native population prior to the Depression: in relation to the total population in Canada, Natives represented 2.5 percent in 1881, 2.4 percent in 1901, 1.5 percent in 1911, 1.3 percent in 1921, and only 1.2 percent in 1931.[44]

As linear as this decline may have been, however, it did not remain a constant feature of the demographic picture, as originally predicted. Indeed, during the Depression years the downward trend not only slackened but began to reverse itself. The 1941 census indicates that there were 35,416 Métis and 126,573 Indians and Eskimo, representing 1.4 percent of the Canadian population.[45] This meant that the total Native population at the end of the Depression was slightly more than it had been twenty years earlier; in fact, this was the beginning of a new Canada-wide trend that would see the Native population explode at rates two and three times that of the national average.

In Saskatchewan, a phenomenal increase was recorded for both the Métis and Indian populations, but given the problems of identifying the Métis in census data, the increase can best be illustrated by the growth in the Indian population. In the province as a whole, the increase in the number of people living on reserves was 9 percent between 1941 and 1946, 15 percent between 1946 and 1951, and 18 percent between 1951 and 1956; and by August 1959 the Indian population had jumped another 21 percent over that of the previous census date.[46] In less than two decades, the population had nearly doubled, from just over 13,000 in 1941 to almost 24,000 in 1959.[47] It was an increase that was more or less general throughout the various census districts and one that accelerated at rates independent of whatever factors influenced the rise and fall of the non-Indian population in the same census divisions. The soaring increase was a result of long-term cultural adjustment and more adequate health care, mirrored in an increasing number of live births and an overall decline in the mortality rate. By the late 1950s, live births per 1,000 Indian population averaged 81.5, compared to an average of only 25.8 in the non-Indian population.[48] By the same token, the Indian death rate in the province dropped from a high of 34.9 per 1,000 in 1942 to a low of 12.2 per 1,000 in 1958, approximating the non-Indian death rate of 7.2 per 1,000.[49]

What all of this meant was that the Indian community produced a relatively large proportion of young, child-bearing adults whose reproductive rate was more than three times that of the non-Indian population; and this, combined with a decline in the number of deaths, produced the population explosion. Moreover, by the late 1950s, it was quite evident that the rapid expansion of the population would continue for some time to come simply because, although the child mortality rate was dropping, it was still almost four times the provincial average.[50] Increased health care in the future would lead to even fewer childhood deaths, and this would further fuel the rate of population increase.

The effect of the demographic change was to place Native society on a collision course with the white population, especially in the southern half of the province. There, most Native communities lacked the natural resources to sustain even existing numbers, and burgeoning population growth only served to exacerbate the problem of underdevelopment in most of those communities. Lacking the economic capacity to absorb the population increase, Indian reserves and Métis settlements became even more tormented than they had been by economic inertia, overcrowded housing, and material destitution. For many Natives, especially the young and ambitious, the only alternative was to leave their home communities in search of employment and the other benefits offered by the small villages, towns, and even cities that increasingly dotted the agrarian landscape. It was an out-migration that was noticeable during the war years and one that accelerated throughout the 1950s. Much of the dispersed Native population remained in the rural areas, but by the 1950s there was also a considerable Native presence in Regina, Saskatoon, Prince Albert, and the smaller service centres of the south; so much so that the so-called 'Native problem' was more and more defined as an urban phenomenon.[51]

Thus the 1930s and 1940s ushered in a somewhat more enlightened attitude about the causes of poverty and underclass development; equally important, this occurred concomitantly with demographic and related changes that, for the first time, brought the Native face-to-face with the wider provincial society.

Métis Poverty and Government Responses

It was in the closing years of the Great Depression that the Saskatchewan government first began to take notice of the Native situation. At the time, the Liberal Party led by Premier William Patterson was in power in Regina. There were few in government who had any appreciation of the nature or extent of the problems faced by the Native community and fewer still who understood the difference between the Métis and Indians, either in a cultural or legal sense. Indeed, in the initial stages of 'discovering' the Native fact in Saskatchewan, the provincial government seemed almost totally in the dark and only faintly grasped the extent of its own legal responsibility for the Métis as citizens of the province. The existence of a Métis problem, in fact, was somewhat of a revelation, underscoring the decades of Native neglect.

The genesis of the issue was to be found in the self-interest of municipal councils, which, under severe financial constraints, became disconcerted over the congregation of Métis people in their districts. Of special concern was the ever-increasing number of people described by local officials as a shiftless and disease-ridden group of paupers, often found squatting on road allowances in makeshift shacks. Indians, per se, were not defined as part of the problem because, constitutionally, they were wards of the federal government, and as such the responsibility of the dominion. But this was not true of the Métis who were like any other provincial citizens in that they could claim various forms of local assistance if they were able to prove that they were ongoing residents of the municipality. Because of their poverty the Métis did not contribute to the tax base of the local government, but also because of their poverty they had the potential to overburden the social assistance programs administered by the municipality. The Métis had one of the highest incidences of disease in the entire province, and at the same time they figured prominently in burgeoning demands for welfare assistance. They were also vastly over-represented in provincial crime statistics, especially in the category of crimes against property, including theft and break-and-enter. Although local officials were not without sympathy for the Métis themselves, their more immediate concern was their financial inability to deal with the problem. It was an arguable point that, given the Métis' poverty and transience – and hence their questionable municipal residence – the plight of Natives represented a special set of circumstances, the amelioration of which was the direct responsibility of the provincial government.[52] And this was precisely the message communicated to the Ministries of Social Services and Municipal Affairs.

Had these problems remained merely a matter of local concern, the whole issue would have been swept under the carpet, as it had been for decades. But the steady growth of the Métis population, combined with the financial constraints imposed on the municipalities by the Depression, made Métis poverty an irrepressible provincial concern. Equally important, the issue was picked up by the popular press and carried into the political arena. In 1939, for example, George Dulmage, reeve of the Rural Municipality of Orkney (near Yorkton), took up the issue of Métis poverty and circulated petitions that he presented to the provincial government.[53] Three years later, he was back in the news when, in an address to the annual meeting of the Yorkton and district Board of Trade, he lambasted the abuse of 'Indian Half-Breeds.' Referring to a congregation of 150 Natives just south of Yorkton, Dulmage described the Métis as a homeless,

Map 1 Southern half of Saskatchewan

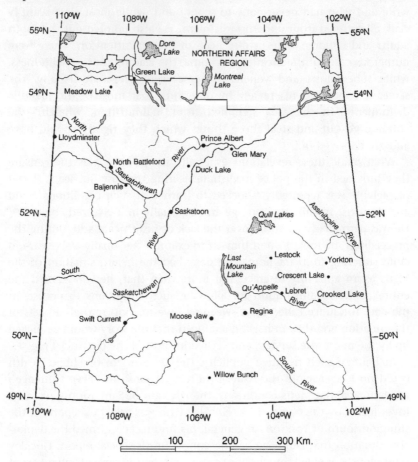

disease-infested group living in mud huts, and he called upon the board to do something.[54] Among other things, his address kindled a response by Major Peaker and the Council of Yorkton who interviewed three provincial cabinet ministers on the matter.

Even more explosive was an account carried in the *Yorkton Enterprise* in 1942.[55] It concerned the trial of a thirteen-year-old Métis child who had been arrested for break-and-enter and theft of a horse and buggy. Ultimately, he was found guilty and sentenced to an indefinite term in the Moosomin industrial school. But the real story had to do with the extenuating circumstances uncovered in the court proceedings. In the teenager's defence, Sergeant Charles Carey of the RCMP reviewed the history of the Métis families located in the Crescent Lake area from which the boy had come. He noted that in wintertime they lived in shacks little better than stables and in summer in tents going from place to place as nomads. There were at least forty children who could neither read nor write and who had never gone to school and, while most were scantily clad, all suffered from undernourishment. He also pointed out that both adults and children were in dire need of medical attention. There were numerous cases of the dreaded trachoma, the leading cause of blindness, while tuberculosis and venereal disease were prevalent. Finally, the sergeant concluded his review by observing that most of the juvenile delinquency in the area stemmed from malnutrition, wherein 'the children go out and steal those things which they rightly should have and are deprived of.'[56]

What made these revelations especially newsworthy was the censure they inflamed in the police magistrate hearing the case. Justice S. Potter of Melville was reportedly 'shocked to learn that such conditions could and did exist in this day and age and especially in a civilized country.'[57] He was particularly incensed over the lack of health care and, during the proceedings, he took it upon himself to examine personally a six-year-old child suffering from trachoma. He described the health situation of the Métis as an appalling disgrace, but more than that, he condemned the entire public administration for allowing such conditions to persist. In the end, the judge called for a sweeping investigation into all aspects of the situation and this, in itself, guaranteed that the story would be picked up by the main wire services and carried in most of the provincial presses.

In light of such negative publicity, the Department of Public Health could no longer avoid the issue. In direct response to Reeve Dulmage's revelations about Métis conditions, the Division of Sanitation sent in an investigator by the name of J.E. Hockley who was asked to report on the situation south of Yorkton. In general, his findings confirmed the deplorable situation that Dulmage had described. In his special report, Hockley scrupulously avoided any attempt to make moral judgments about what he observed; instead, he confined his comments to objective descriptions of the conditions under which the Métis were living. His concluding observations nevertheless left little doubt about his overall impression. 'It has been my privilege to visit homes of Indians, Métis and Whites,' he said, 'but I do not recollect having ever seen such signs of poverty or greater evidence of being improvident, as these homes.'[58]

Likewise, and seemingly in response to Justice Potter's indictments, health officials intensively surveyed the living conditions of the Crescent Lake Métis. A year earlier, the Sanitation Division had investigated the settlement, but a month after Potter's pronouncements, this was followed up with an investigation by the Division of Communicable Disease, and two months after that by a TB survey.[59] All three reports confirmed the abnormally high rate of health problems, although there was little evidence of the kind of malnutrition identified by Sergeant Carey. Perhaps the most telling commentary on the Crescent Lake situation, however, was contained in the concluding paragraphs of the TB report, filed by Dr. A.B. Simes of Fort Qu'Appelle:

> There were two other matters, which may not be within the jurisdiction of any Tuberculosis Survey, but they can hardly be passed off without mention. First the conditions under which these people live. While I did not visit all the homes, from those that I did visit, it would be very difficult to find words to portray a true picture of the existing filth and overcrowding, under which these people are existing. Secondly, one cannot but be astonished, to be repeatedly told without exception, when a child of school age was asked what school do you attend, that they had never been in school. This hardly seemed possible in an area only ten or twelve miles from one of our Cities.[60]

These and other such reports were important because they confirmed that the emergent outcry in the press was justified and not merely political posturing by would-be reformers looking for a cause. They also represented, within the provincial bureaucracy, a growing and irresistible concern that some action be taken.

Pressured by public opinion, the Patterson government responded to the issue with little enthusiasm or resolve. As early as 1936, the premier himself had admitted privately that his government had been unable to evolve a satisfactory policy, and that remained more or less true of the Liberal administration to the very end. Individual ministries and departments were left to their own devices in initiating stop-gap measures, designed primarily to soften criticism of the government. Not untypical was the fact that, in 1938, the minister of municipal affairs, the Honourable J.R. Parker, appointed a one-man commission as a 'First step aimed at a permanent solution of Saskatchewan's half-breed problem.'[61] The man chosen for the appointment was W.E. Read, whose only qualification for the position was that for some fifty-eight years he had owned a general store at Fort Qu'Appelle, through which he had come to know hundreds of Métis personally. The minister insisted that the commission would be invaluable in providing the information necessary to get the Métis off the welfare rolls and into a thoroughgoing rehabilitation program. But in substance, the appointment seems to have been little more than a public relations exercise, aimed at quelling the dissatisfaction of the municipalities. It was certainly no accident that the initiative came from the minister of municipal affairs.

The lack of government policy was nowhere better illustrated than in the field of education. Initially, departmental officials disavowed any responsibility for the Métis, partly because they saw the Métis situation as a larger social and economic problem, and partly also because they mistakenly believed that the Métis were someone else's responsibility. As one education official put it,

> It is difficult to make any helpful recommendations on the matter which would not involve considerable expenditure of funds. However, my opinion is that the education of these children is only one phase of a larger problem. So long as the Dominion government maintains Indian reserves in the midst of white settlements there will be half-breed children. It is possible the Dominion Government should make inquiry into the whole question of the social and economic position of the half-breeds in the Dominion. The settlement of the economic position of these people would no doubt bring with it the solution of their educational problems.[62]

At the same time, department officials had no idea of how many Métis children were unschooled, or even how many Métis there were in the province. From a survey of the Métis population conducted in the spring of 1938, it was estimated that there were perhaps as many as 3,500 Métis children in the province; however, mirroring the inadequacy of the calculation, the estimate was based on a total Métis population of only 6,000, when in fact there were perhaps twice that number, if not more.[63] Moreover, for some time there was confusion in the department over the proper terminology that should be applied to the Métis and even over how the term itself should be defined. In departmental correspondence, the term 'half-breed' persisted despite its pejorative connotations and the fact that it was unacceptable to the Métis themselves. And as late as 1942, the superintendent of schools for Prince Albert found it necessary to write the deputy minister of education indicating that he was not clear 'as to what was meant by the expression, Métis children.'[64] In response, the deputy minister admitted that he was not in a position to define the term.[65]

As ill-prepared as the Department of Education was to deal with the Métis question, it could not avoid doing something simply because, to many observers, education was at the heart of the matter. It quickly became apparent that Native children had been systematically excluded from provincial schools, and this was offensive for a number of reasons. The province had been steadily moving toward a compulsory, universal education system. Training in basic literacy was accepted as the lowest common denominator of an informed society, and the fact that the education system had simply bypassed a whole class of people logically provoked public condemnation. At the same time, the exclusion of Native children offended egalitarian sentiment because it not only exposed the gap between the rich and the poor but also implied the existence of racism. To many, the only possible solution to Native problems was to place Métis children in schools as a first step in integrating them into mainstream society.

This perception was reinforced by other factors as well. One consideration was the demands of Métis parents themselves. Because Native society was underclassed and suppressed, Métis parents were seldom in a position to articulate their concerns publicly. Nevertheless, some parents, often through the Métis Society of Saskatchewan, did make representations to the Department of Education, pleading that their children be schooled.[66] Another factor was that various departments within the provincial bureaucracy were drawn into the issue. The Health Department got involved because the prevalence of communicable diseases among Métis children had a bearing upon their admission to local schools and sometimes upon their expulsion. At the same time, police reports from rural detachments increasingly made mention of the appalling conditions under which the Métis lived, including the fact that their children were largely unschooled. What all of this meant was that, as ill-prepared as education officials may have been, they had no choice but to deal with the matter.

The earliest stirring in the Department of Education occurred in 1939. In October, Mr. Joe Ross, representing the Métis Society, called personally on the director of school district organization, N.L. Reid, to demand that something be done about the large number of unschooled Métis children south of Lestock and east of Punnichy.[67] Reid immediately contacted the inspector of schools for the Govan District and instructed him to investigate the situation, but, at the same time, he admitted to the inspector that he did not know what could be done for the children, even if the complaint were found to be justified.[68] The inspector's report, in fact, did confirm the accuracy of Ross's statements, but even then Reid's only response was to reiterate that he did not know what could be done.[69] By implication, these preliminary findings called for a provincewide investigation of the educational facilities available to Métis children, but no such survey was conducted until almost three years later.

Even so, school officials were well aware of the structural barriers that operated systematically to debar Métis children from schools. One aspect of the problem was that existing schools had been built mainly to satisfy the needs of Euro-Canadian families, at least when they were grouped in sufficient numbers to warrant the construction of such facilities. Métis settlements, however, were usually only semipermanent and even seasonal; individual families and groups would regularly take up residence at one location during summer months, often in an attempt to pick up work as farm labourers, and then move somewhere else for the winter. Even when their residence was more or less continuous, their poverty normally guaranteed that they lived a marginal existence, socially and physically isolated from the main areas of population concentration and at least several miles from the nearest school. Under these circumstances, school officials lacked the authority and inclination to require parents to register their children. At the same time, the parents themselves did not always value education, and even when they did, they seldom had the resources to transport their children to school on a daily basis.

Even more oppressive was the existence of widespread racism. Throughout the province, racial bigotry had been a constant companion to social and economic development and it was not confined to Euro-Canadian society nor targeted exclusively at Native people. Visible minorities of every description, but especially those who seemed less likely to conform to white, Protestant, Euro-Canadian stereotypes, bore the brunt of such prejudice. Natives figured prominently in that category, but Ukrainians, Mennonites, and other minorities were also singled out for abuse. It was no accident that, in the 1920s and 1930s, a chapter of the Ku Klux Klan operated in Saskatchewan as an expression of Protestant white supremacy and received considerable support in certain quarters for its anti-French and anti-Catholic hatred.[70] Even within the Native community, racial and class intolerance was often evident. A 1941 school report on the largely Catholic community of St. Vital noted that 'Apart from the division between the Roman Catholic and Protestant in the town, there is among the Catholic element a division between whites and the breeds and a further division between the high caste and low caste breeds.'[71] Likewise in 1943, a school superintendent's report on the Qu'Appelle Valley concluded with the remark that Métis people in the district 'seem to be looked down upon by both the white people and the Indians.'[72] What all of this suggests is that, while Native people generally were the object of racial bigotry, there was a descending order of discrimination, with the most depressed and neglected segments being the most victimized. As such, it was the Métis in particular who bore the collective weight of intolerance.

Within the context of the school issue, racism was expressed overtly in attempts by local trustees and ratepayers to discriminate against Métis children. Superintendents' reports were replete with references to the fact that the Métis were not welcome and that Native parents had been discouraged from sending their children to school. The excuse commonly cited was that Native children represented a health hazard. As a 1942 health report on the Crescent Lake area noted, 'The difficulty now is that many of the children of school age do not go to school because the trustees and rate payers of the organized schools object on account of the filthy condition of these children and the possibility of spreading disease.'[73] Likewise, according to a 1943 school superintendent's report,

'These children are not wanted in Tipperary School, Kenlis School and Pheasant Plains School. Some parents even threatened to take their children out of school if more of the Métis attend. On the surface this seems to be a very narrow and bigoted attitude, but i[f] we examine the matter more closely from the point of view of health and cleanliness, they may be, at least partly, justified.'[74] In reality, the health issue was little more than a smokescreen for racial and class prejudice. Confirming this was a 1941 superintendent's report on Pebble Lake School District No. 316. The report mentioned a meeting with Mr. Dennis Buckle, the chairman of the district council. Buckle was quoted as saying that the Métis children were infected with trachoma, itch or scabies, lice, and fleas, and that if the Department of Education allowed them to remain in the school the other children would walk out.[75] The report then went on to explain how local officials had manipulated Métis parents by shamelessly using the medical regulations as a gimmick to exclude their children: 'Mr. Burke [the school teacher] stated that the children were not actually excluded from school but in reality the children were excluded. Mr. Burke stated that should a half-breed child attempt to come to his school it would at once be necessary to apply the health laws and regulations and exclude the child from school until a medical certificate was produced and that the parents would not secure such a certificate, and that on account of the home conditions such a certificate would be of little value anyway.'[76] The implication, of course, was that local officials knew that Métis parents lacked the wherewithal to secure the certificate and that, even if parents were able to do so, supposed substandard health conditions in their homes could still be used as an excuse to exclude their offspring. As a matter of school policy, Métis children were denied admission precisely because they were Native, not because as individuals they were proven health risks. Indeed, even when their health status was medically certified, they were still excluded on the grounds of class-based presumptions about their unacceptable living standards.

Faced with pressures to counteract this situation, the Department of Education hesitatingly devolved a school policy. It was a policy that unfolded in only piecemeal fashion but that, in its most succinct form, aimed at Métis integration. This was to be accomplished by desegregating the existing school system where possible, and by devising culturally specific curricula to meet the special needs of Métis children where appropriate.[77] To do this, the department had no choice but to assume full financial responsibility. Among the first schools to receive special funding was St. Vital Roman Catholic Separate School District No. 3. In 1941, the school had an enrollment of some 150 students, more than a third of whom came from Métis families who paid nothing in school taxes.[78] In compensation, the school received a special allocation of $200 per year, and there was some talk of a $1,200 grant for the development of 'a modified curriculum with considerable vocational or handwork' training for Métis students.[79] At the time, the Department of Education justified the funding as 'temporary relief to the symptoms ... of economic maladjustment,'[80] but within a year or two, special funding had become the cornerstone of its Native school policy. The formula that now came into effect was that school districts would receive a special grant of $2 per month, to a maximum of $20 per year, for each Métis child in regular attendance at school. There was a proviso that the total grant from all sources could not exceed $700 if there were some non-Natives in attendance, nor exceed $800 if the school were exclusively Métis.[81] Thus, earlier notions about federal financial obligations finally evaporated, and the province now assumed full responsibility for the education of Métis people in Saskatchewan.

Although school integration was a generally accepted goal, it was also acknowledged that this was not always possible, nor even desirable, and that certain forms of segregated education were appropriate. This idea seems to have stemmed in part from the example of Indian reserves as well as Métis colonies in Alberta, and in part also from an appreciation of the difficulty of rooting out racist attitudes. The understanding was that, if Métis children could not be integrated into the local school with a minimum of friction, then perhaps the best solution was to relocate Métis families, grouping them into distinct communities and providing them with separate educational facilities. As in the case of Indian reserves, colony-like settlements for the Métis offered the possibility of developing self-help and community programs; at the same time, they maximized the ability of officials to manipulate the social and economic environment in order to produce the desired changes. Central to the entire scheme, of course, was the need for a tailor-made educational curriculum, one that would school Métis children in the skills they would need as adult labourers and farmers. For the most part, it was assumed that the primary task of education was to make the Métis productive members of society, but it was also understood that the curriculum, as an instrument of integration, must be appropriate to a working-class station in life.

The idea of Métis colonization was never embraced by the Patterson government as general policy, but it did result in a limited experiment in resettlement at Green Lake, located in the Ile-à-la-Crosse district in what was described as the 'extreme north.'[82] The idea seems to have grown out of a meeting in 1939 between the minister of education and the director of the Northern Areas Branch, and eventually it came into being as a joint venture by both government agencies.[83] The project itself involved some 125 Métis families living in the immediate area of Green Lake. These were people who had been displaced from their lands, largely owing to the inroads of white settlement from the South. In response to the Depression, the provincial government had organized a scheme to take unemployed southerners and move them into the North where they could live off the land. In the Green Lake district, these newcomers not only preempted control over the better lands and most of the hay leases but also impinged on wildlife resources. As a consequence, the local Métis population was displaced from its land patrimony and traditional liveli-hood.[84] To address this problem, the Patterson government now intro-duced the Green Lake Relocation Project, a Métis colonization experiment predicated on five essential elements.

First, in order to reestablish the Métis landbase, white settlers were removed from the area by exchanging their lands for comparable land in the more settled areas. In turn, Métis families were moved on to the vacated lands, each being allocated a forty-acre plot, held on a ninety-nine-year lease from the provincial government.[85] Families received some assistance in putting up farm buildings and breaking a small piece of land for gardening and growing feed. As well, many received a piece of farm machinery as well as some livestock, granted on a credit basis according to the amount of work each family contributed to the community.[86] For those more interested in wage labour than in farming, there was the option of receiving a small plot of land in the hamlet of Green Lake itself, but clearly the main thrust of the scheme was to get the residents into mixed farming, or at very least gardening.

Second, a large central farm operated directly under the control of the provincial government was established in the centre of the district. Essen-tially, it was an imitation of the abortive 'model farms' established on

Settlers at Green Lake. (Saskatchewan Archives Board R-A7447)

Indian reserves in the Canadian West in the early 1880s. In the initial stages, it comprised a section of land, but almost immediately it was expanded to two full sections and equipped with all the necessary machinery for large-scale farming.[87] It was worked by Métis heads of families under the supervision of a white farmer and work crew, and in theory it was designed to teach the Métis the most up-to-date farming techniques and to supplement the livestock feed requirements of the settlement.[88]

Third, it was deemed 'absolutely essential to have the full co-operation' of the Catholic Church.[89] The original idea of a Métis colony seemingly stemmed from the work of Father E. Lacombe, OMI;[90] this, combined with the fact that most Métis were Catholic, made it logical that the church would play an important role.[91] It was the Sisters of the Presentation of Mary who were commissioned to staff the school and set the moral tone for the settlement, and it was one of their members who acted as a professional nurse under contract from the government.[92]

Fourth, a school was established in the settlement as the cornerstone of integrationist policy. Very early on, the directors of the project realized that, if the Green Lake experiment were to fulfil its purpose, energies must be focused on the children through a specially modified curriculum. The parents, it was understood, had only a limited potential for improvement. As the director of the Northern Areas Branch explained, 'I do not expect that we will be able to make farmers out of them, but by growing good gardens and farming on a small scale to supplement their meager trapping and fishing returns the present adult generation will certainly be uplifted.'[93] By comparison, it was believed that Métis children could 'be molded in such a way ... that they will be able to go out in the world and make their own living, eventually being absorbed.'[94] This could only be done, however, by departing from the normal school curriculum. While the goal of basic literacy was not specifically forsworn, an altered curriculum geared to 'moral and manual instructions' was thought to be the key to upgrading the Métis standard of living and making individuals self-supporting.[95] It was for this reason that the boys were given classroom instruction in manual training, including woodworking, as well as practical lessons in carpentry from the project carpenter. By the same token, girls received formal classes in household science, including sewing and knitting. Much of this took place in the community hall, purposely built near the school and outfitted with a fully equipped kitchen and canning plant in order to emphasize the applied aspect of home economics.[96]

Finally, unlike Indian reserves throughout the West or Métis colonies in Alberta, the Green Lake experiment was not grounded in formal legislation. In 1940, the area was designated a Local Improvement District (LID), directly administered by the LID Branch of the Department of Municipal Affairs, but there was no attempt to make it a Métis homeland

School building, teacherage, Northern Areas Branch Office, etc., at Green Lake. (Saskatchewan Archives Board R-A4874-1)

or to define it legislatively. By design, Green Lake was to be an administrative experiment through which various provincial services would be delivered to a specific disadvantaged group. There was no intention of making the colony a permanent or even long-term scheme; its existence as a special government project was to be only an interim stage in its eventual evolution to municipal status.[97]

As an experiment in social engineering, the project at Green Lake held implications for Native policy generally. It certainly was one of the earliest and most concrete examples of the fact that, as ill-prepared as the province was to deal with Métis problems, the long-standing indifference to the Native plight was no longer possible. Although in some ways it was modelled on the concept of an Indian reserve, Green Lake in a very real sense represented a new departure in Saskatchewan social development: not only was it aimed specifically at a group who had been virtually ignored in the past but it also mirrored a growing recognition that only through government intervention and new initiatives could a solution be found.

The very idea of population relocation, even if not innovative in its own right, was new in its application to the province's 'forgotten' people; it also had implications for future development, especially in the southern half of the province where Métis poverty was most visible. While some officials doubted that southern Métis could be persuaded to move north,[98] the idea of grouping those Métis into distinct settlements along the lines of Green Lake was not without influence. As one education official put it, 'The education problem is only one phase of a larger problem. If the Métis could be taken in hand, perhaps after the manner of the Green Lake experiment, and made economically self-sufficient, the educational problem would at the same time be solved.'[99] In fact, as early as 1941, such a colony, founded and operated by the Catholic Church with the tacit support of the provincial government, was already in existence at Lebret, in the Qu'Appelle Valley, and at least some officials in the Patterson government were paying lip service to the notion that additional settlements should be set up in other parts of the South.

Thus, by the time the CCF swept to power in 1944, the Métis fact in Saskatchewan had assumed a certain public profile, at least within the central to southern portion of the province where the bulk of the population was concentrated. There was little public awareness of what was happening in the northern parts, nor any real appreciation of how Indians, as federal wards living within provincial boundaries, figured into local Native issues. By and large, those issues were defined in terms of the problems posed by a fragmented and marginalized Métis community in the organized municipalities of the South. Within that context, the plight of Métis people was neither an all-pervasive provincial concern, nor a dangerous political liability. But it was a moral issue that had the capacity to inflame outrage in those who believed in social justice, as well as a social and financial issue that increasingly tormented municipal and school officials. In response, the Patterson government had taken only the most tentative steps toward devising a solution but, as events would show, the thinking that emerged during this era was part of the legacy left to Tommy Douglas and his new government.

2
The CCF and the Evolution of Métis Policy

In June 1944, Tommy Douglas and the CCF won the provincial election with an impressive majority. The party captured some 53 percent of the popular vote, compared to only 19 percent six years earlier, and was elected in forty-seven of the fifty-three ridings.[1] These results, in fact, represented a striking show of support for the Baptist minister and his band of socialists. They also embodied a massive rejection of the Liberal Party, which, with the exception of a one-term Conservative government during the late depression, had enjoyed continuous power in Saskatchewan. The Douglas victory not only consigned the Liberals to the opposition benches but also relegated the Liberal Party to an obscurity that would last for the next twenty years.

During the election campaign, politicians of every political stripe had almost completely ignored the Native fact. Tom Johnston, the CCF candidate for Touchwood, did talk about Métis rehabilitation, but he was the exception.[2] The plight of the Métis was a moral issue that had insinuated itself into parts of the public administration, but overall it had little bearing on the electoral process. Numbering fewer than 12,000 in a population of 900,000,[3] the Métis were a marginalized minority largely cut off from political participation and power. Moreover, the election took place in an atmosphere that did little to heighten interest in Native issues. Fascism in Europe was crumbling, the Allied troops were mounting their final assaults, and Saskatchewan farmers once more were turning their attention to the whole issue of farm security. Like the other parties, the CCF adopted an electoral strategy that emphasized themes that made sense to a farm community struggling for ownership of the land and a decent return on investment. The party's 'nine-point program' pledged new labour legislation, an overhaul of the school system, industrial development through public ownership, farm security legislation, and a system of socialized health.[4] Likewise, the leader of the party, in his whirlwind tours, stressed those issues that played well to a farm audience: the virtues of rural life, patriotism, the need for a health-care system, and the economic lot of the farmer.[5] Douglas and his followers conducted their campaign with all the fervour and commitment of an evangelical crusade, but they did so largely without reference to the Native community.

This did not mean, however, that the Douglas government was indifferent to Native concerns. The new government was sworn in on 10 July 1944, and was plunged immediately into a period of confusion and disarray. The outgoing Liberal administration, seemingly in an act of vengeance, had destroyed ministerial and other documents that would have made the transition smoother. At the same time, Douglas and his ministers were entirely new to running a government and their own inexperience exacerbated the situation. Nevertheless, slowly but surely the new administration took control and in the process was brought face to face with the realities of Native life. Like the Liberal government before it, the CCF could not ignore the poverty and abuse afflicting Métis and Indian peoples nor could it sidestep the growing public demand that a solution be found. But unlike the Patterson government, the CCF responded with an enthusiasm and commitment that added urgency to the whole issue. Concern for the Native community was generated both by the administrative dictates of the day and by a socialist philosophy predicated on the notion of government assistance to the disadvantaged.

The government's commitment, in fact, was reflective of a more broadly based sympathy for the Native in the CCF as a whole. On 19 July, just after the party took office, the CCF held its Annual Provincial Convention. The meeting represented a grass roots assembly at which more than 200 resolutions, forwarded from constituency conventions across the province, were to be debated and voted on.[6] Like conventions everywhere, it was an opportunity for the party faithful to express their concerns and advance policy priorities. It was clearly recognized that government could not implement everything the resolutions called for. But, stirred by socialist rhetoric and fresh from a first-ever electoral victory, delegates fully expected that the convention's resolutions would serve to guide the government in implementing its reform program in the legislature. As might be expected, the resolutions were addressed to a range of topics near and dear to the farm community – returning soldiers, cooperative farming, farm debt legislation, the nationalization of electric utilities, and health care. However, contrary to what party conventions had done in the past, delegates also passed a resolution calling for assistance to the Métis people:

> **Whereas**, we have many Indian Reserves in Saskatchewan, inhabited by the Métis people, these same people living without any schools and medical care, many of their children being diseased and blind, under the present conditions none of the children in the reserve being allowed to

attend any of the adjoining schools, there being at this time 52 children of school age on the Little Bone Reserve who are now unable to attend any schools,

therefore Be It Resolved: That we request the Provincial Government to take the necessary steps to see that these Métis people be given proper treatment and care, so that they can associate with other people.

Be It Further Resolved: That scholarships be granted to the Métis people so that they can educate themselves adequately to take their place in the legislature and other places and represent their own people. – Carried.[7]

What is interesting about this resolution, apart from it being the first of its kind, is that it was actually a reverberation of public opinion, stemming from the past. Little Bone, in fact, was another name for the Crescent Lake area. It was there, it will be recalled, that the Métis lived in absolutely deplorable conditions – conditions that, two years earlier, had been condemned by the *Yorkton Enterprise*, indicted by Justice Potter, and investigated by two branches of the Health Department. It is reasonable to assume that the resolution had been brought forward from the Yorkton constituency where public opinion had been so inflamed over the situation, but the fact that it was endorsed by a provincewide convention spoke to a more broadly based concern in the CCF that the problems of the Métis be addressed. The solution implied by the resolution was an integrationist model based on self-help, education, and political activism, all of which were in keeping with the ideological propensity of the membership.[8]

Further steeling the government's commitment was the fact that the Douglas regime simply 'inherited' a preexisting and administratively confused problem. The carryover of the Native issue can be traced through the bureaucratic paperchase from the Patterson government to the new Douglas government. In May, for example, two months before Douglas took office, the RCMP investigated a case in Indian Head involving break-and-enter and eventually arrested a Métis by the name of Fred Fayant.[9] The arresting officer noted that the individual had fourteen children, none of whom had ever attended school. The provincial school act stipulated that all children living within a three-and-a-half-mile radius of a school were required by law to attend; but since this particular family lived more than four miles from the nearest school, the officer concluded that the parents were not in violation of the law. He nevertheless deplored the fact that 'these children [were] denied the privilege of obtaining the required education so relevant to their future welfare in the community.'[10]

The matter was thought to 'be of a sufficiently serious nature,' so the officer's report was forwarded both to the deputy attorney-general and the director of the Child Welfare Branch.[11] Child Welfare insisted that it could not act without a formal complaint of child neglect, so it referred the matter to the School Attendance Branch of the Department of Education.[12] By this time, the new CCF government was in place but, largely unaffected by the change in government, the matter continued to make its way through the bureaucracy. In July the chief attendance officer asked for information from the rural municipality in which the Fayant family lived. To his surprise, he was informed by the secretary treasurer of the municipality that the education department itself, only a year earlier, had investigated the status of Métis children living in the area.[13] The report eventually was dug up and dusted off and then seemingly forwarded to the new minister of education, W.S. Lloyd.

Lloyd, in office for only a few weeks, was not in a position to act and so he asked for more information, particularly in regard to the notion that Métis children were being excluded from schools due to the prevalence of disease.[14] Eventually, both he and the premier, who also held the health portfolio until 1949,[15] received health reports on the Métis south of Yorkton and in the Crescent Lake area where the Fayant family lived. The reports had been prepared more than two years earlier by the Department of Public Health but had never been acted upon. In forwarding the reports, the deputy minister of health pointed out gratuitously that, while the Métis and Indians in the two areas needed medical attention, they after all were the responsibility of the municipalities and that the only real solution was rehabilitation, especially by providing education facilities.[16]

And so the whole sorry episode had come full circle. Initially, the Métis in the southern half of the province had been defined as the responsibility of the municipalities and now almost a decade later the provincial bureaucracy was still trapped in the same mindset. Various provincial departments had taken the time to look into the matter and even submit reports, but nothing had come of it because the problem was always seen as some other department's headache. The Douglas government, in fact, had inherited a bureaucracy paralyzed by inertia. The civil service lacked ministerial direction but, more than that, it lacked the collective will to deal with Native issues in a coordinated and effective way. The challenge for the CCF would be not only to find a solution to Native problems but also to develop an administrative focus through which government intervention would be effective.

To make matters worse, there were few lessons to be learned from outside Saskatchewan. Other provinces had done almost nothing to address Native issues or, for that matter, to acknowledge the existence of a problem. Even in Manitoba and Alberta, where circumstances were similar to those in Saskatchewan, few reforms had been introduced, and those that did exist had little appeal or relevance in the Wheat Province. On the contrary, developments in Saskatchewan were often seen as precedent-setting and worthy of emulation elsewhere. During the early war years, for example, officials in Manitoba had come to the conclusion that an academic education for northern Natives dependent on hunting and fishing was not entirely appropriate, and to find a solution to this problem they had petitioned the Patterson government for information on the experiment taking place at Green Lake.[17]

By the same token, in contrast to Saskatchewan, officials in both Manitoba and Alberta defined the so-called 'Métis problem' as a northern issue, rather than one rooted in the established municipalities of the South. This was made explicit during an interprovincial conference held in Regina in the late 1940s to discuss Native rehabilitation. According to Ivan Schultz, Manitoba's minister of health and welfare, the Métis problem in his province was exclusively a provincial matter in that it was situated largely in the unorganized areas of the North and had little to do with the municipalities of the South. Underscoring the limited nature of Native reform there, he said that the main solution to the problem had been to cooperate with the federal government in building hospitals and recognizing various trapping and fur rights in the North.[18]

Similarly at the Regina conference, A.C. McCully, the supervisor of Métis rehabilitation in Alberta, insisted that the Métis and Indian problem in that province was mostly a northern one, although he did admit that some preliminary concerns about the problem had been raised by municipalities in the South. Nevertheless, as he pointed out, the main solution was the creation of Métis settlements in the northern part of the province.[19] These settlements, initially numbering close to a dozen and later reduced to eight, had been created by the Social Credit government of William Aberhart during the closing years of the Depression. In theory, the settlement scheme acknowledged the Métis as original inhabitants of the land and thus gave them preference over whites in regard to hunting and fishing in the area. But, in practice, the settlements were never rationalized as a matter of Aboriginal right; they were seen solely as a rehabilitation project, meant to assimilate destitute Métis into the regional farming community, under the heavy hand of government control. During the Depression, social assistance money had been scarce, so setting aside land for rehabilitation in the North – particularly land that was not yet wanted by white settlers – was an attractive alternative to burdening the treasury. At the Regina conference, McCully maintained that the Métis were under no compulsion to live in these settlements,[20] but his silence about what government assistance might be available for those who chose otherwise spoke volumes about the limits of government reform. In point of fact, the Ewing Commission, which had recommended the establishment of such settlements in its 1936 report, made it quite clear that Métis who did not join a colony would surrender all further claims to public assistance.[21]

Thus, on coming to power, the Douglas government was confronted with an irrepressible need to act on Native reform; however, there was little in provincial experience, whether within Saskatchewan or elsewhere, that provided a well-defined prescription for government reform.

The Métis Society

An added pressure on the new administration, although as it turned out not a very effective one, was the Saskatchewan Métis Society (SMS). The society supposedly represented all Métis in the province and was meant to act as a lobby, accomplishing collectively what Métis could not do individually. When Douglas came to power, the SMS immediately made representations requesting government assistance.[22] The Douglas papers contain a number of letters from members of the society, as well as sympathetic replies from the premier. The CCF, which owed its origins to democratic mass organization, had a natural inclination to support the activities of such an organization. The premier, in particular, believed that if disadvantaged groups were to receive assistance, the government would have to work with a representative body that could identify the needs of its constituents and support the reforms initiated by the province. It was for this reason that, very early on, the Douglas government openly encouraged – some say pressured – Indians in the province to organize a provincewide association through which they could relate to both the provincial and federal governments.[23] The same enthusiasm, however, was never shown for the Métis Society, despite the fact that the need for cooperation was just as great. There is little evidence that the government did much to support the activities of the SMS, either through encouragement or through financial assistance, and still less evidence of any notion of partnership with the society. The reason for this paradox can be found in the checkered history of the society itself and in the self-interest of the CCF. In all, four factors were at play.

First, by the summer of 1944, the SMS's organization was in shambles. The evolution of the society can be traced to informal meetings of southern Métis in Regina in 1931; to the creation of an association known as 'The Halfbreeds of Saskatchewan' in the mid-thirties; and finally to the formal incorporation of the SMS in 1937.[24] The idea behind the organization was to create a provincewide collectivity that could speak with one voice in demanding government assistance and a redress of historical wrongs. Most of the original leadership came from those living in or near Regina and included people like Joe McKenzie, Joseph Ross, Henry McKenzie Sr., and Joe LaRocque.[25] These were men of vision who, despite

Joseph Z. LaRocque (centre) and family, May 1947. (Saskatchewan Archives Board R-A7987)

the inertia generated by the Depression, set out to turn things around. This was not the result, however, because the society was plagued by insuperable difficulties.

At the heart of the problem was the strategy the society initially adopted. Many believed, based on the testimony of elders, that the federal government's Scrip Commission twenty-five years earlier had not fully paid for Métis land surrenders and that scrip should have been paid to subsequent generations.[26] Hence, although the society recognized the need for Métis education and relief, land and the issue of Aboriginal rights became its main raison d'être and informed a major portion of the political consciousness of the membership. The main strategy was to present a petition to the federal government, and to that end the leadership approached Zacharias Hamilton, secretary of the Saskatchewan Historical Society. Hamilton was a newspaper man and unsuccessful real estate speculator.[27] Married to a Métis woman, he also had taken a special interest in Native history, often conducting collaborative research with other amateur historians from the Native community.[28] Hamilton agreed to assist the SMS and eventually secured the support of A.T. Hunt and J.A. Gregory.[29] The two men were members of the history society but, more important, both were Liberal MLAs. Seemingly as a result of these connections, the Métis Society eventually obtained a $10,000 grant from the Patterson government in order to press its land claim against the dominion.[30] In 1940, the society contracted with the law firm of Noonan and Hodges to prepare, in cooperation with Zacharias Hamilton, a land claims brief.

By this time, however, it was already painfully apparent to some that the·society's strategy had been a mistake. The land claims issue was predicated on the understanding that the main responsibility for the Métis rested not with the provincial government but with the dominion. Indeed, at a meeting with the premier and senior officials, the SMS leadership even conceded that, temporarily at least, it would be putting aside demands for reforms that were mostly of a provincial nature.[31] This was tantamount to absolving the province of all responsibility for addressing the everyday problems of the Métis. Patterson, undoubtedly sensing the opportunity to offload the whole matter onto the federal government, probably had no hesitation in making the $10,000 grant, although even then he refused to intercede with Ottawa on behalf of the SMS. Moreover, nobody outside the society itself believed that there was a legal case to be made. Hamilton himself had already concluded that, while moral arguments could be made, the federal government was under no legal obligation to recognize Métis Aboriginal rights as a basis for additional compensation.[32] The predominant point of view generally was that, if the Métis had had rights by virtue of their Aboriginal status – and even that was in doubt – then those rights had already been extinguished by the Scrip Commission process. Unfortunately for the SMS, the law firm it had hired was even more damning in its appraisal of the case, completed in 1943. Essentially, Noonan and Hodges concluded categorically that the Métis did not have, nor had they ever had, any Aboriginal rights enforceable in the courts.[33] Indeed, while they agreed with Hamilton that the Métis had a moral claim, they insisted that even that claim had already been settled by the dominion government.[34] In effect, they were 'telling the Métis that their strategy ... had been a mistake.'[35]

All of this was a shattering blow to a society that, since its inception, had identified so closely with the Aboriginal rights issue. On the one hand, the SMS had given the province a mandate to ignore the Métis; on the other hand, it had commissioned a brief authored by lawyers who privately repudiated claims against the federal government. There was already a widely held belief in the Métis community that nothing would be done by government in any event, and this cynicism was compounded by a deepening sense of frustration and demoralization in the membership. Although Noonan and Hodges did prepare a brief meant to support Métis land claims against the federal government, in effect the whole land claims issue only served to exacerbate the already tentative state of the Métis Society and contributed in no small way to its near disintegration in 1943.

Second, and related to the issue of tactics, was a leadership problem. When war broke out in Europe, hundreds of Métis volunteered for overseas service and this had the effect of siphoning off some of the more forceful and articulate leadership. Where this was not the case, potential leaders refused to take on the job because they lacked the education and financial means to play an active role. And still others, identifying with white society and denying their Native heritage, refused to have anything to do with the SMS. As Joe Ross explained,

> There were all kinds of good leaders but they didn't seem to want to come forward ... there were many who didn't want to have anything to do with the SMS for various reasons. Many felt the politicians would destroy it anyway. Another thing is they felt the Métis people weren't reliable. There were all kinds of people who wouldn't admit they were Métis – couldn't talk to them at all – they wouldn't have anything to do with you. A lot of these people felt 'Well, I'm doing fine. Why should I be bothered with anything like that?'[36]

Such a situation was bound to weaken the society, and among the consequences was a leadership that tended to be co-opted by sympathetic whites outside the Métis community. The trust placed in Zacharias Hamilton was but one symptom of the fact that the SMS leadership lacked the political consciousness and acumen to make a difference. Indeed, by the early forties, the leadership had all but resigned itself to a course of inaction.[37]

Third, there were deep divisions in the membership. From the outset, there was a split between the South and the North, which, according to Joe Ross, 'held back the Métis Society for a long time.'[38] In the southern part of the province, most Métis spoke either French or English and were closely tied to a way of life dominated by white settlers; however, in the North, they often spoke only Cree and their way of life was much closer to that of the Indian, subsisting off the land.[39] This meant that communications between the two regions was sometimes difficult, if not strained, and that each had problems and priorities not always shared by the other.[40] It was for this very reason that in 1943 the northern Métis organized a rival collective known as the Saskatchewan Métis Association (SMA).[41] Another divisive factor was the willingness of the leadership to tolerate outside influence. Indicative was a letter penned by Toby McGillis, from the Willow Bunch local, to Joe LaRocque, past president of SMS:

> why do you have Englishmen run your business for you, you are supposed to be educated enough to run your [own] business affairs. When as you know, they are mostly working for themselves ... We don't know

half of what's going on having them going ahead to do as they like. In Alberta I heard they would have never gotten their land, if they hadn't gone ahead and speak for themselves ... now they have what they wanted already but we don't seem to make any headway.[42]

The only explanation Ross could offer, somewhat apologetically, was that no one could be found in the Métis community to provide the necessary leadership.[43] Still another cause of division was the rivalry between Regina and Saskatoon. The original leadership had been closely associated with the Queen's City but, when it entered a period of dormancy in the early forties, it was preempted by a new group located mainly in Saskatoon.[44] In 1941-2, the Saskatoon group pronounced the old executive defunct and, in violation of the SMS constitution, held an annual convention at which a new slate of officers was elected.[45] Although this raised the ire of the Regina faction, the Saskatoon group ultimately prevailed, but not without causing considerable disenchantment in the South.

Fourth, the Douglas regime may have found the SMS leadership politically suspect, at least in the initial stages. For some time, the Catholic Church had actively pressured the Métis to vote Liberal and until 1940 the society had been presided over by two presidents – Joe LaRocque and Mike Vandale – who were active Liberal supporters.[46] At the same time, the main strategy of the SMS executive had been to court Liberal politicians in order to present their case to Ottawa. It was precisely for this reason that the society had worked so closely with Hamilton and his Liberal friends and that the business of the SMS became so intertwined with Liberal Party politics. LaRocque, in particular, was notoriously partisan and openly campaigned for the Liberal Party, even at SMS meetings.[47] This may also explain why the CCF did little to attract the Métis vote during the election of 1944. In May, Joe Ross, one of the original organizers of the SMS and a member of the CCF, wrote to the party secretary, A.O. Smith, and advised him that the Métis could swing the vote in as many as five constituencies. To that end, he also recommended that a committee of Métis be set up to advise the party on a platform.[48] The idea in turn was passed on to Douglas and five sitting CCF MLAs, but in the end it was never acted upon. Douglas seemingly did not like the idea of Métis advisors and instead asked John Brockelbank and two other colleagues to draw up a pamphlet that could be circulated among the Métis.[49] There is no evidence the pamphlet was ever created, nor was Ross invited to be part of the process, although he did receive a letter from the party asking him to draft an open letter to the Métis inviting them to support the CCF.[50] The party's indifference may have been a calculated response to a relatively unimportant minority; however, it may also have reflected the perceived partisanship of the SMS.[51]

And so, when Douglas came to power in the summer of 1944, he was confronted by a Métis organization that lacked credibility on a number of counts. Neither the premier nor his cabinet were opposed to the society as a would-be voice for an oppressed minority, nor were they ever openly hostile to the lobby that the SMS represented. In fact, soon after its election, the CCF granted the society $500 so that a Métis delegation could go to Ottawa to present the Noonan/Hodges brief to the federal government.[52] Nevertheless, there is little evidence that the Douglas government went out of its way to bolster or reinvigorate the SMS. As had been expected, Ottawa said no to the Métis brief, thereby reaffirming provincial responsibility for the Métis; however, even then, the Douglas government made little effort to work with the SMS.

Certainly one consideration was the integrity of the organization. Douglas could not afford to support publicly a society whose character and representativeness were at issue in the Métis community itself. But that is not the whole explanation. The CCF was intrinsically egalitarian and, as such, committed to integrating the Métis, as citizens of the province, into mainstream society. The commitment stemmed not from a recognition of Métis ethnicity or even Aboriginality but from the notion that the Métis were a disadvantaged group who, like the Mennonites in the province, desperately needed government assistance.[53] It was acknowledged that as a visible minority the Métis historically had been oppressed by racism and discrimination, but it was never understood that salvation was to be found in an enhanced ethnicity, such as represented by the SMS. Indeed, the Métis would be liberated from their desperate situation not by a renewed sense of Nativeness, which would only perpetuate their segregation, but by integrating them – in fact, assimilating them – into society as competitive and fully functioning citizens. While this might entail a recognition of the special cultural needs of Métis school children, education itself was seen as a tool of integration, not of Métis ethnic enhancement.[54] It was precisely for this reason that at no time did the Douglas government ever experiment with even minor forms of self-determination or acknowledge the national Aboriginal status of the Métis. This was clearly illustrated in 1952 when the Green Lake Co-operative Association was advised by the resident director of the Saskatchewan Marketing Services not to include the word 'Métis' in the name of their organization. As he explained, 'I strongly urged them not to use the word ... since we are looking forward to the day when all citizens of Saskatchewan are of equal status, regardless of race, colour and creed. I therefore urged them not to brand themselves with any name indicating special race or colour.'[55] The renunciation of Métis ethnicity explains why the CCF did little to encourage the political organization of the Métis and why the government maintained an arms-length distance from the

SMS. Moreover, because the Métis were a provincial responsibility, there was little benefit – and some liability – in encouraging a Métis organization that had the potential to obstruct CCF reforms.

Despite these considerations, the Douglas government could not simply ignore the SMS, although initially it tried to do just that. In 1945, Fred DeLorande, from Monto Nebo near Saskatoon, was elected president of the society and almost immediately raised the issue of SMS involvement in reforms contemplated by the government. In May, he sent a letter directly to Douglas and, among other things, offered to meet with the premier in Regina.[56] He suggested that, as leader of the Métis association, he was deeply interested in the welfare of his people and had information that would be useful. He added, however, that it would be necessary for the government to pay his train fare to Regina at a cost of $19.[57] He waited more than six weeks, but received no reply, not even an acknowledgment of his letter. Consequently, in a somewhat more strident tone, he penned a second letter to the premier, complaining that he was being ignored in matters directly pertaining to the Métis. Specifically, he had learned that the government was going to examine Métis education, but without his input, and he questioned 'why [the government] should go over [his] head.'[58] Again he received no reply, so in June he sent off yet a third letter addressed to the premier. Finally, in midsummer, he received a reply from O.W. Valleau, the minister of social welfare. The minister informed him that he was looking into the matter of a conference with the Métis, but added that should such a meeting take place, the Métis delegation would have to pay its own expenses.[59]

Not to be put off, DeLorande lobbied E.L. Bowerman, MP for Prince Albert, as well as G.P. Van Eaton, MLA for Shellbrook, both of whom wrote letters to Douglas asking that the province meet with the SMS.[60] By this time there was new urgency to such a meeting because the area around Monto Nebo had been hailed out and Métis farmers were hurting financially. Moreover, DeLorande was now arguing that the government owed the Métis Society thousands of dollars, the balance left from the $10,000 Patterson grant. DeLorande reasoned that the government had paid Noonan and Hodges $7,000 for their services, as well $500 in support of the Ottawa delegation, thus leaving a balance of $2,500 still owing to the society.[61]

Douglas's response was less than enthusiastic. In late summer, he sent replies to both Bowerman and Van Eaton thanking them for their concern. He nevertheless informed them that the government had no immediate plans for a conference with the Métis and that should such a meeting be scheduled they would be informed in due course.[62] In September, both Bowerman and Van Eaton took up the issue once more, again insisting that only a conference could deal with the outstanding

Métis issues, some of which dated back twenty-five years. Bowerman pointed out that he was aware the government was not contemplating a conference, but nevertheless insisted that such a meeting was necessary. He even suggested that the provincial government should pay at least some of the expenses to have DeLorande, if not the entire executive of the SMS, attend such a meeting.[63] Douglas responded to this latest pressure by informing the two politicians that he had taken up the matter with the minister of social services and other members of cabinet 'and hope[d] to get some immediate action on same.'[64] That the premier had, in fact, referred the matter to cabinet is not entirely certain, however. A full two months later, Douglas sent an interoffice memo to Valleau advising him that DeLorande was the man who heads 'one of the Métis associations' and asking him to contact DeLorande to discuss Métis problems.[65] Had the conference been under active consideration, it would hardly have been necessary to introduce DeLorande's name, especially in such a vague way, to the minister under whose auspices the meeting was to take place.

For the time being, the premier's promise to consider a conference eased the pressure to act immediately. The government also dealt with the other two outstanding issues by simply dismissing them as a charge against the government. In November, Bowerman was informed by the premier that the question of hail damage was not a provincial responsibility and that the matter should be referred to the Federal Department of Agriculture.[66] And as to money owing the Métis society, Valleau looked into the matter and found that, of the original $10,000 Patterson grant, $7,000 had been paid out to the lawyers who had prepared the brief and the remaining $3,000 had simply reverted to treasury. As he explained to Douglas, 'the grant originally was made for the express purpose of assisting in the preparation of their case, and since it did not require the entire amount it cannot be assumed that the balance is owing to anyone.'[67]

The question of meeting with the SMS, however, would simply not go away. In November, the CCF held a convention in Saskatoon and both Douglas and Valleau agreed to meet DeLorande in the Bridge City to discuss Métis affairs. The meeting, however, never took place because the premier became ill and returned to Regina prematurely.[68] The matter dragged on through the winter months and into the spring of 1946 when finally it was revealed why Douglas was hesitant to meet with the SMS. In a letter to DeLorande in May, the premier outlined his reservations and asked for information:

> The government is desirous of giving every consideration to the claims of your people. It has been difficult, however, to ascertain the representatives of your organization in this province. It appears that it has not

been functioning very actively in the past, and I would strongly suggest that every effort be made to revive your activities.

I would also like to receive official representations from your organization in the form of a brief or otherwise, setting out your aims and objectives for the purpose of improving the conditions of the Métis population in this province. When this is received I shall be in a better position to work out some scheme whereby the conditions of your people may be improved.[69]

What Douglas did not say in the letter was that the government had already decided to convene a Métis conference. Interestingly enough, however, it was not to be a meeting with the SMS per se but rather it would be a convention for Métis people at large. With that in mind, the premier sent out a circular letter in mid-July inviting the Métis throughout the province to attend a meet with the government in the Regina Court House on July 30.[70] Delegates would be required to pay their own expenses, but the timing of the one-day convention was meant to coincide with the capital's fair week, which normally attracted Natives from outside the city.

The meeting was attended by government officials and some thirty-one Métis delegates from both the southern and northern portions of the province.[71] The chair of the conference was Dr. Morris Shumiatcher, the main legal counsel for the Executive Council and Douglas's chief advisor and troubleshooter concerning Indian and Métis affairs.[72] As a child, Shumiatcher had visited the Sarcee Reserve outside Calgary and had rubbed shoulders with Indians at annual fairs; his high school teacher had been John Laurie, secretary of the Indian Association of Alberta and a man with whom he continued to share an active interest in Native issues.[73] Shumiatcher's position with the CCF increasingly called upon him to act as liaison between the Native community and the government, and it was in that capacity that he now presided over the proceedings of the convention.[74]

From the very beginning, it was evident that old tensions in the Métis community had not abated. The morning session was taken up by a heated exchange over whether the Métis Society, as currently constituted, should be maintained or scrapped in favour of a new, more representative organization. From the perspective of officials, this was an all-important issue because government would deal only with an association that could speak with authority on behalf of the wider Métis community.[75] Almost immediately, a motion of no confidence in the SMS was introduced by Mr. Knudson of Regina, and the subsequent debate revolved around the implied notion that the society had been hijacked by northern representatives in and around Saskatoon.[76] The motion was defeated, in theory

Morris C. Shumiatcher when legal advisor to the premier, ca. 1947.
(Saskatchewan Archives Board R-B2580)

confirming the SMS as the official representative of Métis people in the
province. But the old divisions resurfaced once again. This time at issue
was the internal operations and constitution of the Métis Society and
especially provocative was the appointment of a small Advisory Committee to liaise with the government. Southern delegates insisted that
committee members should come from Regina because of the proximity
to government; northern delegates demanded that the committee be
made up of representatives from the executive of the SMS located in
the North.[77] In the end, a compromise was reached. It was agreed that
delegates would choose an Advisory Committee but only on a temporary
basis. This would give the Métis Society an opportunity to elect the
membership of the committee at its annual convention, scheduled for
the following October. It was further agreed that the interim committee
would be composed of five elected representatives from across the
province as well as the president of the SMS as an ex officio member.[78]
Although the impasse had been circumvented, old animosities remained.

The conference was also devoted to social and economic issues. Delegates spoke to particular concerns or problems experienced by individuals
and groups in their regions and, in some cases, made lengthy statements
for the benefit of government officials. They called for a Royal Commission into the deplorable conditions experienced by the Métis; they
appealed to history and decried the systematic plunder of Métis lands;

they called for government assistance in schooling their children; they asked for better housing and health services; and, above all else, they pleaded for their own land in order to make a living and recover their independence.[79] One delegate recommended settling the Métis on five- to ten-acre plots along the lines of the colonization system already established at Green Lake.[80] But he also recommended that, where individuals had sufficient business acumen and experience, Métis people be given the opportunity to develop commercial gardens, large-scale farms, mink ranching, and industries such as canning.[81] The recommendation spoke to the oft-repeated demand in the Métis community that, as important as small-scale subsistence farming might be, commercial and business opportunities should also be made available.

In his speech to the convention, the premier promised to be brief because the intent of government was not to talk but to listen to what the Métis themselves had to say. His main hopes, he said, were that the convention would create a non-partisan, non-sectarian organization that could speak with one voice for the Métis of Saskatchewan; and that delegates would 'give to the Ministers who are responsible, particularly Mr. Valleau, minister of social welfare, and his officials, some ideas, your reaction to various proposals, so that they may be able to sit down and work out a long term policy for the rehabilitation and re-establishment of the Métis people.'[82] In keeping with the tenor of his speech, Douglas insisted that any conclusions the government had arrived at were only tentative and anything done only experimental in nature.[83] In all, government spokespeople insisted that they had no political purpose in mind and that they were there to listen to what the Métis themselves had to say as a basis for formulating policy.

As it turned out, the 1946 convention was the last real attempt to breathe life into the Métis Society during the Douglas years. Only months earlier, the government had provided financial assistance, and even applied pressure, to bring about the union of three competing Indian associations. But in the case of the Métis, there was little evidence of the same determination. Douglas seemingly viewed the Métis convention as a last-ditch effort and, when nothing came of it, he did little to renew the initiative. The October annual meeting of the Métis Society never took place and this all but sounded the death knell of the organization.[84] In November, two members of the Métis Advisory Committee petitioned the government for a $1,000 grant 'on account of the deteriorated condition' of the SMS.[85] However, because the two men did not speak for the Métis society, nor even for the whole Advisory Committee, the request was refused.[86] In 1947, Malcolm Norris, a one-time provincial organizer of the Indian Association of Alberta and now a field officer for the CCF in northern Saskatchewan, attempted to revive the Métis Society but ultimately abandoned the effort as hopeless.[87] Two years later, Joe Ross made a similar attempt with the same results.[88]

Thereafter, the SMS remained a cherished goal of Métis leaders but, as a fully representative and functioning association, it existed in name only. This meant that the SMS was now eclipsed by the recently organized Indian association, the Union of Saskatchewan Indians (USI). Although the USI sometimes included Métis concerns in its representations to government,[89] for the most part the Métis now lacked organizational expression. That guaranteed that they would be denied input into the reform program brought forward by the CCF.

Métis Reform

That the Douglas government would respond to the problems of the Métis was never in doubt. The southern Métis were among the most disadvantaged group in the province, but, more than that, their poverty was highly visible because, unlike in the far North, development and the bulk of the general population were concentrated in the southern half of the province. For a government whose slogan was 'humanity first,' the CCF could not ignore a people whose poverty was so blatant. The conditions under which they lived were completely anathema to the principles underpinning much of the humanist doctrine publicly espoused by Douglas and others; and they represented an embarrassment to a party whose political principles and rhetoric cast the CCF as the champion of the underclassed.

Also not in doubt was the fact that the Métis were clearly the responsibility of the provincial government. The federal government's inevitable rejection of the Noonan/Hodges brief served only to confirm what Douglas had already accepted: that constitutionally the Métis were subjects of provincial jurisdiction.[90] Equally accepted was the fact that the problems were of such magnitude that they could not be offloaded onto the municipalities. As late as 1949, a meeting of the Regina branch of the Canadian Association of Social Workers reiterated that 'the [Métis] problem should not lie at a local level because the financial burden rests too heavily on the municipality.'[91] In Douglas's mind, there was no doubt that arrangements would have to be made to ease the financial, if not the administrative, burden placed on municipalities where congregations of Métis were most pronounced.

Murray Dobbin has argued that the CCF had no special programs for the Métis in the South,[92] but this assessment is entirely inaccurate. It stems from a failure to appreciate the internal workings of the social assistance program introduced by the Douglas government. During the Patterson era, social relief had been crassly manipulated as part of the patronage system mobilized to win elections.[93] This meant that voters who refused to support the government often found their relief cut off soon after the election. Moreover, municipalities tended to operate in such a way as to minimize benefits and to shame those who asked for assistance. It was a system that the CCF found absolutely abhorrent and one targeted almost immediately for reform.

Before 1944, social aid had been referred to as direct relief and came under the jurisdiction of the Department of Municipal Affairs.[94] The relief program was financed jointly by both the municipality and the province, but was administered by the former. The province normally increased its grant to municipalities with unusually high concentrations of relief recipients and assumed full financial responsibility for indigents who could not meet the municipal residency requirement of one year. The province also paid all of the relief costs of those who lived in parts of Saskatchewan where municipalities had not been organized, including the Local Improvement Districts (LID) and the Northern Administration Area in the far North. One problem was that municipalities found it difficult to deliver an adequate relief program because they lacked the financial resources. This was exacerbated by the fact that often those municipalities least able to pay their share of the costs had the highest number of indigents.[95] As a consequence, municipal officials commonly took the view that relief should not be given to anyone already receiving other forms of assistance, such as mothers' allowance or old age pensions.[96] They also actively discouraged relief applications, often by publishing the names of recipients in a deliberate effort to socially stigmatize those on assistance.[97] Of all the municipalities, the City of Saskatoon had a reputation for being among the most heartless when it came to relief applications.

Douglas was bombarded with complaints over the demeaning and inhumane way the relief system was administered, and so, not surprisingly, only four months after coming to office the government created the Department of Social Welfare and Rehabilitation (DSWR). This introduced a whole new focus on the proper administration of what was now called social aid. As of January 1945, recipients of mothers' allowance and old age pensions, as well as their dependants, were given free medical, dental, and nursing services, a coverage that could not be found anywhere else in Canada.[98] Moreover, the province now took a more direct hand in standardizing the delivery of services. As a guide for the municipalities, the DSWR drew up a minimum social aid schedule and, although adherence was only voluntary, the new schedule did establish a benchmark for a minimum level of service throughout the province.[99] It also redefined and enlarged the role of provincial field staff. Rather than concentrating on the financial relationship between the province and municipalities, social welfare officers were now asked to guide municipalities toward a more professional and adequate delivery of services, to intercede with municipalities on behalf of applicants who had been turned down or received insufficient aid, and to work with families to make them self-sufficient once more.[100] And there was now a far greater tendency on the part of the province to assume 100 percent of the responsibility for indigents neglected by the municipalities.

The importance of the DSWR should not be overstated – the reform of the welfare system was limited by budgetary constraints and related staff shortages. It was only near the end of Douglas's term, when the Unemployment Assistance Agreement between the province and the federal government was signed, that federal transfer payments provided badly needed assistance.[101] Nevertheless, the creation of the DSWR and related measures were important because it extended the welfare safety net to encompass a much wider clientele, including the Métis people. Like other underclassed people in the province, Natives as individuals were embraced by a more humane system of social assistance, predicated on human dignity and right. And as a mobile and displaced minority living on road allowances, the Métis now became the target of welfare assistance financed entirely by the province.

It was within the context of its social welfare policy that the Douglas government evolved its main solution to Métis problems – colonization. Natives as individuals could always go through the normal channels of applying for welfare from the municipalities. But where there were large groups, receiving 100 percent of welfare from the province, the idea of congregating and relocating them into exclusive Métis settlements seemed logical. W.S. Lloyd, within weeks of taking over the education portfolio, was among the first in the new administration to articulate the notion. As minister of education, he had fallen heir to the perception that lack of education was at the root of Métis problems. In reference to the Métis south of Yorkton and to the public stir caused by Justice Potter's findings, Lloyd sent a memorandum to the premier in which he hinted at the idea of a colony: 'I notice in going over our file a number of letters and newspaper clippings which speak in a very condemning fashion of the treatment of the Métis in this area. While it is definitely a problem of education and adequate facilities for education, I suggest that that is not the primary problem and it would seem to be desirable to do something to centralize these people a bit in order to provide educational facilities on a reasonable scale.'[102] Lloyd's suggestion, of course, was anything but original. In a generic sense, colonies were part of the bequest inherited from the Patterson government. No sooner had Douglas taken office than he received petitions from residents at Green Lake asking him to continue the project started by the Liberals.[103] At the same time, the predominant opinion in departmental records, such as they were, was that, although only in existence for a few years, Green Lake had considerable promise and warranted imitation in other areas.[104] Moreover, that colonization could be applied successfully in the South was itself attested to by the existence of Lebret, a Métis settlement in the Qu'Appelle Valley operated by the Oblates. Given the lack of alternatives and the inexperience of the new administration, the existence of two prototype colonies, increasingly touted as the answer to Métis ills, was bound to be persuasive.

Equally important, the idea of colonies meshed with the philosophical predilections of the CCF. Even before 1944, the party had abandoned most of its left-wing rhetoric in the interest of being elected and, once in power, it jettisoned the remaining socialist trappings in favour of a liberal reformist, or populist, posture.[105] There was no attempt to destroy the class structure, nor any impulse to subvert the normal operation of the market economy. On the contrary, a main goal of populist philosophy was to strengthen that economy by curbing vested interests that prevented small businesses from being competitive. Most of the farmers who supported the CCF believed that poverty and destitution were the products of an economy distorted by monopolists and financiers and that it was the legitimate role of government to liberate the individual from the clutches of such interests.[106] At the same time, many in the CCF were animated by a heightened sense of Christian humanitarianism, often personified by the premier himself. Douglas and others in the CCF believed fervently in the canons of Social Gospel, based on the New Testament emphasis on establishing the Kingdom of God on earth. It was a philosophy premised on the doctrine of love and it proclaimed the sanctity of cooperation as opposed to competition; hence, it represented an explicit rejection of the 'survival of the fittest' ethos through which big business rationalized the gap between the rich and poor.[107]

Colonies, as a rehabilitation scheme for the Métis, were entirely in keeping with this thinking because they were seen as a way of making the Métis competitive in mainstream society. By removing the Métis from the road allowances and grouping them into distinct settlements, the government would be able to manipulate the environment to maximize local community development. The understanding was that, if the Métis could not integrate individually, they might do so collectively through the creation of economically viable, self-sustaining communities. Through proper training, self-actualization, and cooperation, they would evolve as a community of farmers contributing to the regional agrarian economy. The scheme seemed all the more realistic because it was widely assumed that the Métis, as Natives, shared the Indians' reverence for collectivist principles. In practice, this meant that the Douglas government, while in many ways replicating the Green Lake scheme, sought to impose its own philosophical stamp on the development of colonies.

This was reflected in the infrastructure within which colonies were administered. Morris Shumiatcher favoured the creation of special enabling legislation to deal with the Métis situation. At one time, he had done some legal work for the Indian Association of Alberta and was generally familiar with Aboriginal rights issues.[108] He pointed in particular to the fact that in the thirties Alberta had passed the Métis Population Betterment Act, thereby creating formal Métis settlements, and argued that the legislation had 'gone some way in solving the problems of these people.'[109] His recommendation, however, was never acted on simply because the idea of creating legislatively sanctioned ethnic enclaves contradicted the goals of the CCF. Douglas never saw Métis colonies as long-term Native homelands, as implied by the Alberta legislation; on the contrary, they were to be short-term experiments designed to meld the Métis community with the wider population. For that reason, colonies in Saskatchewan were created and operated as temporary rehabilitation projects under existing welfare legislation. This meant that the day-to-day administration and delivery of services to the colonies were overseen by the DSWR. The only exception was Green Lake, which, because of its peculiar position in the far North, remained under the jurisdiction of the Local Improvement Districts Branch of the Department of Municipal Affairs, as it had been under the Liberals. Policy for all colonies, in theory, was determined by the cabinet, initially acting on the advice of Morris Shumiatcher and later on that of a coordinating body known as the Committee on Minority Groups (CMG). The latter, created in 1959, was chaired by the premier and made up of representatives from the various departments delivering services to needy minorities, especially Indians and the Métis and, to a lesser extent, the Mennonites. In practice, Native affairs policy was closely associated with Douglas himself. Both Shumiatcher and the CMG reported directly to the premier and it was through him that recommendations were filtered and interpreted for the benefit of cabinet.

Whereas Green Lake represented the northern limit of the government's colonization policy, the CCF assumed control over the Lebret colony and made it the flagship of Métis rehabilitation in the South. Under a previous agreement with the Patterson government, the Oblates had operated a farm about a mile north of the village of Lebret for the purpose of employing and training Métis labourers.[110] In 1945, the CCF purchased the farm from the order, assumed direct control over its operation, and expanded the holdings to two sections. The intent was to make the farm a 'model' of mixed farming techniques through which the Métis would be integrated into the farm community. It functioned as a 'work and wages' enterprise, providing adult employment for an average of nine families and supporting about sixty-five people.[111] In addition, Lebret was

Lebret Métis farm, 1946. (Saskatchewan Archives Board R-B12,457-8)

designed as a support agency for the development of other colonies in the South. Not only did government personnel from Lebret offer advice and direction for colonization elsewhere, but also Lebret's heavy machinery, livestock, and crops were used to aid development of those colonies during the start-up phase.[112]

Although there were approximately thirty municipalities containing sizable Métis enclaves, it was only in those areas where the problems seemed especially acute that additional settlements were established. By the late 1940s, there were colonies at Crooked Lake, Lestock, Crescent Lake, Baljennie, Willow Bunch, Duck Lake, and Glen Mary and they, along with Green Lake and Lebret, contained about 2,500 Métis residents.[113] For a time, Métis settlement seemed like the only solution and so, not surprisingly, municipal council and field workers pressed for an extension of the colonization projects. Nevertheless, throughout the Douglas era, colonies remained relatively small in number, and in many respects never evolved much beyond the experimental stage.

Central to the creation of a colony was the establishment of a school, administered directly by the Department of Education but financed by the DSWR. In some cases a new school was built and in others an older building was hauled to the site. There was also one instance where the children were bused to a nearby village school comprised mainly of Métis children.[114] Close to the school, lots were divided off and assigned to incoming families on a long-term lease. In addition to housing classroom instruction for the children, the school building was designed to serve the wider interests of the community, providing facilities for recreation, adult education classes, and meetings of every description. The school, in fact, was meant to be the birthplace of community identity and development.

By design, the curriculum tended to be 'culture specific' and fashioned as an instrument of integration through which Métis children eventually would be absorbed into the workforce. Unlike the Patterson government before it, the CCF administration believed in adult education and the possibility of improving the outlook and standards of the older generation; but like its predecessor, it also believed that the greatest potential for Native integration rested in the education of the children.[115] That potential, however, could only be realized through an altered school curriculum that would acknowledge the cultural differences and special circumstances of the Métis.[116] In practice, this translated into a school system that aimed at basic literacy but emphasized vocational training appropriate to the rural economy. There was no expectation that Métis children would aspire to the professional ranks, nor were even the most accomplished students earmarked for anything but additional vocational education.[117] The curriculum, in fact, had a very definite race and class bias.

Cooperatives, combined with a self-help philosophy, were generally seen as the means to effective community development in the colonies. In keeping with social democratic understanding, Métis families were encouraged in every way possible to maximize their own potential through active participation in community-based activities. Special agents appointed by DSWR as well as representatives from the Department of Co-operatives acted as instructors and organizing agents in mobilizing collective community action.[118] The first step was usually the organization of a savings union, with each member required to make a small deposit on a weekly basis, no matter how small the amount. The fund eventually was used to finance community projects, including cooperative gardens, woodcutting, livestock raising, and winter fishing. As an incentive to cooperative organization, the government normally provided various kinds of assistance, including long-term interest-free loans to finance the purchase of land or members' homes.[119]

Among the most ambitious schemes were attempts to organize farm production cooperatives. After the Second World War, cooperative farms had sprung into existence in various parts of the province and, although they were never that successful, in their heyday they were perceived as an important innovation in allowing small landowners to participate in large-scale farming.[120] In the case of the colonies, only two such farms were created – the Lacerte Co-op (Willow Bunch) and Blanchard Co-op (Lestock) – and neither proved viable for precisely the same reason farm cooperatives did not do well elsewhere: large-scale land development required massive capital, a high degree of managerial skill, and a renunciation of private ownership. In the Métis colonies, as elsewhere, all three were seldom present.[121]

The Failure of Métis Colonies

During the first decade of operation, colonies were portrayed as a huge success by the provincial government and that was the impression communicated to both the popular press and the various branches of government. In reality, the scheme was laced with administrative and structural problems that, despite efforts to overcome them, continued to persist. By the mid-1950s, serious doubts were being raised about the viability of Métis colonies, and by the end of the decade, the CCF administration had largely abandoned colonies as a solution to Métis marginalization. The excuse commonly cited was that colonies were prohibitively expensive,[122] but this was only one of many problems.

Of fundamental importance was the fact that the CCF had misinterpreted what Métis people wanted. It was simply assumed that an agrarian existence was the most appropriate means to Métis self-sufficiency, and even as late as 1954, the premier was still insisting that 'only in this way can they ever hope to make a decent living and to become part of our society.'[123] In actual fact, many in the colonies were more interested in wage labour than in working the land, and this was true in virtually all settlements. Indeed, in Green Lake the indifference to farming was so pronounced that in the late 1940s the LID Branch completely revamped the land allotment system.[124] Under the new scheme, a forty-acre plot was granted to settlers for only a thirty-three-year term, with the possibility of leasing an adjoining forty acres once the clearing and breaking of the first plot – a task performed by government crews using machinery from the Central Farm – had been paid for by the lessee. Thereafter, the actual farming operation on the various plots was carried out, not by the lessees, but by the government on a share-crop basis. The families who held the leases stood to gain a small income, assuming there was some profit after the government had deducted operating costs and any outstanding rents owed by the lessee. But essentially, although lessees might be employed as farm labourers, they were no longer expected or encouraged to farm their own lands as independent producers.

A similar kind of problem figured into the widespread failure of the various cooperative programs. Departmental reports clearly indicate that, despite government incentives and prodding, the Métis found most co-op ventures, especially production cooperatives, an alienating and unworkable experience. Typical was the Lebret winter fishing co-op. By 1956, after two seasons of operation, there were only a handful of members; before the fishing season began, two members decided not to participate and a third took a job on the railway; this left only two members who then proceeded to buy out the interests of the others at 'depreciated value' and transform the operation into a private venture.[125] Likewise, the Blanchard farm cooperative at Lestock seems to have been in crisis almost from the very beginning. The Métis co-op purchased a quarter section of land from the DSWR through an agreement calling for a $400 down payment and thirty annual payments of $500. The co-op was able to come up with the down payment, but could pay only a portion of the first annual payment and quickly fell in arrears.[126] Within two years, the land was returned to the government and the farm co-op transformed into a house-purchasing cooperative.[127] To explain the failure, some Métis pointed to the fact that members on welfare did not fully commit themselves to making the farm a success because they feared that their social aid would be cut back,[128] while bigoted whites in the town of Lestock blamed the improvident character of the Métis.[129] The real explanation, however, was that cooperative principles were largely anathema to what the Métis themselves wanted.

Production cooperatives, in particular, were often torn apart with infighting, bickering, and sometimes an inability to distinguish between private and cooperative property. In the Blanchard cooperative, meetings were stormy and ructious affairs and this was especially so on one occasion when it was discovered that some individuals had been using co-op machinery for private gain.[130] Such problems were endemic to cooperative organization, especially during the start-up phase, and the Métis were no different than people elsewhere. What was different was that the continuing poverty of the Métis not only enhanced social tensions but also acted as a barrier to mobilizing effective labour. At Lestock, for example, the Blanchard members commonly ran up bills at the local stores during the winter months. To pay them off, employable males had no choice but to leave the colony early in the spring in order to secure wage labour, and this meant that the only people left to carry on the farm operation during the summer were 'unmarried mothers, widows or those who are physically unable to carry on the work.'[131] Also at play was the fact that the most active and most ambitious members were not interested in farming cooperatively. What they wanted was to own their own land or develop their own business, and when they found out this was not possible they simply quit the colony and moved on. In the case of Blanchard, almost all of the original members left the colony within the first year or so, and as DSWR reports admitted, they 'have improved their lot a good deal by so doing.'[132] In all colonies, there was considerable unhappiness over the lack of opportunity to develop privately owned and Métis-controlled businesses. According to an official at Green Lake, 'Many of their complaints may be imaginary; but some of them are justified. The root cause of dissatisfaction is not so much policies or specific actions of individuals, but the growing wish of the natives to run their own businesses.'[133] The fact was that cooperatives very much ran against the grain of what most aspiring Métis wanted. And those who tried to make a go of the cooperatives were often those least able to provide the labour and commitment needed to make the co-op a success. Cooperatives, like farming itself, represented one more example of the government's misreading of Native society.

The unwillingness of government to individualize some of the economic activity in the colonies stemmed from something other than an ideological commitment to collectivist principles. In point of fact, government functionaries – especially at the local level – doubted the competence of the Métis people. This was clearly indicated in the discouragement of elected advisory councils in the colonies and of individual business activities.[134] Commenting on the Canwood district, local DSWR reports insisted that the Métis lacked the value system necessary for success and that they could not benefit from government programs unless they were constantly supervised.[135] The pessimism about the Métis character in general was a constant refrain in numerous field reports and explains why the government, despite petitions from the Métis for a loan system to finance farm purchases and small businesses,[136] did little to assist Métis entrepreneurship outside the cooperative movement. In a stereotypical way, officials tended to see Métis as being only manual labourers, lacking the attributes needed for upward social mobility, and, in at least one instance, this had the effect of widening race and class divisions. During the late fifties, the LID Branch encouraged white people to move into Green Lake in order to operate stores, cafes, filling stations, and other small businesses.[137] In effect, the Métis were systematically excluded from the more remunerative activities and relegated to the role of waitresses, janitors, and other forms of casual labour in the service industry.[138] The fact that no attempt was made to include the Métis in the business community was a clear reflection of the class limitations of the government's rehabilitation program and, in the end, it served to inflame racial tensions in the community.

Another problem was that the purpose of government policy was not always honoured at the local level. It was one thing to have the cabinet determine policy but it was quite another matter when it came to having local officials implement that policy in a way that did not violate the intent. In the mid-fifties, for example, the government decided to take a number of families from Lestock, Glen Mary, and Baljennie in the South and relocate them at Green Lake in the North. The families came from areas that had a weak economic base and, even when employment for farm labourers was available, officials suspected that the Métis were being exploited as cheap labour.[139] Also, there was concern about inbreeding and the possibility that the limited gene pool was causing health problems.[140] The intent was to relocate the families in the Green Lake settlement where there were greater opportunities for wage labour, as well as a wider and more varied social context for marriage. The families themselves were closely consulted; a delegation from each community was sent to Green Lake to check out the advantages; and families were given free transportation and various incentives, including money, homesites, building materials, and assistance in breaking the land for gardens. And yet within two years of their arrival, many of the families had left Green Lake and returned to their former districts. In the case of Lestock immigrants, Green Lake officials blamed the failure on their 'nomadic nature,' but the real reason was contained in a confidential memorandum to the director of rehabilitation from a DSWR supervisor who had been asked to look into the matter. According to the supervisor, the man in charge at Green Lake believed that the newcomers were a 'shifty bunch' who could not be relied upon to stay and so had done very little to assist them in getting started. As he put it, 'although I have no proof of this, these people were not really given all the encouragement they might have been, and consequently felt that they were not treated the same as the others, thereby forcing them to leave.'[141] The incident speaks to the fact that, as well meaning as the relocation scheme may have been, the arbitrary and capricious actions of local officials sometimes undermined the intent of government policy.

Not all distortions of policy, however, happened without full departmental compliance, and in some instances rehabilitation policy took second place to expediency. Departments delivering services to the colonies were under constant pressure to trim expenditures and this occasionally had the effect of victimizing the very people for whom programs were meant. In 1955, the DSWR revealed that the LID Branch, with the full knowledge of the Municipal Affairs Department, had been purposely restricting welfare benefits in Green Lake. Not only had the branch actively discouraged social aid applications but, for those receiving various kinds of 'categorical assistance,' such as mothers' allowances and old age pensions, it had been paying out fewer benefits than recipients were entitled to by law.[142] The ostensible purpose for these practices was to reduce social aid costs,[143] but given the fact that such costs were automatically billed back to the DSWR, it seems unlikely that that was the real reason. On the contrary, it is entirely possible that the policy stemmed from the fact that, as one of the largest employers in the Green Lake area, the LID Branch stood to benefit directly from a restricted welfare system. The Branch owned a central farm, centralized farm operations on the plots, a winter logging operation, and a summer milling business, and in each case financial viability was dependent on modest wage demands. According to DSWR reports, past practices of the branch had had the effect of suppressing wage scales in the area,[144] and it may well be that restricted welfare was meant to keep employable adults in the labour market as well as to reduce wage expectations. This may also explain why the Métis from Lestock had found Green Lake unacceptable as a relocation centre.

An even more troublesome problem had to do with the weak economic base of the colonies. Generally, colonies were located on marginal lands that had been purchased by DSWR from private owners or leased from other government departments. The inability of the land to sustain meaningful development became increasingly apparent, especially in contrast to the burgeoning economic opportunities in other rural areas and in the cities. In the late 1950s, there was a dramatic increase in cottage development in the Qu'Appelle Valley owing to better highways from Regina and 'Monday closings,' and this acted as a magnet drawing the Métis away from Lebret in search of summer employment on the beaches.[145] Likewise, the development of industries in the urban areas, especially Regina and Prince Albert, led to a veritable exodus of Métis from rural areas to the cities. Officials at Willow Bunch said that as many as two-thirds of the Métis population had left the area and similar findings were reported for Crescent Lake and Lestock.[146] The result was that colonies increasingly became repositories of unemployed and unemployable dependants subsisting on government programs. During winter months, when there was less demand for casual labour, there was a slight reversal in the trend in so far as 'unemployed employable' Métis often returned to the colonies in search of social assistance and a place to stay until the spring.[147] But colonies never evolved into economically self-sustaining communities and this was as true of Green Lake as it was of the southern colonies. The only real difference was that at Green Lake the migrants moved not to the cities, but to the far North before returning to the colony for the winter months.[148] Nevertheless, the result was the same: the persistence of poverty, dependency, and social problems for those who remained.[149]

The inevitable conclusion drawn from all of this was that colonies did not work. The government, of course, attempted to put the best face on the situation and, as late as 1964, even recommended to the Indian Affairs Department that the Green Lake model be adopted as a formula for the evolution of Indian reserves to municipal status.[150] Well before that, however, the enthusiasm for colonies had waned. The change was denoted in the contention that there was no short-term solution to the Métis problem and in the admission, at long last, that not all Métis wanted to be farmers. The new orthodoxy also condemned colonies as a form of segregation that perpetuated Métis poverty. As the director of rehabilitation concluded in 1960,

> It would seem that the objectives for these people can only be accomplished over a long period of time – probably several generations. If humans are the produce of their hereditary nature and the environment in which they live, there is not likely to be a quick road to success for these people.
>
> Many people automatically think in terms of rehabilitation farms of various kinds for them, either as co-operative ventures or work and wages projects. I don't believe that all Métis are natural agriculturists [sic] any more than non-Métis are.
>
> I have considerable apprehension about long-term results of the concentration (deliberate or not) on the government's part of Métis people in such areas as Lestock, Crescent Lake, Green Lake, etc. These people are segregated from the community at large and the economic base of the area or [at] least that portion available to them can only continue their depression.[151]

The strategy now adopted by the government was to desegregate Métis society by accelerating migration from the rural areas to the towns and cities, with the ultimate goal of urban integration. In 1959, there was some talk about the DSWR taking over the administration of Green Lake and maintaining it as a colony, but the proposal was squarely rejected by the director of welfare: 'Our policy as regards depressed groups such as this, is designed to help them leave the Métis community and become part of the larger community. We would hesitate to take on a project of this kind and maintain a policy on segregation ... This is foreign to our philosophy as our programs are designed to integrate Métis with other people.'[152] Those who remained in the rural areas as depressed groups would be supported as welfare recipients, but the whole concept of special settlements was now forsworn as government policy. Wisdom dictated that pre-apprenticeship and vocational training appropriate to city life would be the new focus of Métis education, although academic training for some students was also sanctioned. The benchmark of success was now the extent to which Métis children were leaving the rural areas for employment in the cities. As a report on Lebret proudly proclaimed in 1960, 'there are no children on the project not going to school. All of the older children are employed away from the valley. Most are in our cities in steady employment.'[153] The change in policy was a repudiation of rural-based rehabilitation and it was the first step toward redefining the Métis problem as an urban phenomenon.

3
Provincial Indian Policy

While the Douglas government introduced reforms targeted specifically at the Métis, it clearly understood that the Métis could not be dealt with in isolation. By 1944, there were some 14,000 Indians in Saskatchewan,[1] and although constitutionally they came under the jurisdiction of the federal government, first and foremost they were also citizens of the province. Douglas saw the problems that afflicted Indian society as the mirror image of those that tormented the Métis, and he believed that, before any lasting solution could be achieved, the problems of both peoples would have to be addressed in tandem. In the South, Indian reserves often included people who were technically Métis and almost invariably were bordered by Métis settlements. Intermarriage between the two groups was common and, in a cultural sense, there was almost nothing that separated them. A similar situation was true in the burgeoning urban centres in the South. To the same extent that the Métis were leaving the rural areas in favour of the cities, Indians increasingly were migrating from the reserves to Regina, Saskatoon, and Prince Albert in search of wage labour and the amenities of urban life. There, both groups made common cause and subsisted as a marginalized and underemployed class, increasingly subject to the scrutiny of urban welfare officials. Likewise in the North, despite the existence of Indian treaties, only a few Indian reserves had actually been set up. This meant that, notwithstanding Indian Act definitions of who was an Indian, the everyday existence of the Métis was little different from that of the Indian who worked the trapline or otherwise lived off the land. Thus, the Douglas government came to the conclusion that reform would be meaningful only when the Indian was incorporated into the government's rehabilitation policies.

Among other things, this was emphasized at a meeting of government representatives from the three prairie provinces called together in Regina in the summer of 1949 to discuss problems of the Métis across the West. The Honourable John Sturdy, chairing the meeting as Saskatchewan's minister of welfare, opened the discussion with the observation that 'many Métis follow the cultural and economic pattern of the Indian and that the Métis problem and that of the Indian is [*sic*] ... much related.'[2] He later emphasized 'that the native Indian and the Métis group constitute a related and common problem, which indicated that simultaneous action was required for their economic and social improvement.'[3] In turn, delegates debated the merits of dealing with Métis issues separately and ultimately agreed with Sturdy, concluding that the Indian and Métis problems were one and the same.[4]

The interface between the Indian community and the CCF government was personified by the premier himself. In July 1945, a year after taking office, Douglas was invited to a Pipe of Chiefs ceremony on the Assiniboine Carry-the-Kettle Reserve near Montmartre. During a special ceremony, the premier was made a chief of the Assiniboine Nation and named 'We-a-ga-sha' or Chief Red Eagle. His wife, among others, was amused by the enormous feathered headdress placed atop the diminutive frame of the premier,[5] but Douglas himself took the matter seriously. In his address, he refused to accept his appointment as an empty honour and promised that, as chief and premier, he would do everything in his power to improve the conditions under which Indians lived.[6] According to Morris Shumiatcher and others, Douglas's commitment was more than public posturing,[7] and this assessment is borne out by the attention Douglas gave Indian affairs during the course of his premiership.

Ceremony at which Premier Douglas was made a chief of the Assiniboine Nation, July 1945. Right to left: Brigadier G.A.H. Trudeau, T.C. Douglas, Chief Walkingsun, Fred Dundas, and unidentified chief. (Saskatchewan Archives Board R-B658-1)

Chief Walkingsun presenting 'pipe of chiefs' to Premier Douglas, July 1945.
(Saskatchewan Archives Board R-B658-3)

Mrs. Douglas holds 'pipe of chiefs' on occasion of Premier Douglas being
made a chief of the Assiniboine Nation, July 1945. (Saskatchewan Archives
Board R-B2911)

From a policy perspective, the main goal of the government concerning Indians was integration into mainstream society, the same principle that underpinned Métis reform. The Indian was seen as an oppressed minority whose abject poverty and marginalization were certainly equal to, if not worse than, that of the Métis. In the CCF's critique of the situation, Indian misery was seldom attributed to the neglect and racism that figured so prominently in the analysis of the Métis problem, although policy analysts were not unmindful of those factors. On the contrary, the main indictment was leveled at the federal government and the abusive administration of the Indian Affairs Branch.[8] According to this thinking, Indians had become the victims of an uncaring and brutal bureaucracy, which, armed with the authority of the Indian Act, kept the Indian in a perpetual state of poverty, ignorance, and subservience. The result was an Indian society subsisting as a kind of social backwash, cut off from the educational opportunities and social services that people in Saskatchewan had come to expect. The solution was to loosen the grip of Indian Affairs in order to free the Indian from the stifling and enervating paternalism of the federal bureaucracy. The Indian then would be free to integrate into mainstream society, playing a significant role in provincial society and benefiting from provincial programs. Such integration, however, did not presuppose cultural and political assimilation. It was understood that, as a precondition to effective integration, Indian cultural uniqueness and a certain degree of 'self-government' would have to be confirmed and strengthened. As Morris Shumiatcher put it: 'The Indian must first be free to develop his own culture and not merely to imbibe ours; to learn his own history, and not to rely on our interpretation of it; to practice his own religion, and not to be coerced into another; to devise his own means of self-government, and not be cowed by ours.'[9] Whether the same could be said of those who, for whatever reason, had lost Indian status was less certain and remained a moot point in the CCF analysis. For these people, integration might well imply assimilation, as in the case of the Métis.

To place this Indian policy in a North American perspective, it is important to appreciate that, intellectually, the Douglas government was far more attune to the American 'New Deal' Indian policies of the 1930s than to US postwar reconstruction policies. In 1932, Franklin Delano Roosevelt had been elected to the American presidency on the promise of a New Deal. For millions of Americans suffering the worst effects of the Great Depression, this meant massive relief programs along with a rehabilitation of the nation's faltering economy. But the New Deal did not stop there. It was also extended to the treatment of Indians through the appointment of Herald L. Ickes as secretary of the interior and of John Collier as commissioner of Indian Affairs. The latter, in particular, had been a longstanding Indian rights advocate and in 1923 had organized the American

Indian Defense Association (ADA). The ADA was committed to a complete reformation of Indian policy through which Indians could regain control over their own lives. It demanded an end to the massive alienation of reserve lands, termination of the Americanization (assimilation) of Indians, improved education and health services, self-determination and the reestablishment of tribal governments, and affirmation of Indian cultural integrity.[10] With these goals in mind, Collier and Ickes were determined to reshape the face and substance of American Indian policy.

Much of the Ickes-Collier New Deal was effected by executive order. Americanization and the sale of Indian lands were officially terminated. Both Ickes and Collier dramatically increased the number of Indians employed in the Bureau of Indian Affairs and sent instructions to field workers that the culture and history of Indians were to be respected and treated as equal to that of any non-Indian group. In addition, in residential schools, solidly condemned for their intolerance of Indian culture, Indian children were no longer required to attend Christian services, and in many cases they were transferred to community day-schools where they could be closer to families and their cultural base.[11]

What could not be done by executive prerogative was accomplished by congressional legislation. In 1934, Congress passed the Johnson-O'Malley Act permitting the federal government to more effectively contract with states and territories to provide educational, medical, and welfare services to Indians. Then, as a kind of crowning achievement in the New Deal process, Congress in the same year approved the Indian Reorganization Act (IRA), otherwise known as the Wheeler-Howard Act. The IRA promoted cultural pluralism by guaranteeing Indians their right to traditional religion and lifestyle. It called upon Indian tribes to establish written constitutions through which they could set up municipal or 'home rule' governments on the reserve. Within that context, provision was made for either traditional tribal forms of government or democratically elected ruling bodies. The IRA also encouraged the formation of business corporations for managing tribal property and set up revolving funds to provide capital for Indian businesses. Finally, the IRA not only ended the alienation of Indian lands but also established an annual appropriation of $2 million so the secretary of the interior could buy lands for the purpose of restoring lost tribal estates.

The IRA was meant to reverse long-standing Indian policy and its passing into law was hailed by John Collier and others as 'Indian Independence Day.'[12] The New Deal, however, never realized its full potential as an engine of change in Indian society. One factor was the extent to which Ickes and Collier alienated the vested interests associated with the old order. Bureaucrats in the IAB were disinclined to share power with their Indian charges and often proved reactionary. Christian missionaries charged that the reformers used federal moneys to finance 'alien' religions and practices, returning Indians to 'degrading tribalism' and a 'blanket culture.' Within that context, Collier on more than one occasion was called on the carpet before the House Committee on Indian Affairs to answer charges of 'atheism, Communism, and sedition.'[13] Likewise, western congressmen opposed the reforms because they had to answer to constituents who wanted cheap and easy access to surplus Indian lands. Indeed, even a surprisingly large number of Indians railed against the changes introduced by the New Deal. In many cases, these were Americanized Indians who held their lands individually and were opposed to the idea of returning to communal control and tribal governments. But by far the greatest factor in curtailing the achievements of the New Deal was the outbreak of the Second World War. Under the constraints of war, programs were systematically gutted and, by the time normalcy had been restored in the aftermath of war, Congress and American sympathy had swung back to a conservative position. Starting in the late forties and accelerating through the fifties, Congress now officially adopted a 'termination' policy. This was predicated on the withdrawal of all federal services to Indians, the destruction of tribal lands, and the coerced assimilation of Indians into the American melting pot.[14]

There is no doubt that, in a philosophical sense, the Douglas government had more in common with the New Deal reforms than with the terminationist policies of the 1950s. It would be a mistake, however, to argue that the CCF consciously aped the work of Ickes and Collier. It is true that the premier sometimes called for a 'new deal for Indians,'[15] but the phrase itself was not meant to encapsulate specific policy. It is also true that brief references to American reforms can be found in the Douglas papers. In addition to a journal article on American Indians written by John Collier, for example, there are briefing notes on the IRA, penned by Morris Shumiatcher to assist the premier in preparing a speech for a meeting of Indians in January 1946. Shumiatcher pointed out that 'the policy of the United States towards its Indians is in marked contrast to that of the Canadian Government,' and then went on to outline briefly the main principles and content of the IRA.[16] Douglas undoubtedly applauded the liberal and democratic reforms embraced by American legislation, especially the emphasis on Indian cultural integrity and political self-government at the reserve level. However, there is no indication that the Douglas government ever drew up a detailed blueprint based on the ideas of Ickes and Collier. American reform measures served to reassure Douglas and Shumiatcher that Canadian policy was retrogressive and backward. But Douglas's views on Indians were conditioned more by the Canadian experience and his own liberal democratic ideology than by developments in the United States.[17] Also, there was little reason for the

CCF to articulate views on American reforms simply because, as long as the provinces lacked jurisdiction in Indian Affairs, it would have been premature and pointless for the CCF to evolve a specific legislative program. Hence, within the ambit of CCF emphasis on Indian integration, the main thrust of provincial policy initiatives was to question the efficacy of federal jurisdiction and to channel and orchestrate opposition to existing federal practices that operated against that integration.

Indian Organization

A central premise of CCF policy was the need to organize the Indians of the province into a single association through which Indian grievances and concerns could be voiced. Unlike a Métis association, an Indian organization would serve the interests of the provincial government in that it could articulate Indian grievances and demands and, in doing so, legitimize provincial concerns pertaining to the federal administration of Indian Affairs. The problem was that, when Douglas assumed office, the Indian community in Saskatchewan was badly fragmented into a number of competing Indian organizations, some with a regional focus, others with a national or international focus.

One was the Association of Indians of Saskatchewan (AIS). The AIS was a recently organized provincial association whose genesis can be traced to a meeting of some thirty Indians in Regina in the summer of 1944. According to Zacharias Hamilton of the Saskatchewan Historical Society, the new organization was led by some of the best-known Indians in the province.[18] The president was a decorated hero from the First World War, Sergeant Joe Dreaver, chief of the Mistawasis Band near Prince Albert, and widely regarded by Treaty 6 Indians as their hereditary chief.[19] Most of the membership, representing five of the nine Indian agencies in the province, as well as most of the executive of the organization, came from the southern part of the province and consisted of so-called 'progressive farmers.' They included veterans from the Piapot and Assiniboine Reserves, Hector Brass and his wife, Eleanor, from the File Hills Agency, Joseph Ironquill, and Dan Kennedy. The latter, whose Indian name was Ochankugahe, was an Assiniboine from Carry-the-Kettle Reserve. He was described by Hamilton as 'an exceedingly successful, progressive farmer and probably the best educated Indian in Saskatchewan.'[20] Kennedy was instrumental in organizing the founding convention of the AIS and later came to form a close personal association with Tommy Douglas, freely corresponding with the premier on a number of political and personal issues.

The AIS was organized around postwar demands for better schools for Indian children, greater Indian control over reserve life, better health care, and a redress of veterans' grievances, particularly the unequal treatment

Moise Dumont, Chief Dreaver, and Wasecat (left to right) in costume during the royal visit to Regina, 1939. (Saskatchewan Archives Board R-A7668)

of Indian and white ex-servicemen.[21] At the same time, the association was badly divided over the issue of the franchise. Most Indians were not allowed to vote in either provincial or federal elections and this was often interpreted by Kennedy and others in the AIS as a form of inferiority and segregation imposed on Indians.[22] They saw the vote as an instrument of emancipation, integrating Indians into a heterogeneous Canadian nation. Their views seemingly reflected the worldly perspectives of returned veterans and those who had become relatively successful in white society. On the other hand, there were those in the AIS who equated the vote with an attack on Indian nationhood and treaty rights as part of a general attempt to absorb Indians into the provincial population.[23] For them, the franchise meant assimilation and a denial of Indian nationhood, not emancipation or even integration. And they were anything but reassured when the AIS, in drawing up its constitution, made provision for non-Indian associate membership. This meant that whites could become non-voting members, entitled to take part in discussions and hold honorary executive positions in the association.[24] For the opponents of the franchise, associate membership in the AIS by non-Indians was itself testimony to the general trend toward assimilation writ large in the vote. Hence, from the beginning, the AIS was deeply divided over one of the most fundamental political issues of the postwar period.

Dan Kennedy demonstrating use of an Indian prayer pipe, 1947.
(Saskatchewan Archives Board R-A26,447)

A second organization was the Protective Association for Indians and
Their Treaties (PAIT). It was born in the years following the First World
War, when members of three reserves in the Qu'Appelle Valley – Piapot,
Pasqua, and Muscowpetung – organized themselves into what was known
as the Allied Bands.[25] The leaders were Ben Pasqua and Andrew Gordon
from Pasqua, Henry Ball and Abel Watetch from Piapot, and Pat Cappo
and Charles Pratt from Muscowpetung. The focus of their concerns were
the activities of Indian Commissioner Graham whose administration of

the Soldier Settlement Act had the effect of eroding Indian land holdings. By 1932, Graham had been replaced as Indian commissioner and in the following year the Allied Bands changed its name to the PAIT.[26] By the mid-1940s, the association was led by Chief John Gambler and reportedly had between five and six thousand members situated on eighteen reserves.[27] The membership was drawn from the Pelly agency in the west-central portion of the province as well as from three agencies in the South.[28]

As its name implied, the association's main focus was protection of treaty rights and this had the effect of excluding those Indians, such as the Sioux who had migrated to Saskatchewan from the United States, whose ancestors had never signed treaties. Its platform also included the protection of Indian lands and resources, as well as better education for Indian children on reserves.[29] The organization was not diffident about expressing its concerns and had a long history of circumventing the local Indian Affairs bureaucracy in order to appeal directly to Ottawa. In 1928, the Allied Bands had sent a delegation to Ottawa calling for a Royal Commission to inquire into the whole administration of Indian Affairs;[30] in 1945, the PAIT, with the assistance of Morris Shumiatcher, drew up a brief outlining its concerns and grievances and presented it to the minister of Indian Affairs in Ottawa.[31]

At the international level, there was the League of Nations of North American Indians (LNNA), essentially an American organization with affiliates in Canada, including both the Métis and Indian associations of Alberta.[32] It came into being during the Depression largely through the efforts of Lawrence Twoaxe, a Quebec Mohawk from Caughnawaga Reserve who had since relocated to Oakland, California. By the mid-1940s, the Canadian league secretary and national organizer was John Laurie, also the secretary of the Indian Association of Alberta.[33] The LNNA was supportive of attempts to organize the Indians provincially as a first step in affiliating with the international body and, to that end, held organizational meetings in Regina in the mid-1940s.[34] This international organization, however, seems not to have had much influence in Saskatchewan, in part because its activities were preempted by still another organization, the North American Indian Brotherhood (NAIB).

The president of the brotherhood was Grand Chief Andrew Paull, whose exceptional work on behalf of the Allied Tribes of British Columbia had made him an influential figure in Indian circles. Joe Delisle of Caughnawaga was vice-president, while Henry Jackson of Christian Island served as secretary. The NAIB was an international organization with its membership coming mainly from Canada and some affiliates in the United States, including the Indian Defense League of America.[35] At the national level, it claimed to have an extensive membership stretching through all provinces and as far north as the Arctic Circle. Its main objective was to lobby Parliament and the Canadian government 'to secure a new deal for the aboriginals of this country.'[36] By the mid-1940s, NAIB energies were being channeled into demands for a revision of the Indian Act, income tax exemptions, old age pensions paid by the dominion, Indian representation in Parliament, and a Royal Commission to inquire into the whole state of Indian Affairs in Canada.[37]

In Saskatchewan, the brotherhood achieved a following among certain segments of the Indian leadership, including the influential John Tootoosis from Cutknife in the Battleford area. Tootoosis, described by one journalist as a 'walking encyclopedia' about everything pertaining to Indians, was the grand nephew of the revered Chief Poundmaker and a man widely respected for his commitment to organizing Indians. Originally, Tootoosis had been associated with the League of Indians of Canada, founded in Sault St. Marie (Ontario) in 1919, mainly as a result of the efforts of Fred Loft.[38] A decade later, Treaty 6 Indians in both Saskatchewan and Alberta formed their own organization, known as the League of Indians of Western Canada (LIWC). Tootoosis was elected secretary and organizer for the prairie region in 1932 and president in 1934. Eventually, the LIWC split into the Alberta and Saskatchewan chapters and slowly slid into oblivion, the Saskatchewan Branch ceasing to exist after 1942.[39] A year later, a move was underway to create a new central organization, which subsequently became known as the North American Indian Brotherhood. Tootoosis, along with five other delegates from Saskatchewan, attended the founding national conference of the NAIB held in Ottawa in 1944; shortly thereafter he committed himself to the brotherhood, organizing a Saskatchewan Branch of the NAIB in the same year.[40]

From the perspective of the CCF, none of these organizations was acceptable in its own right. Whereas the two provincial associations represented competing and divisive forces, the two international organizations threatened to detract from the special concerns associated with Indian development in Saskatchewan and exacerbated already existing disunity. Douglas was not opposed to pan-Indian organizations per se and in fact pledged his support to both the LNNA and the NAIB.[41] His primary concern, nevertheless, was the creation of a representative provincial organization that could work with government to address the problems unique to the province.

Douglas's commitment to the creation of a single provincial Indian organization was in lockstep with what was already happening in the Indian community itself. In August 1946, the Association of Indians of Saskatchewan held a convention in Regina City Hall council chamber and, among other things, endorsed the idea of uniting Saskatchewan

Portrait of John Tootoosis.
(Saskatchewan Archives Board
R-A7662)

Indians into one organization through which their concerns and views could be communicated to Ottawa. In due course, Chief Joe Dreaver, president of the AIS, petitioned the premier to sponsor a meeting of Indians from across the province for the purpose of organizing a representative association. As he explained, by using the offices of the premier he hoped to avoid the impression that the AIS was attempting to impose itself on the other organizations: 'I personally wrote to him [Douglas] asking him for his assistance because of the fact that if I had asked the executive of the other organizations to attend a meeting where I was going to unite them they would have thought I was trying to submerge them in my organization. We had to get outside assistance, a man who had been an honorary chief of the tribe and ask him personally to assist us.'[42]

Douglas, undoubtedly sympathetic to a cause that also satisfied the political interests of his government, was quick to respond. In December 1945, he issued an invitation to the Indians of Saskatchewan to meet in Regina to put aside their differences and unite in a common cause.[43] His invitation decried the fact that, although the federal government had recently announced its intention to establish an inquiry into Indian Affairs, it had not yet taken any action. In anticipation that such an inquiry would eventually take place, his main plea was that all the tribes of the province be represented at the meeting and that some common ground be found. As he explained, 'If the Indians of Canada are to play their part in the process of reconstruction and are to share in the benefits of the post-war era, it is necessary that they first sink their local differences in order to achieve common ends. Only with a strong and united voice can they express themselves and adequately present their just demands for fair and equal treatment with other citizens.'[44] The premier's invitation, in fact, cast doubt on existing associations as agents of reform and called for a fresh initiative in Indian organization.

The Regina meeting was held in the Legislative Building on 4 January 1946. It was attended by more than fifty Indian delegates, mostly representing the southern Cree, Assiniboine, Saulteaux, and Sioux, although some came from as far north as Prince Albert.[45] It was a matter of comment in the local press that most delegates had adopted the white man's hairstyle and clothing, although two men had braids, half a dozen wore khaki military uniforms and service ribbons, and three councillors and two chiefs wore the Queen's uniform.[46] The latter had been given to each chief when Treaty 4 had been signed in 1874 and had been carefully preserved and handed down to subsequent generations. The meeting was also attended by leading lights in the CCF party who seemingly set the agenda and dominated the proceedings. Although Indian delegates were given every opportunity to debate the issues,[47] it is difficult to escape the impression that the meeting unfolded in a way that had been predetermined by CCF officials.

Delegates were officially welcomed on behalf of the province by Morris Shumiatcher who was subsequently chosen chairman of the conference.[48] The thrust of his opening remarks was to argue the need to establish a single organization to represent all Indians in the province. Delegates were also welcomed by Joe Phelps, the minister of natural resources. Phelps pledged that the provincial government would end the exploitation of Indians in the fur business and in the marketing of furs and fish on which Indians were dependent.[49] Then, seemingly in an effort to contrast provincial practices with those of the federal government, he announced that two Indians would be appointed to a provincial game advisory committee, currently in the planning stages.[50] Finally, Phelps expressed his opinion that Indians should be given full citizenship rights, including the right to vote, as a prelude to having representation in the provincial legislature.[51]

Immediately following the minister's speech, the premier addressed the conference. Douglas reiterated his plea for unity so that Indians might speak with a united voice in demanding their just rights.[52] Based upon briefing notes prepared by Morris Shumiatcher, he emphasized the importance of securing their education and health rights from the federal government and pledged that his government would do everything in its power to assist them in making their case to Ottawa.[53] He also conveyed the message that the province was quite prepared to take a more active part in an area that traditionally had been the prerogative of the federal government. As he put it, while Indians were commonly seen as the responsibility of Indian Affairs, he was not content to see Indians endure privation and hardship if these abuses could be prevented.[54]

Many of the Indian delegates were undoubtedly suspicious of the organizing role played by government officials. The extent to which such fears were evident is difficult to determine because, whereas some of the discussion took place in Cree and to a lesser extent in Saulteaux, only the passages in English were later published and even then only in abridged form. Nevertheless, it was undoubtedly out of deference to the existence of such suspicion that officials went out of their way to reassure delegates that the CCF had no hidden political agenda and that the proposed provincial association would be entirely Indian run. The point was emphasized particularly by G.H. Castleden, CCF Member of Parliament for Yorkton: 'the organization will be yours, not ours. We have no desire to dominate it. You have the decision to make; you have the power; you have the opinion, and we are offering our co-operation and our assistance.'[55] Such statements were a tacit acknowledgment that not everyone welcomed the heavy hand of government.

Appropriately, the motion to create a single provincewide organization was introduced by Chief Joe Dreaver, president of the AIS. The main points of contention were raised by Ahab Spence, who described himself as 'a bush Indian,' or Woodlands Indian from the North.[56] Spence, a Cree Anglican minister and a teacher at Little Pine Reserve in the Battleford area, said he was unfamiliar with what the southern organizations represented and noted that only the AIS and PAIT were represented at the meeting, Tootoosis and others from the NAIB being absent. Specifically, he wanted to know if all the existing organizations were 'for the welfare of the Indians, or have they different ideas?'[57] The subtext of the question

Portrait of George H. Castleden, MP for Yorkton, January 1956. (Saskatchewan Archives Board S-B4852)

spoke to the divisions in the AIS and elsewhere over the issue of the franchise and the assimilation some thought it represented. It drew an immediate disclaimer from Chief Dreaver who insisted that, contrary to what some believed, his organization was not committed to the enfranchisement of Indians. Chief John Gambler also responded, arguing that while the AIS and the PAIT were as different as 'daylight and darkness,' the ultimate aim of the Protective Association was to help Indian people.[58] Spence said he was reassured by Dreaver's response and recommended that, in the interest of unity, the meeting proceed to vote on the motion. In due course, the motion was carried unanimously.

The new provincial organization was to be known as the Indian Federation of Saskatchewan (IFS). It was designed not to offend existing organizations, in that all Indians could join the IFS and at the same time retain membership in existing organizations. A draft constitution, copied from that of the recently organized Indian Association of Alberta,[59] was drawn up but not formally adopted. During the debate, Ahab Spence had reminded the conference that northern Indians were not represented at the meeting, and Castleden, after consulting with Shumiatcher, concluded that it would be a mistake to proceed with the constitution without consulting the northern chiefs. In turn, Castleden persuaded delegates to defer both the adoption of the constitution and the election of officers, pending a meeting

Reverends Ahab Spence, Edward Ahenakew, and Stanley Cuthand (left to right) at a synod meeting in Edmonton, 1956. (Saskatchewan Archives Board R-B7063)

with northern representatives at a later date. In the meantime, the conference agreed to set up a steering committee that would study the draft constitution and liaise with a northern committee that Castleden planned to organize as a prelude to a meeting of northern chiefs at Duck Lake.[60]

The two-day conference confirmed almost everything Douglas had hoped for. The creation of an effective Indian organization was a cornerstone of CCF policy and, although IFS existed in name only at this point, its tentative existence was an important, if only preliminary, step in that direction. In addition, delegates passed a number of resolutions explicitly denouncing the administration of Indian Affairs. They condemned the Indian Act as being outdated but, at the same time, insisted that specific amendments be contingent on Indian consent; they demanded the establishment of day-schools located on the various reserves as well as access to higher education; they wanted old-age pensions for Indians on a par with those for white people; and they called for Indian veterans' benefits comparable to those received by other Canadians.[61] Moreover, because much of the discussion focused on an indictment of Indian Affairs policy, not surprisingly, delegates were entirely of one mind in drafting a petition calling for the dominion government to establish a Royal Commission to inquire into the administration of Indian Affairs.[62] The petition was to be circulated through the Indian community for signatures and then forwarded to Ottawa.[63]

Red Eagle, the premier, became the man of the hour and received warm accolades for his efforts on behalf of Indians. Chief Joe Dreaver lavished praise on Douglas during the conference, arguing that he had done more for Indians since taking office than Indian Affairs had done during the past seventy years.[64] John Laurie, who appeared at the conference as the representative of the Indian Association of Alberta, praised in particular the premier's efforts in bringing Indians together, noting by comparison the hostility of the Alberta government to such initiatives.[65] And even after the conference had concluded, Douglas continued to receive letters congratulating him for having united the Indians of the province.

In point of fact, the Indians of the province were not as united as many thought and this was dramatically demonstrated at the Duck Lake conference held on 10 January 1946, a week after the Regina meeting. This second conference, dominated by delegates from the North, was held in St. Michael's Residential School in the small hamlet of Duck Lake, about forty-five miles north of Saskatoon. The meeting was convened by two leaders from the Duck Lake area, Chief Gamble of Beardy Reserve and Chief Almighty Voice of One Arrow Reserve, and was closely associated with the membership of the North American Indian Brotherhood. It had originally been planned for late December, but in light of the Regina meeting it had been rescheduled to the second week in January so that the northern chiefs could consider the issue of a single provincial organization.[66] The proceedings were attended by eighty-two Indian delegates and chaired by John Tootoosis, an executive member of the North American Indian Brotherhood.[67] In addition, G.H. Castleden and his fellow MP Max Campbell (CCF, Battleford) were on hand to represent the provincial government in its support of the IFS.

It was evident from the beginning that the solutions worked out in Regina were not acceptable in the North. In the first place, delegates took exception to some of the resolutions passed in Regina and reintroduced to the Duck Lake meeting by Mr. Castleden. For example, according to the Catholic *Indian Missionary Record* – which was not an unbiased observer – delegates resented the Regina motion in favour of day-schools on reserves because of the scurrilous notion, advanced by non-Indians, that sectarian residential schools off the reserve were inferior and abusive.[68] As a post-conference press release put it: 'The general feeling of the meeting was that we Indians at this meeting were not interested in outside political interference and that remarks made regarding methods used by Indian agents and Indian residential school principals did not meet with enthusiastic reception and a number of our Indian spokesmen resented and corrected these slighting remarks.'[69] The reference to outside influence spoke to an even more explosive issue. Early in the proceedings, Chief Donald Gamble demanded that the deliberations be limited to Indians only.[70] This was a direct challenge to perceived domination by government officials and was directed specifically at Mr. Castleden, representing the provincial government. In the end, Castleden requested and was granted observer status, so that he could act in an advisory capacity on the issue of a new provincial organization.[71] Finally, and the clearest indication of the mood at Duck Lake, the delegates debated and then rejected the creation of the Indian Federation of Saskatchewan. John Tootoosis was the most vocal critic of the new organization and in the end he carried the day. He argued that the only organization recognized by Indian Affairs was the North American Indian Brotherhood and that, if Indians wanted the Indian Act revised, they would have to throw their weight behind one organization for all Indians in Canada – the NAIB.[72] Also at play was the inference that the proposed new organization was being pushed by outside white people who were meddling in Indian matters. According to conference spokespersons,

No doubt some southern Indians were easily led into committing themselves at the Regina conference due to the numerous organizations among the bands. However, more solidarity of purpose in regards to membership in the North American Indian Brotherhood organization was encountered at the Duck Lake meeting and the suggestion by some of the white people regarding the forming of a provincial federation did not receive the warm reception anticipated.

The draft constitution drawn up at the Regina Indian conference was ... turned down. The northern Saskatchewan Indians do not wish to endorse this draft ... Being members of the North American Indian Brotherhood organization we would like this misunderstanding made right because we did not accept or recognize the federation.[73]

The rejection of IFS as a tool of provincial officials was one of the earliest and clearest indications that Indians in the province resented attempts by white trainers to manage their affairs. Such resentment had the potential to seriously strain government-Indian relations, but at the time officials showed little concern.

Douglas was undoubtedly disappointed by events at Duck Lake and later maintained that the comments carried in the *Indian Missionary Record* about the proceedings did 'not give a true picture of the attitude of the Indians ... toward unity.'[74] At the same time, the premier was too astute a politician to allow the northern chiefs the last word on the issue. Evidence suggests that he had anticipated resistance from the northern chiefs and had developed a contingency plan meant to sidestep any opposition to a provincial organization. This was intimated in the actions taken by Castleden to head off disaster during the Duck Lake proceedings. Acting on Douglas's authority, he announced to delegates that the government planned to hold still another conference, this time in Saskatoon, for the purposes of considering and adopting a draft constitution for a new federation.[75] As an added incentive, he also made it known that the province would pay the expenses of delegates attending the next meeting.[76] This latest initiative was in blatant disregard of majority opinion at Duck Lake and it was duly denounced by conference spokespersons as 'outside political interference.'[77] Nevertheless, Castleden's manoeuvre effectively outflanked the opposition and, as it turned out, set the stage for the birth of a new provincial organization.

The Saskatoon conference was held on 23 and 24 February 1946, in the Barry Hotel. The meeting was attended by nearly 100 delegates from every band in the province and represented the largest gathering of chiefs and councillors in the province's history.[78] Once more, the conference was chaired by Morris Shumiatcher who kicked off the proceedings by reading a message from the premier who had been unable to attend. Tying Indian unity to the benefits promised by treaties, Douglas insisted that, 'Without unity, you are the prey of all; united, you are strong and secure. In federation, you will surely find that strength which will enlarge your lives and help to build for yourselves, and all people, that better, friendlier world spoken of in your Treaty, to last "so long as the sun shines and rivers flow.'"[79] In turn, the unity message was hammered home in speeches by A. MacPherson, Mayor of Saskatoon, Joe Phelps, G.H. Castleden, John Gambler, and Joe Dreaver. Overall, the message was well received by delegates because, by this time, the idea of some kind of provincial association had pretty much been conceded.

Not all opposition, however, had dissipated. The most serious, and the one implied in Regina and articulated in Duck Lake, was the issue of white people interfering in Indian politics. John Tootoosis insisted he understood that the Saskatoon conference was supposed to be an Indian meeting, 'with an Indian chairman to speak our own language, for half of the Indians here do not speak English.'[80] Indian interpreters, in fact, were used during the proceedings, but language in itself was not the only point Tootoosis was making. The real concern was made explicit by Chief Almighty Voice: 'We want to know who this convention belongs to. Does it belong to the Indians or does it belong to the White men?'[81] The question invited a sharp response from Castleden: 'If we left this convention to be called by Indians, it would never have been called.'[82] Castleden then went on to reassure delegates that the only aim of government was to assist with the initial organization of the Indian association, after which the federation would be turned over completely to Indians themselves. The commitment of government not to interfere in the actual operation of the new organization seems to have defused the issue for the time being, but deep-seated Indian suspicions, conditioned by long experience, undoubtedly lingered.

Two other trouble spots remained. Support for a provincial council under the umbrella of the North American Indian Brotherhood remained strong, principally among the northern delegates. To bolster that cause, none other than Andrew Paull, the national president of the NAIB, had been brought in from British Columbia. But Paull's plea for exclusive loyalty to the brotherhood failed to carry the convention. As an outsider, he was undoubtedly at a disadvantage, but more than that, his emphasis on the NAIB to the exclusion of the other two existing organizations limited his appeal and made him seem partisan. The other problem had to do with semantics. A man by the name of Jiggity took exception to the word 'federation' because it implied a direct association with the Co-operative Commonwealth Federation. As he explained: 'We are not well educated. We do not know a lot of these high words and when this word federation is used it means we will be C.C.F., so I think we should use a different word, for instance "Union."'[83] The point was well taken because few delegates wanted to be identified with either the CCF or the partisan politics of white society, so Jiggity's suggestion for a name change was readily endorsed.

The motion calling for the creation of a new provincial association was carried by a large majority, seventy-six to nine. A fourteen-member committee, with Shumiatcher as legal advisor, was struck to prepare a constitution, using as a starting point the same IAA-based constitution introduced in Regina almost two months earlier. The new organization, in effect replacing the abortive IFS, would be known as the Union of Saskatchewan Indians (USI). It was to be a provincewide association whose creation, in theory, did not mean the disbandment of the three original organizations; instead, it would coexist with them. The USI constitution stipulated that the union would 'be democratic and non-sectarian, and shall not directly or indirectly be affiliated to, or connected with any political party.'[84] First and foremost in the Aims and Objectives of the USI was the protection of treaties and treaty rights. This goal not only headed the list of problems the union would address but also figured prominently as the overriding objective of the organization. Although non-Indians could be appointed honorary members of the union, only Indians could be full members with voting rights.

The constitution also called for the establishment of locals in all ten of the provincial Indian agencies and provided for the election of two councillors from each so the organization would be representative of provincewide opinion.[85] The first elected executive included people closely associated with the old organizations. John Tootoosis, who at Duck Lake had spoken so passionately in favour of the NAIB, was chosen president; John Gamble and Earnest Goforth were elected first and second vice presidents respectively; and Gladys Dreaver, Joe's daughter, assumed the office of secretary-treasurer.[86]

The creation of the USI was a seminal development in Indian history, in that the same basic organization has survived in Saskatchewan to

Indians attending organization meeting of the Union of Saskatchewan Indians, Saskatoon, 23-4 February 1946. (Saskatchewan Archives Board R-B834)

the present. In 1958, the name of the association was changed to the Federation of Saskatchewan Indians (FSI) and in the early eighties to the Federation of Saskatchewan Indian Nations (FSIN). The organization born of the Saskatoon conference ultimately would produce a unity of purpose among Saskatchewan Indians and forever change the face of Indian politics. This did not mean, of course, that everyone was happy with the new association. At the local level in particular, the election of chiefs and councillors sometimes invited considerable opposition, with reserves dividing into pro- and anti-union forces.[87] These divisions were often exacerbated by the lingering existence of the older organizations, but none of these organizations proved to be an alternative to the union. Without the active leadership of John Tootoosis, the local chapter of the NAIB lost much of its drive and profile. For a time, local concerns and sometimes regional jealousies continued to be expressed through the AIS and the PAIT, but neither organization recovered its former stature; both eventually slid into obscurity and proved to be of only transitory importance.[88] The province now had a new provincial organization, which henceforth would dominate Indian politics in Saskatchewan.

As a man under whose auspices the USI had been created, the premier once more was credited with bringing unity to the Indian community. His contribution was acknowledged not only in the popular press but also in correspondence from Indian leaders. In a bulletin of the League of Nations of North American Indians, Lawrence Twoaxe, chairman of the National Organization Council, formally acknowledged the role of both Douglas and Castleden in organizing the province's Indians.[89] Likewise, Malcolm Norris, who had been instrumental in organizing the Indian Association of Alberta and who later would work for the CCF as a field officer in northern Saskatchewan, penned a personal letter to the premier congratulating him for 'sponsoring Indian unity' and setting 'an enviable preceedent [sic] for governments.'[90]

While the CCF was instrumental in the creation of the union, its contribution should not be overestimated nor allowed to obscure the important role played by the Indian leadership itself. James Pitsula has argued that the creation of the union was the result of two developments: 'the increased political activism of Indian people caused by their participation in World War II and the support given the Indian cause by the Saskatchewan CCF government.'[91] The problem with this interpretation is that it attributes the union to short-term political activism in the Indian community during the postwar period and, by implication, gives equal weight to the importance of non-Natives. Such an approach has been condemned by writers in the Native Studies field because it speaks to an enduring notion in Canadian historiography that Indian political activism and gains were dependent on the role played by white people;[92] and, by discounting the long-term continuity of Indian struggles, it fails to place the achievements of Indian people in proper historical perspective.

In actual fact, Douglas and the CCF had simply grafted their own political agenda onto a preexisting Indian movement, dating back to the inception of reserves. Historically, Indians had fought a heroic battle to regain and preserve their prerogatives as separate nations within Canada and, to that end, they had made every effort to organize politically. The continuity of purpose can be traced through the so-called 'Autonomy Movement' led by Chiefs Big Bear, Little Pine, and Piapot in the early 1880s,[93] the activities of Loft and the League of Indians after the First World War, and the political associations that came into being in the 1930s and 1940s.

Not infrequently Indians were fragmented and divided in their attempts to organize, not because they lacked a common cause but because the political and social establishment in Canada was aligned against Indian unity of any kind. Whereas all churches rarely found it in their own best interests to have Indian congregations politically organized, the Catholic Church, in particular, actively opposed sectarian organizations that threatened to preempt religious authority. John Tootoosis, himself a practising Catholic, was highly critical of the priests' opposition to his organizing efforts during the Depression and postwar years. At one point, Father Ernest Lacombe, a missionary in the Battleford area, seemingly threatened Tootoosis with excommunication because of his radical views and defiance of the priests.[94] Tootoosis also tells the story about John Henry Agecoutay, a supporter of the USI from Pasqua. Agecoutay seemingly was in hospital when he was approached by a priest with a proposal meant to undermine the union: 'The priest told him ... to start up another organization. They would give him all the money he needed and the missionaries would work for him to organize the Indians and he would be the leader.'[95]

Reinforcing church opposition was the fact that, as a matter of state policy, the Canadian government had historically done everything in its power to divide Indians so they could not make common cause against the oppressive measures administered by Indian Affairs. The illegal pass system, introduced in 1885, was clearly an attempt to prevent Indians from leaving the reserves and organizing politically.[96] Leaders who sought to organize politically were often stigmatized as troublemakers and found their activities effectively suppressed by state agencies, operating under oppressive laws designed for just such a purpose. In 1927, through an amendment to the Indian Act, the federal government made it illegal for anyone seeking to represent Indian interests to solicit money from Indians without the written consent of the superintendent general of Indian Affairs. Even in the best of times, Indian leaders normally found it difficult to organize because their cash-starved constituents were unable to contribute financially. The new amendment now made it illegal to even ask for financial contributions and was tantamount to banning Indian associations of every description.[97] Over the years, it was used as a menacing threat to would-be Indian organizers, including Fred Loft of the League of Indians.[98]

Hence, the creation and evolution of the Union of Saskatchewan Indians must be seen in the larger historical context of Indian struggles to organize, despite the opposition of church and state. The USI speaks to a continuity in Indian history that cannot be explained by merely focusing on a postwar revival of political activism and certainly not by giving equal credit to the CCF. It is true that the CCF funded activities associated with the creation of the union and attempted to dominate the Indian agenda, denoted in the heavy hand of the CCF in conference procedures and the preparation of briefs. As important as this may have been, however, the real contribution of the Douglas government was not about money or legal advice. The seminal contribution of the CCF was its dismantling of the historical barriers to Indian organization through which the Indian leadership was free to fashion and evolve its own political organization. This was exactly what John Laurie had alluded to at the Regina conference in 1946 when he complimented the Douglas government for bringing Indians together, in comparison to the antipathy displayed by the Alberta government. This should not, however, overshadow the fact that the unity movement itself was first and foremost an Indian initiative with long historical antecedents.

It was precisely because the creation of the union was so deeply rooted in Indian political tradition that Indians were often uneasy, if not offended, by the union's continuing association with the CCF. The use of Indian languages, particularly the demand for the use of Cree at both the Duck Lake and Saskatoon conferences, had itself been an attempt to ethnically define the political process. After the Saskatoon conference, Indian leaders as well as the rank and file continued to resist attempts by the CCF to intrude into the activities of the USI. The resentment of Indians was seldom expressed publicly or highlighted in press coverage but its existence was unmistakable. The substance of the complaint was outlined in a letter from E.A. Boden of Battleford to the premier a few months after the Saskatoon conference. Because it speaks to an irritant that would perpetuate troubled relations with the CCF in the future, it is worth quoting at length:

> I am writing you at this time because of a discussion I had recently with John Tootoosis ...
>
> John was rather reluctant in giving much credit to our Sask., government in being interested or helping to solve the problem. I finally found out what the trouble was ... John said that ... so many of his people did

not understand as yet and were very much opposed to the white man telling him what to do or even to suggest a remedy. This is the impression that they have after last winters [*sic*] sessions. John himself said that he was surprised that Castleden was so determined to take over and run the meeting when according to John Tootoosis the Indians themselves were to handle their own meetings. I believe Max Campbell scented this at the Duck Lake meeting and promptly left.

John also mentioned that the Indians were very much disgusted with what was in the press concerning the Indians and the action taken by the Sask., Government on their behalf ... John told me that just recently he had to warn Shumiatcher who apparently was attending one of the meetings lately of the danger in being a little too ready to offer advice to the Indian.

To sum it all up they are not in a mood to have anyone tell them how they should run their affairs. They seem to think that the government or those that were representing the government were trying to lay down all the by-laws and regulations instead of letting them handle that part of the organization. John says that he appreciates very much the interest that you and others are taking in the problems of the Indians but as he said do not make it more difficult for him to get the Indians to co-operate by not properly understanding the Indian, suspicious as he still is of the white man. God only knows that he has every reason to be suspicious of the white mans [*sic*] ways.[99]

Tootoosis was not the only person decrying government interference in Indian affairs. In October 1946, Douglas received a blistering letter from Andrew Paull who, as grand chief of the NAIB, demanded that provincial agents stop meddling in Indian affairs and displaying a hostile attitude to the brotherhood:

It is with a great deal of reluctance and after much serious consideration that I feel compelled to ask you to instruct Dr. Morris Shumiatcher and other members of your group to stop calling meetings, attending meetings of Indians where they attempt to force the Indians to adopt their policies, and who advise the Indians NOT to co-operate in one Canadian organization. Dr. Shumiatcher last year prepared and sent a brief to the [federal] government, representing it to be the wishes of the Indians of Saskatchewan, which was not true.

Recently he instigated the calling of a meeting last month which had to be cancelled by the president John Tootoosis, because it was impossible to get a representative meeting.

Now I am told the others intend to attend a proposed meeting on the 28th. of this month, when it is feared he and others whom he has invited will advise the Indians not to co-operate in one Canadian organization, that he explicitly means our organization.[100]

Paull then went on to say that he had received complaints from Indians in Saskatchewan about interference in their deliberations by white men, especially Shumiatcher, and then concluded by insisting that the premier lay down a strict rule that white men not attend Indian meetings.[101]

There can be little doubt that the CCF government sought to influence, if not control, the agenda of the USI. It probably also believed it was in competition with the NAIB for the hearts and minds of Indian people in the province. Nevertheless, Douglas responded to Paull's letter by simply denying the allegations. The union, he insisted, 'represents a majority of all of the Indians of Saskatchewan, and I am pleased to be able to say that it is functioning in a free and democratic fashion, and remains uninfluenced by any group or organization, whether political or otherwise.'[102] He then largely dismissed Paull's charges as being partisan by implying that the NAIB was ideologically opposed to the formation and independence of the USI: 'I am well acquainted with your activities at the organizational conference of the Union [in Saskatoon], and I feel that, at this point, you cannot validly interfere in the operation of this organization.'[103]

Neither Douglas nor Paull, of course, would have the last word on the issue of interference. USI leadership very early on made it known that it would not tolerate outside influence. The letters from Boden and Paull, nonetheless, seem to have had a chastening effect on Douglas because, from that point on, government officials were far more circumspect in their involvement in Indian organization. The image now consciously cultivated, not always with success, was that of a government working on behalf of a disadvantaged minority, not that of domineering politicians meddling in matters that did not concern them.

Provincial Indian Affairs and Federal Inquiry

The CCF's relationship to both the Indian community and the federal government was administered largely through existing government departments on the basis of expediency. No consideration seems to have been given to enhancing the profile of Indian issues by creating a provincial Department of Indian Affairs. On the contrary, Native matters were dealt with largely on an interdepartmental program basis, seemingly consistent with the view that such matters ran across departmental jurisdictions.

At first, the main focus of Indian Affairs was the office of legal advisor to both the executive council and the premier. This was the position held by Morris Shumiatcher for much of the first decade of CCF rule. By the mid-1950s, the office was occupied by John Sturdy, who by then was

widely known as the government's expert on Indians.[104] How he qualified as such is not entirely certain, but, according to Sturdy himself, he
had for twelve years been a school principal in Fort Qu'Appelle and there
had come to know the Indians 'pretty well.'[105] He also claimed to have
known one member of the Sheep Indians Tribe who, he claimed fatu-
ously, was the 'last of the Mohicans!'[106] In government, Sturdy had served
in the cabinet as minister of reconstruction and rehabilitation from 1944
to 1948; as minister of social welfare and rehabilitation from 1948 to
1956; and now as minister without portfolio, acting as a special assistant
to the premier.[107] In addition, the government sometimes established
special cabinet committees, designed to address particular problems. By
the mid-1950s, for example, the burning issue was whether or not the
Indian should be given the right to vote, and so in 1956 the cabinet set
up a Committee on Indian Affairs, chaired by John Sturdy, to investigate
the whole matter.[108]

By the late 1950s, the government had come to the conclusion that
it needed a more permanent and defined mechanism, and this led to
the creation of a standing interdepartmental committee, known as the
Committee on Minority Groups (CMG). The main purpose of the committee was to assist departments and cabinet in formulating policies concerning minority groups, especially the Hutterite Brethren, Indians, and
the Métis, whose social and economic conditions required study and
action. The committee was mandated to keep a central information file
on the policies and programs of different departments pertaining to such
minorities; to assist in the planning and development of departmental
programs for minorities; to gather and disseminate research data on the
targeted minorities; to liaise with officials, including those from the federal government, minority groups, as well as welfare, voluntary, and religious groups, with a view to exchanging information and encouraging
joint programs; and to assist the provincial Indian organization, by this
time known as the Federation of Saskatchewan Indians (FSI), 'to maintain
a strong democratic and positive organization devoted to the improvement and advancement of all people of Indian ancestry.'[109] The membership consisted of executive representatives of departments concerned with
minority groups as well as special members, including Morris Shumiatcher
(member at large) and William Wuttunee (Indian representative).[110] The
latter, a graduate of McGill law school, was reputed to be one of the
first Indians to practice law in Saskatchewan, and was employed by
Saskatchewan Government Insurance.[111] Reflecting the ever-present influence of the premier, the committee was not only responsible to Douglas,
who chaired its meetings, but also was able to report to cabinet only
through the premier.[112] The director of the committee was Ray Woollam,
a one-time United Church minister.[113] Woollam was responsible for putting

Portrait of William I.C. Wuttunee,
of the Legal Department of the
Saskatchewan Government
Insurance Office, June 1961.
(Saskatchewan Archives Board
61-211-03)

into effect the decisions arrived at by the committee. Among other things, his duties included collaboration with the Indian Affairs Branch in matters pertaining to joint federal-provincial programs, promotion of FSI, and liaising between the FSI and the committee.[114] Woollam, in fact, played a major role in Indian issues near the end of Douglas's tenure as premier.

Within the parameters of this administrative framework, the government dealt with Indian matters in a somewhat haphazard fashion, responding to the exigencies of the day. As might be expected, the views of provincial officials were conditioned by the issues with which they were confronted over time and changed correspondingly as they became more familiar with the Indian scene, and as they became increasingly frustrated in their efforts to effect change. Nevertheless, Douglas and his cohorts consistently expressed the view that the only way Indians would be integrated into mainstream society was through a complete transfer of jurisdiction over Indians from the federal to provincial governments. This view was premised on two related, and only seemingly contradictory, notions about jurisdiction. On the one hand, Douglas insisted that the province de facto had no choice but to deal with Indians who occupied provincial hospitals, jails, insane asylums, and urban centres; on the other, he willingly acknowledged the de jure jurisdiction of the federal government.[115] The latter, in fact, was based on provincial self-interest because demands that jurisdiction be transferred were always accompanied by the proviso that federal funding likewise be consigned to the province. In the interim, Douglas was quite prepared to enter into – indeed, was insistent on – cost-sharing arrangements with the dominion

Ray Woollam, Director of Provincial
Committee on Minority Groups,
ca. 1960. (Saskatchewan Archives
Board R-A11,544-3)

whereby the province would deliver services to the Indian community
on behalf of the federal government. The province was also determined
to play the role of honest broker, informally mediating between the Indian
community and the federal government and, where possible, initiating
minor reforms within the purview of provincial jurisdiction.

A central issue was the demand for a federal inquiry into Indian conditions. It had been in anticipation of such an inquiry that Douglas originally had called Indians together and that the Regina conference had passed
a resolution calling for a petition to Ottawa. The CCF was not prepared
to let the issue die and, shortly after the creation of the USI, mounted a
campaign both provincially and federally. In March 1946, newly elected
MLA Fred Dewhurst (CCF, Wadena) introduced a motion into the Legislative Assembly calling for a federal commission, with Indian membership,
to investigate conditions on Indian reserves, with particular reference to
health, education, social welfare, and civil rights.[116] The debate on the
motion, which was passed unanimously, was little more than an excuse to
air publicly complaints against the administration of Indian Affairs. While
the attack was dominated by the CCF, it was supported by Liberals as well.
The main speakers included the premier, Joe Phelps, Jacob Benson (Last
Mountain), L.W. Lee (Cumberland House), D.Z. Daniels (Pelly), D.M.
Lazorko (Redberry), P.J. Hooge (Rosthern), and R. Wooff (Turtleford).

During the debate Douglas condemned the enervating paternalism of
federal Indian Affairs policy in Canada and, in a cursory and rare reference to other countries, contrasted it with the 'happy relationship'
between Aboriginals and whites in New Zealand and with the 'New Deal'

in the United States under the late Franklin Roosevelt.[117] He then went on to argue that the measure of any society is the way it treats its least fortunate group. In the case of Saskatchewan, he said, 'It is not enough to establish a co-operative commonwealth and to raise the standard of living if there continues to remain like a canker a small, underprivileged, diseased, illiterate minority.'[118] Benson reinforced this notion by insisting that, if federal authorities refused to act, the provincial government should intervene.[119] Phelps chimed in with the demand that Indian jurisdiction and funding be transferred to the provinces and insisted that Indians be given full citizenship rights, including the right to vote and drink alcohol in public places.[120] Whereas Lazorko likened Indian reserves to 'voluntary concentration camps,'[121] Wooff roundly condemned the health services delivered to Indians. He noted that, while the province had taken great strides in eliminating diseases such as TB, contagion continued to flourish on reserves and had the potential to undo all that had been accomplished.[122] And virtually all speakers condemned Indian education facilities as the main deterrent to integration. They took particular issue with the sectarian nature of Indian education wherein churches – mostly Roman Catholic and Anglican – placed religious considerations above training Indians to take their place in society. The only solution, they argued, was that Indian schools be divested of their religious affiliation and placed directly under the provincial Department of Education.[123]

The Dewhurst resolution was applauded in the local press as an appropriate means to 'pressure' federal authorities into action. The *Regina Leader-Post* questioned the wisdom of transferring jurisdiction for Indians to the ten provinces on the grounds that it would cause 'unevenness of treatment across Canada.'[124] Nevertheless, the intent and most of the content of the resolution were warmly supported. Also applauded in the Saskatchewan press was the follow-up action taken by Castleden and his CCF supporters in the federal House of Commons. In May, Castleden placed a resolution on the order paper, proposing a Royal Commission, which would include Indian representation, to study the whole question of Indian Affairs.[125] In due course, the federal government finally gave in to the mounting pressure in Ottawa, Saskatchewan, and elsewhere, and formally announced the appointment of a Joint Committee of the Senate and House of Commons (JCSHC) to inquire into Indian Affairs; but even then Castleden, along with Max Campbell and H.G. Archibald (CCF, Skeena, BC), continued the attack in the House, denouncing Indian Affairs as a 'monument of disgrace to those ... in power.'[126]

The joint committee was mandated to inquire into the Indian Act and to make recommendations for its revision. In general, it was to investigate and report on the Indian administration and, in particular, it was to inquire into a number of areas of special concern: treaty rights and obligations, band membership, the liability of Indians to pay taxes, enfranchisement, the Indian franchise, white encroachments on Indian lands, the operation of Indian schools, and the social and economic advancement of Indians.[127]

The appointment of the committee reflected the fact that, unlike during the Depression and war years when public attention was focused on global issues, the postwar era had ushered in a new social conscience increasingly fixed on the domestic scene, especially the plight of Indians.[128] The committee was also meant as a response to concerns expressed in the House of Commons and elsewhere that the sorry state of Indian Affairs represented a source of potential embarrassment for Canada at the international level. With the growth of the Cold War, the conflict between East and West was being fought increasingly at the propaganda and rhetorical levels, and there was particular concern that the Soviet Union might question the treatment of Canadian Indians in the United Nations Assembly.[129]

The hearings of the committee in 1946 were addressed principally to evidence from Indian Affairs officials, and so there was no request for representations from Indian organizations.[130] That notwithstanding, a number of briefs were presented, including major submissions from the North American Indian Brotherhood and the Indian Association of Alberta. Also noteworthy was a particularly bitter brief from the St. Regis Mohawks. They demanded their treaty rights and denounced a revision of the Indian Act because 'it will never promote our welfare as long as we are on a double chain of pauperism and mental servitude.'[131] Although these briefs were accepted into evidence, the JCSHC nevertheless deferred consideration of them until the 1947 sitting of the committee. It was during that session that emphasis would be placed on the Indian Act, rather than on the administration of Indian Affairs, and that Indian associations and bands from across Canada were expected to make their views known.

In Saskatchewan, the sitting of the joint committee gave new urgency to the brief that would be drawn up by the Union of Saskatchewan Indians. A moot point was the extent to which this document, in reality, was influenced by what was perceived as the union's close relationship with the provincial government. Earlier, in 1945, the executive of the Protective Association had petitioned the government for assistance in preparing a brief for presentation to Ottawa. According to Morris Shumiatcher, the people involved were past supporters of the CCF and were drawn to the government because of the premier.[132] The entire brief, although based on information provided by the association, had in fact been drawn up by Shumiatcher and was laced with CCF notions about democracy.[133] Not surprisingly, this cooperation between the PAIT and

Shumiatcher made it easy for politicians, both provincially and federally, to see the secret hand of the CCF in the brief ultimately prepared by the USI. This was all the more so given that Shumiatcher was the union's legal advisor and that union meetings were housed in facilities provided by the provincial government. Indeed, Douglas freely admitted that he and his government were 'doing everything possible to assist the Indians ... in consolidating their representations in order that they may be placed before [the] joint committee.'[134]

The first draft of the USI brief, in fact, was fashioned by a special USI committee, appointed at the first annual meeting of the union held at Lebret in May 1946, shortly after the announcement of the JCSHC. The USI committee, along with the executive of the USI, met over the next two months and hammered out the main details of the brief; Morris Shumiatcher, as legal advisor, then translated the committee's ideas into a written text. In late October, the draft was ratified by the northern chiefs meeting in Saskatoon and then, in early December, it was submitted to the southern chiefs during a convention held in the Court House in Regina. The meeting in the capital was attended by some forty delegates, almost half of whom were veterans.[135] The government had a certain presence at the Regina meeting, in that the province hosted a dinner for delegates in the legislative building cafeteria and both Morris Shumiatcher and Joe Phelps attended some of the sessions.[136] But officials were careful not to meddle in the proceedings of the conference. According to one newspaper account, despite the government's sponsorship and encouragement of an Indian brief, 'it was felt the Indians themselves should be allowed to carry on. For this reason government officials took no part in the Regina discussions.'[137]

The brief itself was not well received and was not ratified. Especially troublesome was the issue of citizenship rights for Indians. Delegates tended to confuse the 'franchise,' or the right to vote, with 'enfranchisement,' the process whereby an Indian ceased to be an Indian in a legal sense. The semantic confusion was compounded by the fact that enfranchised Indians automatically received the franchise. Also at issue was the long-standing principle that the right to vote carried with it the responsibility of paying taxes, a principle that threatened the tax exemption rights of treaty Indians. Understandably, given the complexity of the issues, compounded by language problems, there was considerable confusion and distrust. In the end, the conference decided not to ratify the brief, opting instead to have it translated into Cree and circulated throughout the province for local input.[138]

It was at this point that the perceived affinity between the CCF and the union proved to be a political liability. At the local level, both Indian Affairs and Catholic Church personnel attempted to intervene in reserve politics, a process especially noticeable in the Duck Lake area. In March, Chief Don Gamble had called a meeting, attended by thirty people from four bands, to prepare a local brief for submission to the parliamentary committee. Although the brief was at odds with the USI brief, in that it supported the continuation of denominational residential schools, many of those who attended the meeting were USI members. The meeting was held in the Duck Lake residential school and was attended by Reverend Father Letour, the principal of the school, and Mr. N.J. McLeod, the local Indian agent. According to affidavits submitted by John Tootoosis to the JCSHC, both men attempted to prejudice the meeting against the union because of its perceived connection with the CCF. At one point, Reverend Letour advised the Indian delegates 'to do away with this Union of Saskatchewan; he said it was connected with the CCF political party. Furthermore, he persuaded the band to have their own agency brief.'[139] At another point, John Eyahpaise suggested that some reference should be made to the brief already prepared by the union, and in reaction the Indian agent insisted that 'those who are in favor of the Union of Saskatchewan Indians or are connected with that CCF outfit had better pack up and go.'[140] In response, most of the representatives left the meeting.

A similar kind of political partisanship was expressed at the federal level as well, this time in the JCSHC itself. Although the committee was composed of members from all political parties, including Castleden from the CCF, it was dominated by Liberals and Conservatives. Even before the USI Regina meeting, Donald Brown, one of the chairmen of the parliamentary committee, let it be known to the press that his committee had no authority to deal with Indians from the prairies.[141] Zachariah Hamilton, secretary of the Saskatchewan Historical Society, characterized Brown's views as 'an unfortunate mistake on someone's part.'[142] He insisted that, only two months earlier, the Honourable J. Glen, minister in charge of Indian Affairs, had told him he hoped western Indians would appear in person at the hearing to plead their case.[143] Brown's statement, in fact, was indicative of a hostile attitude held by some members of the parliamentary committee. According to one newspaper account, 'a considerable amount of wrangling had gone on in the committee's sittings, charges being made that the union had been set up and was controlled by the Saskatchewan government and that it was not representative of Saskatchewan's Indians.'[144] In the end, the committee decided to limit the presence of the USI at committee hearings by identifying the organizations in the province that would be funded to attend the hearings in Ottawa. Initially, there were supposed to be three representatives from the union, as the all-inclusive organization of status Indians in the province, and one from the 'unorganized' Indians. However, the committee finally decided that, in terms of the organizations, it would pay the expenses of one member only from each of the union, the Association of Indians of Saskatchewan, the Protective Association for Indians and Their Treaties, and the North American Indian Brotherhood.[145] This was done despite the fact that both the AIS and the PAIT were now entirely inactive and that their leadership had been co-opted by the union. The idea that the USI was merely the mouthpiece of the CCF was not easily put to rest and would continue to hound the union for some time to come.

The issue of USI representation in Ottawa, along with the problems associated with the Indian brief itself, were finally settled at a union conference in Saskatoon in the spring of 1947. The sixty-odd delegates, angered by the JCSHC's refusal to recognize the union as an all-inclusive body, interpreted the ploy as an attempt to split the USI's membership.[146] Ultimately, they decided to comply with the committee's requirements, but they did so in a way that underscored the representativeness of the union itself: they chose delegates to the JCSHC who in the past had been the undisputed leaders of the old organizations that were now inactive. John Tootoosis would represent the USI; Joe Dreaver the AIS; John Gamble the PAIT; and Ahab Spence, an Anglican teacher from Little Pine Reserve, would speak for the unorganized Indians in the province.[147] It was up to the Saskatchewan branch of the NAIB to send its own representative.

The conference also unanimously ratified an amended union brief. Consensus was achieved by sidestepping the whole issue of full citizenship rights for Indians. In its final form, the brief recognized the need for Indians to assume eventually the responsibilities and duties of citizenship, but nevertheless rejected both enfranchisement and the franchise. It did sanction enfranchisement on an individual basis, but only with the consent of the individual and only after he or she had been sufficiently educated.[148] The brief decried the unwillingness of government to honour the treaty rights of Indians and adamantly called for a fulfilment of treaty promises. It also included demands for educational, health, and other reforms, as well as enhanced self-determination.[149] Unlike eastern Indians, most Indian bands on the prairies had not yet been brought under the Indian Act's 'Betterment' section through which, at the discretion of Indian Affairs, bands could have greater control over their own affairs.[150] The brief asked that Indians be given increased autonomy by exercising municipal-like powers, through which reserves would be schooled in self-government; it demanded decreased power and control from Ottawa; and it asked for representation in Parliament, wherein Indians would be elected by reserve communities on a non-political basis without first being required to enfranchise.[151] In total, the brief contained thirty-five specific criticisms and/or recommendations, many of which were copied verbatim from those contained in the brief of the Indian Association of Alberta.[152]

Although the Saskatoon meeting solved some of the problems confronting the USI, the controversy concerning the union's domination by the CCF remained. A day after the conference, Regina's *Leader-Post* carried an editorial regretting that Indians were divided over the content of the brief and that the Saskatchewan government 'could not have obtained a greater measure of support before proceeding with the brief.'[153] Shumiatcher, as legal advisor to the union, immediately published a disclaimer, pointing out that the editorial mistakenly referred to the Regina brief, not the revised one sanctioned by the Saskatoon conference.[154] He also dismissed the notions that Indians were divided on the issue and that the brief was not based on ideas that had come from the Indian community itself. According to Shumiatcher, these mistaken impressions stemmed from those 'who were anxious to deprecate the ability of the Indians to think for themselves.'[155]

Shumiatcher's disclaimer notwithstanding, the controversy did not go away. On May 6, the four Indian delegates left for Ottawa. On the same day, Shumiatcher wrote to Castleden. He alluded, with a certain paternalistic air, to the fact that the 'boys' had departed Regina and expressed the hope that they would receive a warm reception.[156] He also asked for the support of Castleden, as a member of the JCSHC, in eliciting the necessary facts about Indian life.[157] As it turned out, union representatives received anything but an amicable reception from the parliamentary committee. According to one source, the spectre of politics entered the committee room every time the Indians of Saskatchewan were even mentioned.[158] Castleden was drawn into protracted bickering in an effort to fend off charges that the USI was not representative of Indians in Saskatchewan and that 'it was merely a machine set up by the C.C.F. for propaganda purposes.'[159] When John Tootoosis appeared before the committee on 8 May, debate on these charges took up most of the entire morning and filled no fewer than nine pages of the committee's printed minutes and proceedings.[160]

The committee adjourned around 1:00 p.m. When the sitting resumed in late afternoon, the proceedings were reportedly less confrontational, in that the committee now heard testimony in support of the union. The Reverend Dan McIvor, a Liberal MP from Fort William and a one-time teacher in the Regina Indian Industrial school, appeared before the committee at his own request. His presentation was essentially 'a sweeping character reference' for two of his past pupils, union representatives Chief John Gamble and Chief Joe Dreaver.[161] Immediately after this, James Ostrander addressed the committee with considerable authority. As the inspector of Indian agencies in Saskatchewan and as a man who had married a woman from the File Hills agency,[162] Ostrander was thoroughly conversant with the Saskatchewan scene and spoke to the credentials of the union's delegates: 'I have no hesitation in saying that these four gentlemen can properly represent the Indians of Saskatchewan as far as it is possible to do so. I took all the trouble and time I possibly could to be sure that the representations of the Indians of Saskatchewan were put fairly and justly before this committee, and I have no hesitation in standing behind these four men as being fully capable and fitted to make representations to you.'[163] The Reverend Ahab Spence also denied that the union was merely a front for the CCF, arguing that he never would have joined the delegation had the union's brief been prepared by the CCF.[164] In the end, the union's representatives and brief were accepted by the Committee, although probably with reluctance by some members.

The JCSHC tabled its report in July 1947. During its deliberations, it had held 67 meetings, heard from 102 witnesses, and consulted 153 written briefs.[165] The findings of the committee were important because of the revelations they contained about the deplorable conditions on Indian reserves throughout Canada. But in its own right, the report was hardly revolutionary in its twenty-six recommendations for change. As a matter of some urgency, the committee called for immediate action to remedy certain abusive practices. This included the issuance of rations for the proper and sufficient care of Indians; setting up a claims commission to examine and enforce the terms of Indian treaties; the construction, at once, of a government hospital and nursing station central to Indian agencies in the North; legislation providing permanently for the adequate care of the aged, infirm, and blind; as well as the removal of non-Indians illegally occupying reserve lands.[166] As a long-term goal, the committee also recommended a restructuring of Indian Affairs, with qualified Indians being given preference in hiring at all levels of the bureaucracy. Under this proposal, Indian Affairs would be upgraded from a branch of the Department of Mines and Resources to the status of a separate department with its own minister, deputy minister, and two assistants, one of whom would be an Indian.[167] Indian agents – the subject of complaint in briefs from across Canada – were to be subjected to changes in the method of their appointment, promotion, and control and dismissed immediately if they were found to be incompetent, as Indians alleged.[168] In addition, the committee proposed that a similar joint committee be established at the next session of Parliament and that it be mandated to consider those matters deferred by the present committee.

While these recommendations were meant as a response to Indian complaints, they did little to satisfy the agenda of the provincial government. Essentially, the committee had chosen not only to maintain the bureaucratic status quo in Canada but also to enhance the power centralized in

Ottawa by making Indian Affairs a separate department. Moreover, the committee deferred consideration of matters deemed important by the CCF in the liberation of Indians from their second-class status. Indian education and enfranchisement had a direct bearing on the process of bringing Indians into mainstream society, but neither was dealt with adequately. The report did recommend that, out of deference to complaints about church-run schools, all educational matters should be brought directly under Indian Affairs. Nevertheless, detailed consideration of both citizenship and education was largely deferred.[169] For a provincial government anxious to play a major role in Indian matters, particularly in education and health, the report of the joint committee must have been less than encouraging.

CCF Response to Indian Complaints

For the most part, the relationship of the CCF to Indian issues remained unaltered by the findings of the JCSHC. This was a result of the fact that, whatever might be happening at the federal level, the Douglas government was increasingly drawn into Indian affairs as the would-be champion of an oppressed minority. Indians were encouraged to see the CCF administration as 'their' government and to make demands on it as a matter of right. And when they did so, the premier and his advisers responded with alacrity and commitment to even the smallest request or concern. The Douglas papers are filled with letters and representations from bands and individuals who petitioned the premier for assistance, sometimes in regard to personal problems, other times in reference to Indian Affairs bureaucrats. The premier's office, in fact, became a kind of clearing house for complaints and requests. When the matter fell within provincial jurisdiction, it was referred as a matter of course to the appropriate minister or director for immediate action; when it involved federal jurisdiction, either Douglas, Shumiatcher, Sturdy, or an appropriate minister would write directly to senior federal officials asking that the complaint be investigated.

Matters satisfied within the ambit of provincial jurisdiction were varied and wide-ranging. The executive of the USI routinely asked the premier personally to arrange for facilities in Regina so that it could have a meeting.[170] When a group of Indians from Sintaluta decided to go to Montana to attend a Sun Dance, Morris Shumiatcher arranged for a provincial bus at a special 'club rate.'[171] At one point, the Exhibition Boards of both Regina and Battleford decided to break with past practice and charge Indians an admission fee on account of the prevalence of Indian drunkenness at local fairs; the matter was taken up by the premier at the request of the USI's executive.[172] On another occasion, Dan Kennedy, who had inherited land in Montana threatened with flooding from a government diversion project, asked the government to protect his interests. The premier's executive assistant, H.S. Lee, secured a lawyer in the attorney general's office to advise Kennedy 'unofficially' and recommended a Montana lawyer who might be consulted about the matter.[173] On still another occasion, the province intervened on behalf of Indians involved in making a movie for Twentieth-Century Fox.[174] The movie company had contracted with Indian Affairs to provide food for some 280 Cree Indians from Piapot Reserve, near Regina. The Indians were being used as 'extras' during the filming of a movie about the massacre of Assiniboine Indians in the Cypress Hills in 1873. The food never arrived, however, and in response to urgent calls from the movie producer, the Saskatchewan Department of Natural Resources rushed 450 loaves of bread and more than 100 pounds of meat to the film site.

Even more voluminous were requests that the province intercede with Indian Affairs, a course of action often resented by federal officials. Indicative of the process was a request to the premier from members of the Ochapawace Band in the summer of 1947.[175] Several men from the east end of the reserve, along with Chief Ochapawace, met in the chief's house and passed a number of resolutions, mostly asking for assistance from a seemingly uncooperative band council. In particular, they complained that, in past years, they had had difficulty getting their crops off the fields before the onslaught of winter and, as a solution, they wanted the council to provide 'a complete threshing outfit.' They criticized the impassable state of roads, both on the reserve and leading to town. They also wanted use of one of the two tractors in operation on the band's community farm, as well as an increase in the living allowance for a destitute band member named Little Assiniboine. Finally, seemingly in opposition to a move to replace the existing chief, they demanded that Ochapawace remain in office.

The resolutions represented a criticism of a situation supported by Indian Affairs, so they were not presented directly to local IAB officials but instead hand-delivered to Morris Shumiatcher's office. On behalf of the dissident group, Shumiatcher had the resolutions typed up and forwarded with a covering letter from the premier to C.D. Howe, the acting minister of mines and resources.[176] When more than two months passed without a response, Douglas followed up with a second letter, this time addressed to J.A. Glen, the minister who had been away on sick leave.[177] In reply, the premier finally received a letter from the minister, evidently perturbed by what was seen as Douglas's unwarranted interference:

> Please be advised that all matters covered in the list of grievances presented through you have been fully investigated and dealt with in the ordinary course of administration and all matters settled, we believe, in

accordance with the wishes of the Band as expressed to us in the official and proper way, through the proceedings of the Band Council. In every case the complaints placed before you appear to be from a disgruntled minority of non-co-operative Indians ...

I do not think any useful purpose is served in taking sides as you have in this matter with a disgruntled and non-co-operative group against the Band Council and the majority of the Band which they represent. It would have been preferable to have referred the matter back to the Band Council and the Indian Agent, as the facts have proven that there was nothing in the representations that could not have been and which has now been handled in a satisfactory manner through the usual channels.[178]

Glen's resentment was only slightly veiled by the official nature of the letter and there can be little doubt that his reply was meant as a reprimand to a premier who was being meddlesome.

Douglas was not one to be chastised like a school boy. A week later, he sent off a letter to the minister duly advising him that he was wrong. He pointed out that the resolutions had been drawn up in good faith, out of a sincere attempt to improve conditions on the reserve, and that the meetings had even been held in the home of the chief. Therefore, he said, 'there appears to be no indication whatever that this is a disgruntled or non-co-operative group.'[179] Douglas's assertion, however, was largely bravado and had a hollow ring to it, in that he could offer no rebuttal to the fact that the dissident group had no official standing on the reserve and was clearly at odds with the Band Council. It was probably for this reason that he was quite prepared to drop the matter. On the same day, Shumiatcher contacted the dissidents and advised them that the minister had investigated and dealt with their complaints, adding that if there were additional concerns he would assist them if possible.[180]

The matter did not end there, however. As required, the dissidents committed their concerns to 'the proper channels,' petitioning the local Indian superintendent,[181] Mr. Kearly, for a redress of their complaints. Although Indian Affairs did allocate an additional $2,000 for road improvements in and around Ochapawace, no action was taken to satisfy the other concerns, particularly the need for a threshing machine.[182] In turn, the dissident group drew up a petition and once more called upon the assistance of Morris Shumiatcher. The petition was forwarded to Ottawa, along with a covering letter representing the dissidents as the 'majority' of the band and asking for appropriate action.[183] The response from Ottawa, however, was no more sympathetic than past correspondence had been. Shumiatcher was advised by the deputy minister that nothing had changed since the minister's letter to the premier and that there was 'no justification for the purchase of a threshing outfit for the small group of Indians involved. We are satisfied that Mr. Kearly is dealing properly with the situation.'[184]

In the end, Douglas's secretary acknowledged the deputy minister's reply and at long last the matter was dropped. The incident illustrated the more or less intransigent nature of the Indian Affairs bureaucracy, but also the eagerness and tenacity with which the province was prepared to make representations on behalf of the Indian community. Indeed, the paper flow between Regina and Ottawa increased vastly through the late 1940s and was addressed to every subject imaginable: an aged and ill Indian living on an income of only $5.00 a month; Indian land claims based on treaty entitlement; parents and their ill child left standing in the snow at subzero temperatures waiting for an Indian Affairs doctor who showed up two hours late for the appointment; Indian veterans denied the same rights as non-Native servicemen; an Indian who had lost his railway travel card and could not secure a replacement from the local Indian agent.[185] No matter was too big or too small to draw a sympathetic response from the provincial government, even though the reply from Indian Affairs was seldom encouraging.

Needless to say, Ottawa was less than enthusiastic about the province's intervention and eventually reacted. In the summer of 1949, the new minister of mines and resources, Jas. A. MacKinnon, sent a letter to the premier complaining about the 'unusually large number of letters on file here relating to the administration of Indian Affairs in Saskatchewan received from you and from Mr. Shumiatcher.'[186] In particular, MacKinnon was disturbed by the fact that Indians were petitioning the province instead of submitting their concerns to local and regional officials. He said the practice not only disrupted administrative procedure and destroyed the morale of local officials but also lessened the prestige of officials in the eyes of Indians. He therefore 'suggested' a proper course of action for future reference: urgent concerns could continue to be reported to him directly; but in the case of minor matters, Indians should be referred to the local Indian superintendent or the regional supervisor.[187]

In his reply to the minister, Douglas agreed to the new procedures but left himself latitude to ignore them. He pointed out that Shumiatcher had petitioned ministerial officials directly because he had seldom been able to get satisfaction at the local level and he indicated that, were that to remain true, referral to Ottawa would still be necessary. As he explained, he would ask Shumiatcher 'to direct these matters ... to the proper officials, and should he find it impossible to get any response, to take the cases up with your Deputy Minister.'[188] Apart from the fact that 'urgent' and 'minor' were left undefined, Douglas knew that problems on reserves often stemmed from local bureaucrats who lacked either the will or authority to deal with Indian concerns and he had no reason to believe the situation would change with the new procedures. Should Indian superintendents prove receptive to requests from the province, so much the better; but if not, he was not prepared to surrender his right to represent Indians before officials in Ottawa. His reply to the minister was tantamount to a diplomatic nicety, which, in practice, placed almost no restraints on past practices. The province would not be silenced by administrative procedure and this was underscored in the volume of continuing correspondence between Regina and the capital.

While criticism of Indian Affairs figured prominently in provincial-federal relations, it was by no means the only, or even the most important, factor in the interface between governments. The province's complaints, although often seen in Ottawa as a form of provincial whining, were not without import and served to dramatize deplorable administrative practices. But in addition to this, there also evolved substantive issues arising from political principle and conflicting jurisdictions. Fundamental to the idea of Indian integration was the issue of Indian citizenship rights. To the Douglas government, this meant a delivery of services to reserves comparable to those enjoyed by other citizens because this was the only way Indians could achieve a degree of social and economic equality. The citizenship issue also raised the thorny question of whether Indians should be given the right to vote and consume alcohol legally, as in the case of non-Indians. In most peoples' minds, the franchise and liquor rights were two sides of the same coin and represented the hallmarks of citizenship. Such considerations were philosophically rooted in the political environment and, as it turned out, served in many ways to define the relationship between Regina and Ottawa from the late 1940s through to the early 1960s when Douglas left office.

4
Citizenship Issues

The demand in Saskatchewan that Indians be given full citizenship rights was a result of a number of factors, not all of which originated within the province. Ironically, it did not come from the Indian community itself; rather, it was sustained mainly by white humanitarians, responding in many ways to the same factors that had led Ottawa to inquire into the whole state of Indian affairs in the first place. The postwar social conscience, coupled with the fear of international embarrassment, created a climate of opinion that the federal government could hardly ignore. If nothing else, the JCSHC process was meant to showcase Ottawa's sympathy for a more liberal approach in dealing with Indians, and the findings of that committee served to reinforce the message. In 1948, for example, the JCSHC was reconstituted and eventually submitted two reports, both of which roundly condemned the existing situation. Essentially, the reports called for a revision of all sections of the Indian Act 'to make possible the gradual transition of Indians from wardship to citizenship and to help them to advance themselves.'[1] In one sense, this statement was anything but new, in that theoretically it had always been the goal of government to reshape Indians into citizens. What was new was the accompanying recommendation that, among other things, Indians should be given the right to vote in federal elections.[2] It was a concrete proposal, which, in effect, catapulted the citizenship issue from threadbare philosophy to the realm of practical politics.

Reinforcing the postwar atmosphere was the contradictory nature of Indian wardship. On the one hand, Indians increasingly were making their presence felt in Canadian institutions, especially in the West where their numbers were proportionally high. As early as 1916, for instance, Indian youths in the File Hills agency became increasingly involved in the Junior Red Cross, and by the mid-1950s, Indian residential schools in Saskatchewan accounted for some seventy-three branches of that organization.[3] Likewise, during both world wars, Indians not only volunteered for service at a rate that outpaced all other groups in society, proportional to their total population, but also collectively compiled an outstanding record for service and bravery. Yet, on the other hand, Indians were set apart, if not segregated, by special racial legislation – the Indian Act – through which Indian Affairs ruled reserve life with stifling paternalism and authority. Whereas many whites doubted that Indian status actually conferred any real benefits on Indians, those who believed otherwise saw those benefits as a burden on the Canadian taxpayer. Wardship also meant that Indians were treated inequitably and denied the kind of rights other people acquired by the mere act of being born.[4] The Indian Act, for instance, proscribed Indian drinking with a stringency and punishment far more severe than the regulations governing the use of alcohol by non-Indians. Likewise, although Indian servicemen and their wives were given the federal vote, the vast majority of Indians were not allowed to participate in either federal or provincial elections, a prerogative other Canadians generally accepted as a fundamental human right. For democrats, the restrictions on Indian drinking and voting typified all the worst features of wardship and stood as a monument to the inequality that separated Indians from full citizenship. For that reason, the alcohol and franchise issues became inexorably linked in public discourse and together became the focus of the citizenship debate.

The contradiction inherent in wardship status was writ large in a murder trial in the Court of Queen's Bench in Yorkton in the late 1950s.[5] John Bird, a twenty-year-old Indian from Keesekoosee Reserve, in the Kamsack district, was charged with clubbing a man to death. However, before the trial could get underway, the defence lawyer, G.M. Forbes of Regina, objected to the proceedings on a point of order. He pointed out that none of the impaneled jury was Indian and that the accused was entitled to be heard by a jury of his peers, namely treaty Indians. As he explained,

> It is a long standing principle of British justice that a person is entitled to be tried by his peers and the accused being a treaty Indian should be entitled to be tried by a jury of treaty Indians.[6]

When pressed for an interpretation of the word 'peer,' Forbes defined it as 'one who is equal in standing.'[7] In response, the crown prosecutor protested that he had never before heard such an objection. He said he was inclined to agree that Indians are British subjects, but he insisted that they did not have citizens' rights because they came under the jurisdiction of the Indian Act. Having heard counsels' arguments, Judge McKercher adjourned the proceedings to consider the matter and eventually ruled that the jury had been properly impaneled. From a legal point of view, the objection raised by Forbes was of little importance. It did nevertheless underscore the inconsistencies of Indian wardship and the problems they posed at the social and political levels.

A third factor at play was the belief by many that Indians would never progress until they had achieved citizenship rights. From the beginning, Dan Kennedy was one of the staunchest proponents of the vote for Indians, although he was fully aware that many Indians were opposed because they believed it entailed a loss of treaty rights. In a letter to Douglas, he largely dismissed this fear as being analogous to American slaves refusing freedom after the Civil War because their souls had been crushed by their slave masters.[8] Kennedy insisted that the vote would liberate Indians and in a newspaper article he pointed once more to the American experience to show that Indian fears were unfounded: 'Uncle Sam extended the franchise vote to his Indian in 1924 and they took to it just as naturally as a duck takes to water.'[9] Douglas readily agreed because he saw the franchise as the cutting edge of a more pervasive demand for rights. As he explained to Kennedy, 'if our Indian brothers are to be given the vote they have an equal right to claim all the other privileges which Saskatchewan citizens enjoy.'[10] He also insisted that only by obtaining the franchise would Indians make politicians and others listen to their demands. As he explained to one Indian gathering, 'the wheel that squeaks the loudest gets the grease.'[11]

The final, and perhaps the most fundamental, factor in the demand for Indian citizenship rights was the realization that Indians were not a dying race, as had been assumed. Increasingly it was demographics and economics that made the citizenship issue so important in the eyes of Saskatchewan officials. Starting in the late 1940s and accelerating through the 1950s, speeches, interviews, and interdepartmental memos increasingly alluded to the burgeoning Indian population and its implications for the economy. The most succinct definition of the problem, however, was outlined in a brief submitted by the Saskatchewan government to the JCSHC in 1959. It was prepared jointly by the Economic Advisory and Planning Board and the various provincial departments dealing with Indian matters, under the supervision of the Committee on Minority Groups. It was presented to the JCSHC by John Sturdy and Ray Woollam and represented a digest of Saskatchewan's Indian policy.

The basic assumption of the brief was that the ultimate goal of Indian policy was the complete integration of Indians, as full citizens, into Canadian social and economic life.[12] This was dictated, said the brief, by an exploding Indian population growth that could not be supported economically because of the adverse conditions that existed on reserves. It noted that the population of reserve communities in Saskatchewan had increased by 9 percent between 1941 and 1946, 15 percent between 1946 and 1951, 18 percent between 1951 and 1956, and 21 percent between 1956 and 1959.[13] This meant that, over the entire period, the population had increased from 12,783 to 23,000, driven by a favourable age distribution, declining mortality, and a rising birth rate.[14] Generally, this population could be divided into two broad categories, said the brief. In the North, and representing about a fifth of the provincial population, Indians lived in small groups throughout the broad expanse of forest, lake, and rock, extending northward from the province's forest belt. These people depended mainly upon the fish, fur, and game resources of the wooded northern regions. In the southern half of the province, reserves were concentrated in a broad diagonal band running from the North Battleford-Meadow Lake region on the north-west, to the Manitoba border on the south-east. The main source of livelihood for these people was agriculture.

According to the brief, the basic problem was that Indians lacked the resource base to sustain the population growth. In the North, fish and furs provided more adequate resources than did agriculture in the South and this meant that Indians in the North were less dependent on government transfer payments, but even there the Indian existence was only marginal at best.[15] In the South, the situation was chronic. Between 1941 and 1956, the cultivated acreage of Indian reserves had more than doubled, perhaps approaching the limit of expansion. During the same period, the dramatic increase in population meant that the number of acres per Indian dropped from ninety-four to only sixty.[16] Thus, at a time when existing land could not be made more productive, the amount of land available to each Indian had dropped severely. The implication, said the brief, was 'that the reserves are becoming less and less a possible place to earn a living from farming, and more and more merely a segregated domiciliary area for Indians.'[17] This was self-evident in the chronic lack of income. Whereas the per capita income for Saskatchewan as a whole was $1,245, the average annual income for Indians was only $208, and as low as $165 in one agency.[18] And even then, said the brief, some 30 percent of Indian income came from government transfer payments of all kinds, especially poor relief.[19] What all of this meant was that Indians, both in the North and the South, lacked the resource base necessary to produce a substantial improvement in standard of living. Indian dependence on natural resources, it was concluded, could only perpetuate the chain of poverty and inequality that set Indians apart from mainstream society.

What was needed, argued the brief, was that Indians must be assisted in exploiting the resource base. But more than that, the long-term solution rested in moving Indians out of their old subsistence patterns and integrating them into industrial society and wage labour.[20] In the North, this would entail the commercialization of the fish and fur industries as well as greater participation in activities associated with mining, tourism, construction, fire fighting, and related developments; in the South, Indians would have to leave the reserve to take advantage of wage opportunities found in the towns and cities. The prerequisite to Indian long-term employment, however, was the need to integrate Indians into the range of services provided for the population at large, including vocational training and employment counselling, hospitalization, as well as health and social services.[21] The brief anticipated that eventually all of these services would be provided by the province, with compensatory funding coming from Ottawa, but that joint federal-provincial planning and cooperation would be necessary during the transition period.[22]

Thus, according to the CCF's analysis of the Indian situation, the province's First Peoples would have to become fully functioning citizens as the only means to their economic and social salvation. This conclusion was accepted by the Douglas government as a moral certainty and this meant that the Indians' right to the vote and use of alcohol, the touchstones of citizenship, was axiomatic. In Saskatchewan, perhaps more so than in other provinces, the question was not whether these rights should be recognized formally but how soon. It was a question that hinged not only on whether Ottawa was sincere in its commitment to implement the recommendations of the JCSHC. It was also dependent on what action Douglas and his cabinet were prepared to take within the ambit of provincial jurisdiction.

The Franchise and Alcohol Issues

Although the province could not give Indians the right to vote federally, it did have the power to extend the franchise to Indians in provincial elections. With the exception of Nova Scotia, where Indians had had the right to vote in provincial elections from the time the province came into being, provincial electoral laws across the country were uniformly restrictive when it came to the Indian. Under Saskatchewan law, Indians were specifically excluded from voting, and the definition of who constituted an Indian was broadly based. In law, 'Indian' was interpreted to mean all persons of Indian blood who belonged, or were reputed to belong, to any band or irregular band.[23] The concept of band encompassed anyone who had a property interest in a reserve or shared lands, the title to which was vested in the Crown, and anyone who shared in the distribution of annuities for which the federal government was responsible.[24] Irregular band referred to any tribe, band, or body of persons of Indian blood who had no interest in a reserve or land whose title was vested in the Crown, who possessed no common fund managed by the federal government, and who had not had any treaty relations with the Crown.[25] These definitions effectively excluded all Indians from voting and, in effect, were more restrictive than the Dominion Elections Act. Under federal law, Indian servicemen and their wives automatically received the federal franchise, as did those who voluntarily or otherwise 'enfranchised' or, in other words, legally surrendered their status as Indians.[26] By comparison, there was no provision in provincial law that would allow Indians under any circumstance to receive the franchise.

The idea of giving Indians the provincial vote was seriously considered by the CCF as early as 1947. In that year, the Douglas government passed a provincial Bill of Rights, the first such legislation in all of Canada. The bill, guaranteeing in law the human rights of the provincial citizenry, was clearly at odds with the fact that a sizable portion of the provincial community – Indians – did not have the right to vote. The premier was among the first to acknowledge the inconsistency and he responded by offering the franchise to Indians.[27] However, Douglas also knew there was considerable opposition to the vote in Indian circles and he was not prepared to impose an unwanted reform on would-be voters. He therefore simply referred the matter to the Union of Saskatchewan Indians, asking that the Indian community consider the proposal.[28]

Symptomatic of what was, in fact, widespread opposition to the premier's proposal was the reaction of members of the Sintaluta Reserve where, only a few years earlier, Douglas had been made a chief.[29] They had learned of the proposal from radio and press reports and had seen signs advertising a meeting to discuss the matter. Operating under the mistaken impression that the initiative had come from Ottawa, rather than the province, they responded by denouncing the proposal in a formal statement drawn up by a local notary public. Their message, which they had printed in the *Regina Leader-Post* and broadcast by radio station CKCK, was that they wanted nothing to do with the vote: 'We, the Indians of Sintaluta Indians reserve have seen notices and signs coming into our reserve from the house of commons and have heard listening to radio broadcasting stations of Saskatchewan that Indians be franchised and given the right to vote, a move which we do not wish or wish to be forced.'[30] The statement then went on to challenge the right of the federal government to even raise the issue: 'According to our treaty with the queen in 1873, no authority has been given to any person, white or Indian, to direct signs or have some broadcast. We have our treaty and want to keep our rights and freedom.'[31]

As the Sintaluta statement made explicit, a root cause of the opposition was the perceived loss of Indian rights implied by the vote. As noted earlier, this stemmed from a semantic and functional confusion between the terms 'enfranchisement' and the 'franchise,' a problem exacerbated by the fact that English was not the mother tongue of most Indians.[32]

The terms were further confounded by provincial politicians and lawyers, including Morris Shumiatcher initially, who sometimes used the two terms interchangeably and without due regard for legal distinctions. Moreover, as Douglas pointed out, past experience had taught Indians to be leery of fraudulent reforms promising benefits.[33] This, combined with the dubious meaning and implications of the franchise, quite naturally led Indians to conclude that no change was better than a reform that might endanger what few rights they did possess.

While the USI was prepared to discuss the franchise, the proposal provoked widespread antipathy among the rank and file and garnered little sympathy in the leadership. For that reason Douglas was content to drop the idea, at least for the time being. Three years later, however, the issue was renewed, this time in reference to the course of events unfolding in Ottawa. It was widely assumed that the federal government was planning a major overhaul of the Indian Act in response to the recommendations of the JCSHC, and this created a certain sense of unease in the Indian community. On behalf of the Union of Saskatchewan Indians, Morris Shumiatcher petitioned Ottawa for a review process through which Indians would have an opportunity to discuss the proposed amendments before action was taken.[34] The federal government, however, preferred to keep the Indians in the dark, refusing to release any information until the amendments were introduced in the House. This only heightened the sense of apprehension, especially since it was known that the 1948 JCSHC had recommended that Indians be given the federal vote. That proposal had been roundly condemned by the USI as 'the white man's edge of the wedge' in destroying remaining Indian privileges, and it was feared that the vote would be included in forthcoming amendments.[35]

No group was more incensed over the issue than the Queen Victoria's Treaty Protection Association (QVTPA). QVTPA membership was centred in the Battleford area and encompassed some eight reserves in the central portion of the province near the northern limits of population concentration. At a meeting held in North Battleford in the spring of 1949, the QVTPA vehemently denounced the USI for its unwillingness to protect treaty rights. According to spokespersons, the union was not an Indian organization but rather a creation of the provincial government, which was known to favour the franchise.[36] Henry Chatses of Poundmaker Reserve, dredging up an old issue, insisted that the USI brief submitted to the JCSHC two years earlier had been drawn up by the government's lawyer, Mr. Shumiatcher, and that the union could not be trusted to represent Indian interests.[37] Clearly, the QVTPA's attack on the union was an expression of fear concerning the vote, but it was also motivated by an unrelated issue. Many lived off the land and were unhappy over the fact that the CCF was closely monitoring and regulating the harvesting of wildlife in the northern areas. As important as the franchise issue was in its own right, it also offered these Indians an opportunity to vent their hostility to the new regulations, described as containing 'too much socialism.'[38] It may also be that the QVTPA was motivated by sectarianism. According to Leona Tootoosis, John's daughter, the membership was heavily Catholic and hence was predisposed to dislike the union.[39]

Contrary to the perceptions of the QVTPA, the membership of the USI was not of one mind about the vote, and was divided according to age on the strategy that should be endorsed. In anticipation of sending a delegation to Ottawa to discuss amendments to the Indian Act, the USI held a government-sponsored convention in Saskatoon a few weeks after the QVTPA meeting. Delegates easily reached consensus on the need for some changes in the Indian Act, including better health provisions, educational opportunities equal to those for whites, and better treatment of the youth and aged.[40] The citizenship issue, however, was a different matter. The most conservative group, encompassing the oldest segment of the Indian population, was strongly in favour of maintaining the status quo, fearing that the vote might endanger their treaty money, tax-free land, and other benefits.[41] A second, less conservative, group, including John Tootoosis and other leaders, wanted to concentrate on getting the government to honour existing treaty rights before demanding citizenship. The argument here was that Indians could not trust the white man in a citizenship arrangement if they could not trust him to meet existing obligations.[42] The third group was composed mostly of the youth wing of the organization. Members insisted that full citizenship should not be resisted as an evil, but rather embraced as a means of making the government respect treaty obligations. They also argued that, in the past, young Indians had competed on equal terms with their white peers and could continue to do so if given equal opportunities.[43] In the end, it was the wisdom and experience of the older generations that prevailed. Delegates agreed that the USI should oppose citizenship rights for Indians and that that message would be conveyed to Ottawa by a three-member delegation composed of John Tootoosis (president), Lancelot Ahenakew (vice president), and John Gambler (second vice president).[44]

Within a month of that decision, events were overtaken by developments in Ottawa. In June 1950, the Liberal government of Louis St. Laurent introduced an entirely new Indian Act, Bill 267. Almost immediately, it ran headlong into a torrent of opposition, both outside and inside the House. According to one newspaper, the bill was a 'shamefully inadequate piece of legislation'; according to another, it had the potential to make the prime minister 'go down in history as an inglorious traitor to our native citizens.'[45] A main objection was that, despite government promises to the contrary, there had been almost no attempt to consult Indians about the content of the new bill. The fact that Indian associations and bands received copies of the bill only after its introduction in the House and only two weeks before Parliament was to be prorogued was more than enough to suggest that the promised consultation was a sham.[46] Even more important, the bill was condemned for its lack of real reform. Members who had served on the joint committee were astounded to learn that so few of their recommendations had actually been incorporated into the proposed legislation. As one member put it, 'When I come to examine the act, as a member of the Indian affairs committee, I find myself deeply disappointed. I spent three years of hard work on that Indian affairs committee, as did the other earnest members who were there. To think that after all our efforts, the sum total of our reward is this contemptible thing we have before us today makes me wonder if I do not have to struggle to keep my faith in humanity.'[47] The same sentiment was echoed by the Conservative opposition in the House. John Diefenbaker, with the deftness of oratorical skill for which he was known, denounced the bill as a perpetuation of the old authoritarian regime:

> At a time when throughout the world freedom is being challenged, when the very nature of democracy is being challenged, we have before us a bill that places shackles on a large part of the population of our country, numbering about 125,000. For three years that committee sat. Now the mountain brings forth a mouse. Here we have not what was recommended by the committee but what apparently meets the desires and the wishes of the administrative officials. In its present form of bill it is a perpetuation of bureaucracy over the Indian. It is a denial of his rights. It places him in the position of being a second class citizen under the law. It denies him freedom except with the consent of the minister or with the consent of some official of the Indian department.[48]

With equal skill, Indian leaders themselves denounced the proposed legislation. Apart from the fact that too little time had been allowed to examine the bill in detail, what was known about its content produced a negative reaction in the Indian community. Joe Dreaver, in an article in the *Regina Leader-Post*, expressed his personal disappointment for reasons similar to those of John Diefenbaker: 'It appears my people are to remain manacled to, and governed by, bureaucracy. Should the government decide to retain the smothering protective laws that have kept us down for so long, then the future is indeed dark, without a glimmer of the expected dawn.'[49]

The most detailed reaction, after Parliament had been prorogued, came from the Indian Association of Alberta in a point-by-point discussion of the shortcomings of the proposed legislation. Although the IAA found some aspects of the bill acceptable, for the most part it was condemned as a violation of both the treaties and the good faith in which the government had originally negotiated them. The features of the bill singled out for censure included the centralization of power in the hands of either the minister or governor-in-council, as well as the failure of the bill to endorse Indian self-government; enforced enfranchisement, even of an entire band, at the discretion of Indian Affairs; the arbitrary powers of Indian Affairs in land expropriation and the removal of band members from the reserve; the failure of the bill to restore hunting, fishing, and trapping rights; and the provision that allowed the government to impose the franchise on Indians.[50] In substance, the IAA's response amounted to an almost complete repudiation of the bill.

In light of this opposition, the government found it necessary to withdraw the legislation, the intent being to introduce a revised bill the following session. Plans were also made for meetings with representatives from the Indian organizations so that past problems could be avoided. For example, an informal meeting between W.E. Harris, the minister in charge of Indian Affairs, and representatives of the bands in southern Saskatchewan was held in Regina in November 1950 to discuss plans for a new bill. As it turned out, there was little substance to the meeting in that, according to an organizer for the Union of Saskatchewan Indians, the meeting was too short and dealt with only two controversial issues.[51] This meeting, however, was preliminary to a more formal conference held in Ottawa in late February and early March 1951. It was attended by the minister and deputy minister as well as nineteen delegates, including three from Saskatchewan, representing Indian interests in all ten provinces.[52] Despite the limited number of Indian delegates, the meeting did represent a more serious attempt to consult Indians than had been true in the past. It was perhaps for this reason that the conference unfolded in a cooperative atmosphere, reflected in a marked degree of consensus concerning the new bill.

The proposed legislation had 124 sections and, of these, 103 sections were unanimously supported by delegates; 113 sections were supported by a majority of those present; and only 6 sections were opposed by a majority of the representatives, and of these only two were opposed unanimously.[53] Whereas the two sections totally rejected had to do with the taxation and enfranchisement of Indians, the other sources of opposition for most delegates were the provisions dealing with the use of intoxicants. Although a majority rejected the drink provisions of the bill as drafted, opinion on the proper course of action was nevertheless divided, some preferring total prohibition and others demanding varying degrees of access to alcohol.[54]

In due course, Bill 79, after three days of debate in the House, was passed and became the new Indian Act. In terms of the power relationship between government and Indians, the new act differed in few respects from the abortive Bill 267 or from earlier legislation. Certainly the intent of the 1951 act – the assimilation of and dictatorial control over Indians – was identical to that of the past, while most of the essential elements remained intact.[55] Band councils under the new act, for example, had no more authority to manage their own affairs than they had had under the old act. It is true that some of the more restrictive features of past legislation, including a ban on Indian dancing and ceremonies, were omitted from the new legislation. Also absent were provisions giving the government the power to terminate reserves, to enfranchise Indians without their consent, and to arbitrarily lease reserve lands to non-Indians. Nevertheless, the old authoritarian regime that had ruled over Indians as dependent wards of the Canadian state remained unchanged. Indicative was the fact that over half the provisions in the 1951 act were dependent on the discretion of either the minister or governor-in-council and that the latter was empowered to declare any or all parts of the act inapplicable to any band or individual Indian, subject only to existing treaties and other statutes.[56] The act, in fact, proved to be a grave disappointment to Douglas and those who had expected a new deal for Indians.

That the new legislation did not automatically extend the franchise to all Indians was a foregone conclusion, rooted in previous debates in the House of Commons concerning proposed amendments to the Dominion Elections Act and to the Indian Act. While the government was quite prepared to give the vote to the Inuit, as citizens without wardship status, it denied the same right to Indians. Government spokespeople reasoned that, unlike the Inuit, Indians were exempt from taxation of personal property as long as they lived on reserves and, therefore, should not have the right to vote. This justification was in keeping with British constitutional principles, which suggested that the right of citizens to choose a government stemmed from the fact that they provided the tax dollars necessary to sustain the government. It was also enshrined in the long-standing British and American principles of 'no taxation without representation' and the concomitant notion that there should be 'no representation without taxation.'[57] Hence, the government insisted that only after Indians, on an individual basis, had waived their tax exemption would they receive the right to vote in federal elections, without losing Indian status. The opposition, however, saw little logic in tying the franchise to taxation, pointing out that Indians were not exempted from taxation because they had given up the right to vote but because they had surrendered their valuable land holdings as part of the treaty process. It was also argued, with effect, that many white people in Canada paid no taxes whatsoever and that over 200,000 low-income Quebec farmers paid on average only twenty-five cents in taxes per year and yet enjoyed not only old age pensions and other benefits but also the right to vote, unlike Indians.[58] And M.J. Coldwell, the leader of the CCF in the House, also condemned the government's position because it stood in opposition to the fundamental human principle that all people, no matter what their colour, race, or creed, should have the right to vote.[59] Nevertheless, despite the inherent logic of opposition arguments, the government used its majority in the House to ensure that its position was enshrined in the new Indian Act. Henceforth, Indians would be allowed to vote in federal elections only if they renounced their long-standing right to tax exemptions, which, understandably, few were prepared to do.

While the federal government held firm on the franchise, it was prepared to take a softer line on the use of alcohol, at least to the extent that the matter could be offloaded to the provinces. As a result of an amendment in 1951, Section 95 of the Indian Act provided that any province could petition the governor general-in-council to permit Indians to consume intoxicating beverages in licensed premises.[60] This meant that Indians would still not be allowed to consume alcohol on their reserves, but that they would be able to drink in licensed beer parlours and bars. Basically, what was being said was that the province had to take the initiative – and responsibility – for asking the federal government to bring about the change. In theory, this was perfectly logical, since provincial officials were in a better position to determine the liabilities involved; in practice, it allowed federal officials to bail out, leaving the province to take whatever political flack might result.

In Saskatchewan, as elsewhere, there was considerable support in the Indian community for changing the liquor laws. It came, of course, from the thousands of Indians who wanted freer access to a social climate and drinking pattern that other Canadians took for granted. Surprisingly, it also came from a certain segment of the Indian leadership, both at the social and political levels. A.H. Brass, formerly of File Hills, was active in social welfare councils in Regina and Saskatoon, and he supported legalization on the grounds that it would lead Indians away from using alcohol-based alternatives, such as shoe polish and hair spray.[61] The Reverend Canon Edward Ahenakew, a seventy-three-year-old man from Sandy Lake Reserve and reputed to be the first Cree Anglican minister, made a similar case in the *Regina Leader-Post*.[62] He pointed to the extensive use and abuse of home-brew on most reserves and insisted that, were drinking legalized, it would be consumed in a more moderate and responsible fashion. In addition, he argued that existing laws not only discriminated against Indians and made them feel inferior but also made them appear more unlawful than white people. By the same token, Andrew Paull and the North American Indian Brotherhood were in favour of the province legalizing Indian drinking, largely out of concern that Indians be treated equally. In a letter to Douglas in the summer of 1951, Paull urged the premier at his earliest convenience to implement Section 95, 'so as to eradicate one of the many evils encountered by native Indians.'[63]

The province, however, was not prepared to act. Douglas himself was a committed teetotaler and, although he tolerated the use of alcohol by others, he was not in favour of drinking, whether by whites or Indians. Over and above his own views on the matter, he also knew there was considerable opposition throughout the province. He was virtually inundated with letters from concerned citizens, asking him not to legalize Indian drinking.[64] People had been sensitized to the issue, in part because of stereotypes about Indian drinking, and in part also by press coverage of real events. At the very moment legalization was under discussion, for example, the press was commenting in detail on the trial of a young Indian who had murdered his wife following a drinking party. As reported, the judge in handing down his sentence apologized to Indians for the fact that white men had introduced them to alcohol and then he condemned the liquor traffic as 'a constant menace to and an enemy of the Indian whenever he leaves the protection afforded him on his reserve.'[65] The message drew sympathetic comment from both the minister of social services, J.H. Sturdy, and the attorney general, J.W. Corman,[66] and could hardly be ignored by the reading public when it came to the issue of legalizing Indian drinking. Also at play was the opposition of vested interests associated with the liquor industry. Hotel owners were frightened that drunken Indians might cause violence and drive away business. In a letter to the attorney general's office, the president of the Saskatchewan Hotel Association insisted that his members were solidly opposed to legalization on the grounds that it would not be in the Indians' own best interests. In addition, he pleaded for a formal meeting with the government, to spell out the association's objections in detail, before any decision was taken.[67] Lastly, there was the opposition of the Indian leadership throughout much of Saskatchewan. Local chiefs knew only too well the disastrous effects alcohol had had in the past and understandably they were not anxious to legitimize or broaden its use. It was undoubtedly for this reason that the USI made no move to invoke the provisions of Section 98.

So, for the time being at least, both the franchise and legalized drinking were put on hold. Whereas the former right had been silenced by Indian antipathy and federal intransigence, the latter suffered a state of inertia because the climate of opinion in Saskatchewan, both in the white and Indian communities, was either unsympathetic or divided.

Related Citizenship Issues

The demand for integration of Indians as citizens of the province nevertheless remained at issue and was raised in a variety of contexts. Would Indians continue to be segregated in denominational schools or should the whole education system be restructured, as had been recommended by the JCSHC? If the system were reformed, would Indians be placed in federal schools or integrated into existing provincial school systems? Moreover, would Indian social services be upgraded to a level comparable to that of the provinces? If so, what role would provincial governments play and under what circumstances? These were fundamental questions and, although they lacked the public profile of the franchise and alcohol issues, they had an important bearing on Indian public policy throughout the 1950s.

Above all else, the school question demanded immediate attention. In its brief to the JCSHC in 1947, it will be recalled, the Union of Saskatchewan Indians had roundly denounced parochial schools. The union favoured a better and more extensive school system, based not on the hated residential schools but on regular day-schools operated on a non-denominational basis; however, it expressed little support for the idea of integrating Indian children into the provincial school system, presumably because of the implied cultural assimilation a provincewide curriculum would entail. By the same token, the JCSHC had vehemently rejected the parochial school system but, unlike the USI, it had recommended that Indian children be placed in regular provincial schools wherever proximity to reserves made attendance feasible. This view was wholeheartedly endorsed by the Saskatchewan government. Douglas envisaged a thoroughgoing integration of the province's Indian, Métis, and non-Native student population, based on a cost-sharing arrangement with the federal government. The central idea was that all students in the province, no matter what their racial background or economic status, would have equal access to the benefits of a standardized provincial education. Whereas non-Indians would be supported by provincial tax dollars, the participation of Indian students would be funded by transfer payments from Indian Affairs.[68]

Despite consensus on the need to reform Indian education, the school question – as Douglas pointed out – was one of the most contentious features of Indian administration.[69] Because proposed reforms threatened entrenched religious interests, governments of every description were reluctant to act precipitously, and this was especially true of the Liberal government in Ottawa. Technically, Indian Affairs adopted the school recommendations of the 1948 JCSHC in the same year they were made,[70] but implementation of those recommendations was another matter. According to one source, with an election looming in the near future, the federal government refused to act immediately because of 'the religious overtones' and the 'touchy' nature of the subject.[71] Historically, Indian Affairs had shared a partnership with the churches, especially with the Anglican and Catholic denominations, whereby Indian schools were operated by the churches but built and largely funded by the dominion. The arrangement satisfied vested interests, in that the competing denominations were allowed to indoctrinate their students with their own particular brand of Christian belief; the Indian Affairs bureaucracy was able to maintain its control and authority over Indian schools; and presumably the Liberal government enjoyed the sympathy and support of the denominations during elections, or at very least was not the target of their antipathy. The symbiotic relationship between government and church was based upon a tacit acknowledgment of mutual interest, and this normally meant that government was reluctant to do anything that might be perceived as an attack on religious prerogative. Hence, it was out of deference to the status quo that only after the election of 1950 did the federal government set itself to the task of implementing the school recommendations of the JCSHC and that, even then, the pace of reform was not as dramatic as some have maintained.

The federal government did increase the school budget by more than half a million dollars, earmarked mainly for the construction of new day-school facilities on reserves.[72] There was also provision in the Indian Act of 1951 for the joint education of Indian and non-Indian children. Specifically, the minister of citizenship and immigration – the office now responsible for Indian Affairs – was authorized by the act to enter into joint agreements, for the education of Indians, with provincial governments, public or separate school boards, and religious or charitable organizations.[73] Religious privilege was carefully maintained, in so far as Roman Catholics were entitled to go to Catholic schools, while Protestant children would be able to attend the public schools of a province where it was feasible to do so. The overriding rule was that the teacher would have to be of the same religion as the majority of students in the classroom.[74] At the same time, Indian Affairs officials were quick to suggest that the idea of joint schools was not new and that such a school had been established in the vicinity of The Pas, Manitoba, three years earlier. In that instance, a dominion-provincial agreement had been instrumental in placing eighteen Métis children in an Indian school, located at Big Eddie Reserve five miles north of the town.[75] Thus, although sensitive to denominational concerns, Indian Affairs policy, by the early fifties, did embrace interracial school integration, based on provincial cooperation.

But even then, integration was not always honoured in practice nor was it implemented with the alacrity necessary to satisfy the Douglas government. The Big Eddie experiment notwithstanding, federal officials steadfastly refused to open their schools to white and Métis children. Constitutionally, the dominion government was not responsible for education, apart from the requirement of providing schools for Indians as federal wards. Nevertheless, the Douglas government insisted that, in the interest of cooperation, federal schools should be made available to others where conditions warranted it. That this was not the case was a source of common complaint by the province and figured in a list of 'concerns' drawn up by John Sturdy in the early 1950s. Sturdy pointed out to federal officials that, although the province had made its schools readily accessible to Indian students, Indian Affairs refused to reciprocate where unschooled white or Métis students were involved, a problem especially acute in the far North.[76] At the same time, the declared federal commitment to joint agreements and provincial common schools did not immediately translate into wholesale integration. In 1956, a retired Indian superintendent who had served for nine years at Meadow Lake and Kamsack Reserves proffered that 'it would be a God-send if every school on an Indian reserve burned down.'[77] He was appalled by the segregating and isolating effects of such schools and insisted that Indian Affairs, now recognizing the problem, was starting to have as many Indian children as possible educated with white children.[78] As implied by this statement, school integration was only getting under way by the mid-1950s and was far from complete by the time Douglas had left the province.

This is borne out by statistics relating to Indian enrollment in grades one through twelve in provincial and private schools. Nationally, such enrollment continued to climb steadily throughout the 1950s, representing 6.1 percent of total Indian enrollment in 1950, 11.6 percent in 1955, and 25.1 percent in 1961.[79] In Ontario and British Columbia, where the number of Indian students was greatest and the interracial contact lengthy, the national rate was often surpassed.[80] But on the Prairies, the incidence of Indian student integration fell far below what was happening elsewhere. In Saskatchewan, for example, Indian attendance in provincial and private schools was only 2.3 percent of total Indian enrollments in the province in 1950, 4.4 percent in 1955, and 15.9 percent in 1961.[81] While such figures spoke to an undeniable trend toward schooling Indian children in provincial institutions, the integration lag in Saskatchewan was undoubtedly a matter of frustration to a CCF government bent on taking over Indian affairs and placing all Indian students in provincial schools.

If the Douglas government was disappointed by the pace of educational reform, it was downright dismayed by the drift and direction of social service delivery. The conflict over Indian pensions, statistical surveys, hospitalization, and health care was embedded in the paperchase that took place between Regina and Ottawa and sometimes bordered on an open rift. At issue, of course, was the extent to which either government was responsible for Indians under certain conditions and who should provide the funding and delivery of service. Federal officials took a narrow view, maintaining that their responsibility extended only to those Indians actually living on a reserve. Other Indians, they insisted, were provincial citizens and, like anyone else living in Saskatchewan, had the right to make demands on the province for support. By comparison, the Douglas government saw the federal position as little more than an attempt to offload responsibility to the province. It argued that historically and constitutionally the federal government had been responsible for status Indians and that, while the province was prepared to deliver services to Indians living off the reserves, there should be a transfer of funding from the dominion to the province in compensation. Moreover, Douglas was not above using the issue of Indian social services as a lever to piggyback the Métis into the equation. In effect, he and his ministers maintained that the Métis and Indian problems were two sides of the same coin and must be dealt with in a planned and coordinated matter, including the creation of joint projects shared by the two levels of government. Federal officials, however, were leery of such proposals because they correctly saw it as a ploy through which federal responsibility would be extended to the Métis. As a result, there was little room for federal-provincial cooperation when it came to social services.

One issue that proved to be especially confrontational was the matter of old age assistance and the blind persons allowance. In the spring of 1951, the federal government announced that it would be taking steps to eliminate from federal enactments all barriers to the payment of old age assistance and blindness allowances to Indians.[82] In the following year, legislation to that end was passed in the House. Basically, the program called for joint agreements with the provinces through which 50 percent of the old age assistance and 25 percent of the blind persons allowance would be paid by the province, with the balance coming from the dominion. The programs were meant to standardize benefits across Canada, regardless of racial origins, and were meant to include Indians who, as a specific racial group, had not been eligible for the benefits in the past. Because Indians were a federal responsibility, the provinces were allowed to exclude Indians from the programs, but they had to do so by specifying their exclusion in the provincial enabling legislation that would put the programs into effect.[83] Nine of the provinces, including Saskatchewan, applauded the benefits that would accrue to their Indians communities and passed the necessary legislation without excluding Indians.[84]

The Douglas government, however, sensed an opportunity to get additional benefits from the federal government by objecting, after the fact, to the cost-sharing arrangements. The opening cannon shot was fired by John Sturdy, minister of social welfare, in a letter to Paul Martin, minister of national health and welfare, in April 1952. Sturdy pointed out that, up until the time the dominion wanted the provinces to fund part of the old age and blind persons benefits for Indians, federal authorities had always insisted that Indians' social welfare was the prerogative of the dominion and had resented interference from the provinces.[85] He then went on to suggest that, if the province were to contribute to Indian welfare, then the federal government should assume some responsibility for Métis programs. As he put it,

> We are anxious that the Federal Government continue to assume its full responsibility in these matters and would not consider making arrangements to provide Old Age Assistance or Blindness Allowances to Indians unless and until mutually satisfactory arrangements are made with regard to the general welfare of both Indians and Métis. The problems of Indians and Métis are inextricably bound together and the problems of one cannot be settled without the problems of the other. Wherever there is an Indian reserve there is a contiguous Métis settlement each aggravating the problems of the other. It appears that each of our governments is attempting to deal with the problems of the Indians and Métis in different ways when the only difference between the people themselves in many cases is that some are not legally recognized as Indians although they may have more Indian blood than those of Indian status.[86]

Sturdy, of course, realized that the Métis, like everyone else, would benefit from federal contributions to the old age and blind persons programs. But the point he was making was that the issue at hand was only one of many social welfare areas affecting Indians and Métis as a collectivity and could not be dealt with in isolation or through divided jurisdictions. He therefore requested an urgent meeting in Ottawa with Martin, along with the minister in charge of Indian Affairs and their deputies.

If Sturdy was prepared to play hardball in denying Indian benefits, Martin was quite prepared to reciprocate in kind. In his reply, the minister deftly underscored the complete inconsistency of the Saskatchewan position. Although he was prepared to see the provincial minister in Ottawa, he doubted the value of such a meeting since the real problem was the Saskatchewan government itself. He pointed out that the province could have legally excluded Indians from the two programs when they were originally set up and that, in now refusing applications from Indians, the province was not only in contravention of its agreement with the federal government but also in violation of its own enabling legislation.[87] He then concluded with an unmistakable threat: 'If the Saskatchewan Government persists in taking this stand, the Federal Government will have no alternative but to declare that the agreements have been violated by the Saskatchewan Government, with the result that Federal reimbursement [to the province] will no longer be authorized.'[88] What Martin was saying was that, if the province did not include Indians in the old age assistance and blind persons allowance, he would withhold federal contributions to the two programs for everyone in the province.

In late April, Sturdy did meet with federal officials in Ottawa. There, he outlined the problems and concerns his government had experienced with Indian welfare in the past and pleaded for the creation of a broadly based committee, composed of federal, provincial, municipal, and church representatives, to undertake a complete survey of the situation in Saskatchewan. The thrust of his argument largely ignored legal niceties, which tended to support the federal position, and instead emphasized the practical nature of the problems associated with social services and with conflicting jurisdictions. Federal officials were attentive but noncommittal and steadfastly opposed the creation of an investigative committee. In the end, it was agreed that the provincial minister would draw up a list of his concerns to which federal officials would respond in due course.

Sturdy's written statement was forwarded to Ottawa in mid-May. In it, he cited a number of specific difficulties to illustrate the nature of the problems confounding the province as a consequence of divided jurisdictions.[89] Many of his arguments were based on rather loose, if not inaccurate, interpretations of the Indian Act and the rights of the province to enforce the criminal code. In the corrections field, he pointed to the fact that, once an Indian had committed a crime, he was incarcerated in a provincial prison and provided for at the expense of the province; and yet, because Indian reserves fell under federal jurisdiction, the province had no opportunity to institute crime prevention or to carry out probationary aftercare on reserves. In the area of child welfare, children of mixed blood increasingly were being removed from reserves in keeping with the more stringent definition of Indian status laid down in the new Indian Act. Having spent their whole lives on a reserve, such children often found it impossible to integrate into non-Indian society and were unlikely candidates for adoption. The problem was compounded in the case of illegitimate Indian children whose rights, in law, were uncertain. According to the Indian Act, a child born of an unmarried Indian women was a non-Indian, unless it could be shown that the father was also Indian. Where the status of the father was uncertain, welfare officials were reluctant to give the child over to adoption by Indian parents because the Indian Act also stipulated that the child must have at least a quarter Indian blood. This meant that if it were subsequently determined that the father was non-Indian, the child might not qualify as Indian and would be removed from the reserve by Indian Affairs either before or after the adoption process was complete. Furthermore, the welfare minister maintained that, in implementing old age assistance and other programs for Indians, field workers would have to devote extra time and effort to eligibility screening, means tests, and supervision of the way in which assistance moneys were spent by Indian clients. Sturdy then went on, gratuitously, to criticize the lack of economic development on Indian reserves, particularly the practice of leasing out large sections of reserves to white farmers. He insisted that such a practice was a deterrent to Indian farming because it robbed Indians of the training and experience necessary to make them independent farmers one day. Finally, given that federal officials during the Ottawa meeting had opposed the idea of a representative investigative committee, Sturdy proposed setting up a committee of federal-provincial civil servants who would study Native issues as a first step in a coordinated effort to deal with the problem.

Sturdy's statement was meant to reinforce the notion that Native problems, including those of the Métis, demanded a concerted and broad frontal attack by both levels of government. There was never any doubt that the province was prepared to pay for the inclusion of Indians in the old age allowance and blind persons benefits programs. As the premier explained in a letter to a CCF party member in Alberta,

> We have no objection to paying the pensions to the Indians but we are trying to use the agreement which we are asked to sign as a bargaining weapon to force the Federal Government to deal more intelligently with the Indian problem. As you know, the condition of the Indians on the reserves is a national disgrace and the problem of the Métis people is one which the Federal government has avoided altogether. Our department of Social Welfare is convinced that we can not clean up the Métis problem unless something is done simultaneously about the Indian problem.[90]

It was largely in this context that Sturdy had included in his statement of concerns the need for some joint coordinating body to address Native issues.

Saskatchewan's ploy must have seemed completely transparent to federal officials because they made no effort to compromise. In June, Sturdy's deputy minister received a threatening letter from Ottawa advising him that, unless the province acted at once to include Indians in the old age pension and blind persons assistance programs, it would not be possible to process the programs' federal transfer payments to the province for the previous month.[91] Two weeks later, Sturdy received a reply to his statement of concerns from W.E. Harris, minister in charge of Indian Affairs. Harris's letter, in fact, was a very able, point-by-point rebuttal to virtually every point raised by Sturdy.[92] He pointed out that there was nothing in the Indian Act that prevented provincial corrections and probationary officers from exercising their duties in respect to Indians, whether on or off the reserve. In fact, he welcomed the extension of such services to reserves and promised that his officials would cooperate in every way possible. As far as child welfare was concerned, he maintained that Section 87 of the Indian Act in effect made provincial laws governing adoption, neglect, and delinquency as applicable to Indian children as to anyone else. Moreover, he said, the act clarified the definition of who was an Indian by establishing a register in Ottawa of those who officially had Indian status. Among other things, this meant that there was no uncertainty concerning the status of children. Whether a non-Indian child were adopted by Indian parents, or whether an Indian child were adopted by white parents, the status of the child would not be altered; and in either case, the status of the child would not change the legality of the adoption. In terms of implementing the old age allowance and blind persons benefits programs, he admitted that Indians would require greater assistance than other citizens and, to that end, he promised that Indian Affairs would provide all available resources and records at its disposal to assist provincial field workers. As far as economics was concerned, Harris insisted that, while reserve development was not what he wished it to be, the leasing arrangements on reserves were beneficial: whereas leases were an inexpensive way to get unbroken reserve land into production, Indian bands, to their financial advantage, received a share of the crops until such a time as the leases expired and the lands were taken over by the Indians themselves.

Harris's arguments were tantamount to dismissing the notion that the divided jurisdictions were causing problems for the province. Even more important, however, was his categorical rejection of any proposal that might imply federal responsibility for the Métis. He left no doubt whatsoever that the idea of a joint committee of civil servants was not acceptable because, as he said, it would be 'difficult to visualize the effectiveness of such an organization,' given that Indian Affairs had no mandate to deal with the Métis.[93] Seemingly in an effort to trivialize Sturdy's proposal, Harris suggested that the interface between civil servants of the two levels of government should be even closer than that which could be afforded by a mere committee. Instead, he said, it was more important that field officers from the dominion and province 'labour harmoniously and in full accord towards a common goal.'[94] To that end, he simply referred Sturdy to the Indian Affairs' regional office in Regina, adding, 'I can not help but feel that mutual co-operation between that office and your officials would be much more to advantage than the proposed committee.'[95] The subtext was that Indian Affairs had no intention of being drawn into the problems and financial obligations of the province.

In point of fact, the province's bluff had been called. All that remained was an attempt by the Douglas government to bluster and save face. In mid-July, Sturdy's deputy minister penned a letter to the federal deputy minister of welfare suggesting that the province was considering amending its enabling legislation to exclude Indians from the old age and blind persons benefits.[96] Officially, the point of the letter was to ask whether the federal government would continue to pay the federal share of the costs for other citizens, were the province to exclude Indians from the two programs. In reality, the letter was little more than an implied threat because it had already been established that the province had the right to exclude Indians and still receive federal funding for other citizens. Three weeks later, the Douglas government backtracked even further. In a second letter to the federal deputy minister of welfare, Sturdy's deputy minister this time asked: if the Saskatchewan government were to include Indians in the two programs for the time being, could it amend its enabling legislation later on to exclude Indians?[97] Once more, the question was largely rhetorical and denoted only Saskatchewan's final acquiescence to the conditions imposed by the federal government. In reality, the outcome was never in doubt. The Douglas government was ideologically and politically committed to Indian social reform. To exclude Indians from programs that placed Indians on an equal footing with other Canadian citizens would have been unthinkable and everyone knew it. Hence, the province could negotiate only from a position of weakness.

What Douglas and others did not fully appreciate at the time was that the pensions issue was only the tip of the iceberg in federal offloading. In late 1952, Indian Affairs personnel, including Colonel H.M. Jones, IAB superintendent of welfare services, as well as J.P. Ostrander, regional supervisor of Indian agencies, met with provincial social welfare officials in Regina to discuss problems associated with Indians. The agenda was addressed to many of the problems identified in Sturdy's statement of concerns, outlined the previous spring, but conspicuously absent from the discussions was any reference to the Métis. The meeting was held in strict conformity with the notion that Indian Affairs was responsible for Indians only, and that if provincial officials wished to interface with federal officials, they should do so along established lines of communication, as Harris had insisted. But that was not all. Indian Affairs officials now adopted the position that they were only responsible for Indians living on reserves.[98] In effect, this meant that the province and municipality would now be totally responsible for delivering all welfare services to Indians who had been living off the reserve for a year or more.[99] In theory, such Indians had not only achieved municipal residence but also lost Indian status in the process; and, like other citizens of the province, they were now free to claim assistance under provincial programs. Although entirely legal, the change in Indian Affairs policy must have seemed like a bombshell to provincial officials. It did more than call on the province to assume responsibility for Indians who, in the past, had been taken care of by the federal government: it did so without any hint of financial compensation to the province for the added responsibility.

The province responded officially in a series of letters from J.S. White, the provincial deputy minister of welfare, to Colonel Jones. With little room to manoeuvre, White used the only leverage he had at his disposal: he downplayed the legal rights of the federal government and emphasized the practical need to address Native problems effectively. As he pointed out to the colonel, 'The problems discussed [at the Regina meeting] ... have not been solved nor can they be solved until we can in some way approach them with open minds and place as much emphasis on the social factors involved as on their legal aspects.'[100] The reference to 'social factors' harked back to the old argument that Indian concerns were only a part of a much larger Native problem and could not be dealt with in isolation. To that end, White also reiterated the demand for a committee of federal and provincial civil servants to study the problems of both Indians and the Métis as a first step toward long-range planning.[101] The most substantive issue, however, had to do with money, and on that front White was adamant that, at the very least, the federal government should share in the costs associated with the province assuming responsibility for off-reserve Indians.[102]

Once more, federal officials proved entirely intransigent. With uncharacteristic resolution, the Indian Affairs Branch determinedly confined its responsibility to on-reserve Indians and steadfastly refused to countenance either financial compensation or a committee structure that would entail consideration of the Métis problem. For its part, the province had no choice but to acquiesce again, but it did so grudgingly and with a lingering sense of resentment. The change in IAB policy, in effect, augmented the number of Natives for which the province was now responsible and potentially threatened to overwhelm municipal and provincial welfare resources. The fear was heightened by the lack of statistical information on the number of Indians who might now become provincial charges.

Indeed, the lack of information itself became a separate issue and further exacerbated federal-provincial relations. As early as 1952, John Sturdy had petitioned federal officials to cooperate in setting up a joint commission aimed at examining conditions on reserves, 'particularly among Indians and Métis who are not on 'reserves.'[103] The idea was to compile information on all people of Indian ancestry in the province in order to formulate a systematic and planned attack on Native problems. It had special appeal for the CCF government because it dovetailed nicely with social democratic theory about social engineering and long-term planning. It also found precedent in a similar study conducted in Manitoba.[104] For these reasons, the proposal was periodically revived throughout the 1950s, but generally found little support among federal officials. This may be attributed in part to the fact that provincial proposals often called for a study not of Indians per se but of people of Indian ancestry, which would include the Métis. Understandably, federal officials were reluctant to sponsor any project that might imply federal responsibility for a provincial Native population. The proposal was revived once more when, in 1957, the Liberal Party fell from electoral grace and John Diefenbaker and the Conservatives came to power in Ottawa. The new government, however, proved no more receptive to the idea of a study than had its predecessor. In 1959, the prime minister explained to Douglas that he would not support such a study on the grounds that his own government was contemplating the appointment of a JCSHC to inquire into all aspects of Indian affairs throughout Canada.[105]

Hence, by the late 1950s, a system of Indian service delivery had evolved that did little to satisfy provincial demands. Social services, according to provincial officials, represented a veritable patchwork of confusing and conflicting jurisdictions. In terms of health care, for example, the federal government sometimes denied legal responsibility for Indians, but in fact provided such services for status Indians. The Indian and Northern Health Services Division (INHSD) of the Department of National Health and Welfare assumed complete responsibility, not only for Indians in the North who lived an 'Indian's way of life,' but also for Indians living on southern reserves and those who had been off-reserve for less than one year.[106] In the latter instance, Indians could seek medical attention from one of eight INHSD-salaried doctors or from one of many doctors designated by the division under a fee-for-services contract. But often Indians did not know which doctors they were supposed to consult nor where to find them and, in the case of indigent Indians off the reserve for more than a year, they were seldom aware that medical services were available through the municipalities.[107] To further complicate the matter, by federal-provincial agreement Indians were insurable under the Saskatchewan Health Services Plan. The INHSD paid to the province the personal hospitalization tax for on-reserve Indians and those living in the far North. In theory, the INHSD would not pay the tax for those who had lived off the reserve for more than a year, but in practice exceptions were made when it was felt individuals needed additional time and support to establish themselves off the reserve.[108] In such cases, the individuals were often the subject of dispute between the INHSD and the municipalities as to which level of government should pay the taxes and, as a result, they were commonly shuffled back and forth between jurisdictions.[109]

A similar situation existed in the delivery of welfare services. Under joint federal-provincial agreements, the federal government financially compensated the province when on-reserve Indians and their off-reserve counterparts were the beneficiaries of provincial vocational rehabilitation programs, juvenile and corrections programs, old age assistance, disabled persons allowance, and blind persons allowance. In addition, Indians living off the reserve were eligible for social aid, administered by the municipalities. The problem was that municipalities were opposed to Indians establishing local residence and often pressured Indians to return to their reserves. They were not opposed to administering social aid, which, after all, was fully funded by the province; on the contrary, they were opposed because Indians receiving social aid were also eligible for medical and hospital services, the cost of which was borne by municipal coffers, even though Indians did not normally own property and therefore did not pay municipal taxes.[110]

From the perspective of Douglas and his officials, the system that had evolved was a failure because it ran counter to the all-important provincial goal of integrating Indians into the general population. Indeed, the system operated in such a way that it did just the opposite, in that it encouraged Indian segregation on reserves. Given the confusion and complexity concerning which programs applied to which Indians under which circumstances, Indians were understandably confused and confounded by the whole social services structure, especially if they lived off the reserve.[111] Those who left the reserve to secure wage labour in Regina Beach or Saskatoon soon discovered that municipal officials were less than cooperative and that family health benefits and social security were not easily obtained off the reserve. Often their only choice was to return to the reserve where Indian Affairs services, as inadequate as they might be, were available and well known. This was especially so when federal guidelines increasingly enforced the 'twelve month' rule for off-reserve Indians.[112] According to CCF officials, the whole system conspired to keep Indians on the reserve, effectively divorced from any meaningful economic development and cut off from the range of services promised by full provincial citizenship.[113]

Vote and Drink Reform

Overlapping with social assistance issues was renewed interest in Indian franchise and drinking rights. By the mid-1950s, social reformers, white politicians, and some Indian leaders were once more questioning why

Indians should be denied such basic rights. Their promotion of these rights was driven by the same factors that had made citizenship an issue in the late 1940s. The main difference now was that the Indian franchise no longer seemed like such an alien concept, in that other provinces were increasingly incorporating Indians into the body politic. The provincial vote had been granted to Indians in Newfoundland when that colony had joined Confederation in 1949; it had been extended to Indians in British Columbia in the same year, in Manitoba in 1952, and in Ontario in 1954.[114] There was also living evidence in British Columbia that Indians were perfectly capable of playing a political role beyond merely exercising the franchise. In 1949, Frank Calder made headlines across Canada when, as the first Indian to do so, he was elected to the BC legislature. He won his seat by only six votes, but then went on to win a solid majority in the election of 1952.[115] Calder already enjoyed the distinction of being the first Indian to graduate from the University of British Columbia and his election only added to an already illustrious career. As a member of the CCF party in British Columbia, Calder became a popular speaker at social democratic gatherings in Saskatchewan.[116] In his own right, he personified the role Indians could play in the political arena; more than that, he was a vocal and persuasive proponent of the Indian franchise and drinking rights.[117]

Two developments in particular made citizenship a public issue in Saskatchewan. First, in 1954 and again in 1956, Bill Berezowsky (CCF Cumberland) introduced a motion in the Saskatchewan legislature calling for the government to honour Indian citizenship rights. Like its predecessor, the 1956 motion asked the government to consider the advisability of submitting legislation that would unconditionally extend the provincial franchise to Indians and that would remove from existing legislation any laws that restricted Indian rights.[118] It also asked the province to make representations to Ottawa with the intent of setting up a federal-provincial board or commission to plan programs and policies that would give status Indians the same health, welfare, education, and local government services that other Saskatchewan residents enjoyed. All of this, said the motion, should be done without any abrogation or loss of the Indians' hereditary or treaty rights. Technically, the motion was a private rather than a government initiative; however, it was undoubtedly introduced with the government's blessing and perhaps figured as a safe way for Douglas to test the political winds on the issue. As it turned out, the motion was warmly endorsed by speakers from both sides of the Assembly and passed unanimously.[119] Outside the legislature, the press was equally enthusiastic, and in subsequent interviews the premier went on record to the effect that, if returned to office in the upcoming election, his government would take action.[120]

Portrait of William John Berezowsky,
MLA for Cumberland, 1956.
(Saskatchewan Archives Board
R-B5445-1)

The second development was an amendment to the Indian Act. Five
months after the Berezowsky resolution cleared the Saskatchewan Assembly, the federal government passed legislation broadening the rights of
Indians to consume alcohol. In light of the earlier amendment, passed in
1951, Indians could obtain the right to consume alcohol in public places,
which mainly meant drinking in beer parlours, if the provinces took the
necessary steps to permit them to do so. According to the 1956 amendment, Indians would still need provincial sanction before they could
exercise their drinking rights; the main difference now was that they could
be given all the rights enjoyed by other citizens, including the right to purchase alcohol from a liquor store and to be in possession of alcohol off a
reserve.[121] There was also provision for local options, in that any band by
majority vote could decide not to come under the general law, thereby
maintaining its 'dry' status.[122] The amendment, coming on the heels of the
debate in the Saskatchewan Assembly, served to reinforce the demand for
provincial action and once more made citizenship rights an issue.

While Douglas was willing to bring in the necessary legislation, he was
not prepared to do so without Indian compliance.[123] Both ideologically
and emotionally, he was opposed to imposing measures on an unwilling
Indian community and this was especially so when it came to the use of
alcohol, which he found distasteful for both personal and social reasons.
In addition, a change in the drinking laws was politically dangerous
because it was widely opposed in much of the Indian leadership and
among the electorate. Douglas received menacing letters from constituents who threatened to tear up their CCF cards if the government

gave Indians free access to alcohol.[124] He also received only slightly veiled threats from some Indian leaders who insisted that, at the very least, he should consult the Indian community before effecting any changes in the franchise or liquor laws. This was underscored in a letter from Angus Mirasty of Allingly who demanded that the premier meet with the Union of Saskatchewan Indians before proceeding on the matter. Mr. Mirasty was a USI leader and one of a number of spokespersons for the northern chiefs. He claimed that, at a meeting in Duck Lake in 1953, John Diefenbaker had stated categorically that if Indians got the vote they would have to pay taxes.[125] Echoing the old argument that citizenship rights meant an end to special status and treaty rights, he insisted that he was not prepared to surrender his birthright, guaranteed by the Crown, 'just ... to vote and drink the white mans [*sic*] fire water.'[126] Mirasty concluded his letter with a threat that must have given the premier reason for pause. He maintained that two-thirds of the Indians in Saskatchewan were Roman Catholic and that, if Indians were given the franchise, they would vote for the party supported by the priests – 'and you can be sure it wont [*sic*] be the C.C.F. either.'[127] In point of fact, the letter served only to reinforce what had always been Douglas's conviction, the need to consult with Indians before acting. During debate on the Berezowsky motion in the Assembly, he had made it clear that the government would not bring in legislation until it had convened a conference of Indian representatives to obtain their views and he never varied from that premise.[128]

This is not to say, however, that Douglas was willing to place the citizenship agenda in the hands of Indians. By force of circumstance, pressure was mounting to resolve the issue and Douglas was determined not to be overtaken by events beyond his control. To that end, in the summer of 1956, the cabinet authorized the appointment of a special Committee on Indian Affairs (CIA), chaired by John Sturdy, minister without portfolio. Members included Gordon Campbell, director of adult education, Dr. Lewis Thomas, member at large, John Archer, Saskatchewan archivist, and William Wuttunee, a lawyer employed by Saskatchewan Government Insurance and member at large.[129] By this time, Sturdy was clearly Douglas's point man on Indian issues in general and the committee was established specifically to examine the whole question of Indian citizenship. The committee's frame of reference was drawn up by Sturdy himself and submitted for cabinet approval in October. In its draft form, the mandate called for a sweeping investigation into a whole battery of matters. It included the terms under which the province might take over the entire Indian Affairs administration; an assessment of the relationship between Indians and the Métis population; and the moral, legal, and financial responsibility of the federal government to Saskatchewan Indians.[130] The list, however, was pared down by cabinet to focus squarely on matters pertaining directly to Indian citizenship in the province, although it was understood that the mandate might be broadened at a later date.[131]

The first report of the CIA was drawn up in mid-November and submitted to cabinet in early December. Written in confidence, the eleven-page document offered unusual insight into the thinking of those in the know about Indian affairs. In substance, it is as much a political document as it is a statement of public policy because the committee was asked not only to determine what legislative changes would be necessary to implement Indian citizenship rights, but also to identify the related problems and liabilities that might be contemplated. In all, the report was addressed to four main areas of discussion.

First, on the question of the Indian franchise, the committee reported that it was a relatively simple matter to give Indians both provincial and municipal voting rights and that this could be done without, in any way, adversely affecting their status under the Indian Act.[132] Interestingly enough, however, the CIA recommended that Indians not be given the vote under the present circumstances. Life on Indian reserves, it was explained, was dominated by Indian agents who, often political appointees, had not only a strong bias in favour of the Liberal Party, which had been in power federally for the past twenty years, but also the necessary power to control the lives and destinies of Indians. Because of segregation, bureaucracy, bossism, discrimination, and other 'elements repugnant to democracy,' Indians had been relegated to a perpetual state of wardship, effectively incompatible with citizenship privileges. And as long as Indians were dominated by Ottawa and denied the education, health, social, and other services concomitant to citizenship, said the report, the granting of the provincial franchise would be meaningless. More than that, the CIA argued that the Indian vote would only cause problems for the provincial government without bringing any real changes in the lives of Indians. The reasoning here was that, because Indians were subject to 'the acceptance of gifts and presents' as well as to 'promises which have no basis in reality,' they would tend to vote in such a way that the status quo would be maintained. A case in point, said the report, were the Métis. These people, likewise susceptible to the influence of IAB officials and agents, entertained the perception that the provincial government had done little to improve their conditions over the past twelve years and tended to vote for the Liberal Party, which had been in power in Regina for so long. The CIA therefore concluded that the extension of the vote to Indians would be useless without far-reaching related reforms; and this, it said, could only be done by transferring the entire administration of Indian Affairs to the province, accompanied by a quid pro quo financial compensation for the added responsibility. To that end, it recommended that the province initiate talks with the federal government to determine the possibility and circumstances under which such a transfer might be effected.

Second, on the liquor issue, the CIA recommended against the province unilaterally introducing changes.[133] The amendment to the Indian Act permitted either the provincial government or the bands to initiate the process whereby band members would be brought under the provincial Liquor Act, although in the latter instance the province could veto the Indian initiative for a period of time. The amendment also contemplated the phasing in of drinking privileges: in stage one, Indians would be permitted consumption of alcohol in licensed premises; in stage two, Indians would be allowed to purchase and possess alcohol off a reserve; and in stage three, reserve Indians, by referendum, would be allowed to consume alcohol on the reserve. Of the three options, the committee found the first the most acceptable because of the controlled circumstances under which alcohol would be consumed. The second was deemed especially problematic because, in a province where most Indians lived on reserves, it invited violations of the Liquor Act: Indians would be allowed to possess alcohol but not consume it in their homes on reserves, and this would lead to illegal consumption on highways and in automobiles. The third stage, contingent on the implementation of the second stage, was also found to be troublesome. This was particularly so because the amendment did not require band referenda within a specific time frame and this meant that the necessary enabling legislation could not be put into effect across the province at the same time. The CIA concluded that the whole question created an unfavourable situation for the administration and strongly recommended that, for political reasons, the government avoid precipitous action and leave the initiative to the Indians. 'In this way,' said the report, 'the government will avoid as much criticism as possible ... for any action ... would undoubtedly produce a violent storm of protest.'

Third, the report included an assessment of the political risk the CCF ran in allowing Indians to vote provincially.[134] The central question was whether or not the inclusion of Indians in the electorate would endanger the CCF's hold on power. Sturdy and his committee approached this question by focusing on the results of the 1956 election and factoring into those results what was known or supposed about Indian demographics and political propensities. Based upon the supposition that the Indian turnout would be the same as that of the general electorate and assuming that Indians would vote for parties in the same proportion that the Métis had cast their votes in three polls in the Melville constituency in 1956, the assessment was that the Indian vote would not have substantially altered the outcome. The only possible difference in the results would have been a Liberal gain in Athabaska or perhaps a CCF gain in Turtleford.

Finally, the CIA recommended an interim course of action concerning the citizenship issues.[135] It suggested that, in order to promote harmonious relations with the Indian community, there would have to be a continuous flow of information in both directions. The USI leadership, along with at least two reserves in each of the Indian agencies, should be consulted immediately and, where possible, contact should be of a personal nature in order to engender mutual trust. Once Indians had had an opportunity to appraise proposed legislation on the matter, the government could then hold a series of conferences with the Indians to get their views and, based on the results, determine what should be done next.

The work of the CIA was important in reassuring Douglas and his ministers that, if necessary, the vote could be given to the Indians without disastrous consequences, as long as it was done correctly. By the same token, the CIA's strictures concerning amendments to the Liquor Act undoubtedly had a chastening effect on those in cabinet whose principles sometimes blinded them to political pitfalls. In effect, the committee had flagged the liquor issue as being potentially dangerous, and thereafter Douglas and his ministers redoubled their efforts to be circumspect on the matter. Ever present in the political stratagem followed by government was the hand of John Sturdy who increasingly influenced cabinet policy on the matter and oversaw relations with the Indian community. In January 1957, Sturdy was authorized by cabinet to approach the minister of Indian Affairs to ascertain whether Ottawa would entertain a proposal concerning the transfer of jurisdiction for Indians to the province.[136] In a subsequent meeting in Ottawa, he was assured by J.W. Pickersgill that the dominion, in fact, did favour such a transfer – eventually – but nothing ever came of it.[137] Sturdy was also authorized to convene a conference of Indian representatives to discuss the issues. This mirrored the fact that, in December 1957, the cabinet had made the decision to proceed with the Indian franchise, but only after consultation with Indian representatives.[138]

The invitation for Indians to meet in conference was drafted by Sturdy and amended by cabinet.[139] It contained an unequivocal statement that the government wanted to give the vote to Indians and that at the next session of the legislature it would give consideration to amending the Elections Act to that effect. It noted that Indians in other provinces were now exercising the franchise and that the right to vote would in no way jeopardize either treaty rights or legal privileges under the Indian Act. The main purpose of the conference, said the invitation, was to discuss the franchise before the government proceeded on the matter. But also included in the page-long invitation was a one-sentence statement that amendments to the Saskatchewan Liquor Act should also be discussed.

The two-day meeting would be held near the end of October 1958 in Valley Centre, Fort Qu'Appelle, and was to be attended by the chief and one councillor from each reserve throughout the province. The cost of travel, accommodations, and food for all delegates would be covered by the government.

As might be expected, Sturdy was anxious to keep his ear to the ground in preparation for the conference. Among other things, he arranged to have Bill Wuttunee visit as many reserves as possible during the summer months to sell the idea of voting and drinking reform. Wuttunee, it will be recalled, was a member of the Committee on Indian Affairs. In order to keep the CIA fully apprised of the situation, Wuttunee was to act as a kind of roving ambassador, submitting weekly reports to the CIA on his activities and on the political mood of the Indian community.[140] His findings clearly indicated that Indians were deeply divided over the issue, as they had been in the late 1940s. Among the supporters of the franchise was David Knight, chief of James Smith Reserve.[141] The opponents included John Tootoosis, president of the USI. Tootoosis was seemingly against the vote because he saw it as the first step in a would-be assault on Indian special rights.[142] According to Wuttunee, Tootoosis's eloquence was an important factor in making the government's message a tough sell and, for that reason, he recommended that special effort be made to get the chief on side because he would be persuasive in convincing others. Also among the opponents was William Joseph of Big River Reserve. Joseph was president of the Queen Victoria Treaty Protection Association, which, at the time, was at odds with the USI on a number of issues. He was attempting to raise money from QVTPA supporters, located mainly in the north-central part of the province, in order to visit England for an audience with Queen Elizabeth. He argued that Indians constituted a nation with a special relationship to the Crown and that, without the consent of that nation, there could be no transfer of jurisdiction over Indians either from England to Canada or from the dominion to the provinces.[143] He also denied the widely accepted doctrine of the day that Parliament was supreme and in theory could terminate both treaties and reserves, if it chose to do so.[144] It therefore followed that Joseph was hostile to the notion of provincial citizenship, including participation in elections. At the root of the QVTPA's opposition, of course, was the belief that citizenship would mean the end of treaties.

The divisions identified by Wuttunee proved to be a portent of what would happen at the 1958 conference.[145] In all, some 103 chiefs and councillors from 57 of the 61 reserves in the province registered for the opening session on 30 October. Serving as the chair of the conference, Sturdy described the Qu'Appelle meeting as the largest and most representative provincial conference in the history of Saskatchewan and perhaps of the

Premier Douglas speaking to Indian chiefs and councillors at a conference held at Valley Centre, Fort Qu'Appelle, October 1958. The conference was held to get Indians' views on liquor and the franchise. (Saskatchewan Archives Board R-B8435-1)

nation. Douglas was on hand to deliver the keynote address and took pains to reassure his audience that the government would not act on either the franchise or alcohol issue without the approval of Indians themselves. Also present were Senator Gladstone, an Alberta man and the first Indian ever to be appointed to the upper house, Albert Thompson, one of the founders and leading lights in the Manitoba Indian Brotherhood, and Frank Calder, MLA for Atlin, British Columbia. All three were in favour of Indian citizenship rights and in fiery speeches argued the importance of Indians playing a more important role in the political and economic life of the province. To create a 'bottom up' discussion of the issues, delegates were divided into five panels, each of which was chaired by an Indian leader and included a member of the committee on Indian Affairs for 'consultative purposes.' In turn, the views of each panel were reported in both Cree and English to the plenary session of the conference.

The reports made it quite evident that many were still opposed to both voting and liquor rights. Some claimed that, although they had had a change of heart and now supported the measures in light of new information, they nevertheless were duty bound to oppose the measures because they had been so instructed by their constituents. Faced with apparent failure, John Sturdy countered with a proposal that would allow the issue to remain open. He suggested to the conference that, although

Frank Calder, Senator James Gladstone, and Premier Douglas (left to right) at an Indian conference in Valley Centre, Fort Qu'Appelle, to discuss the liquor and franchise problems, October 1958. (Saskatchewan Archives Board 58-523-02)

a vote could be taken on each issue, the conference by resolution could defer a decision to a later date.[146] In due course, the delegates were persuaded to do just that. Resolution 1, introduced by John Tootoosis and seconded by Chief J. Pinay, was passed by a large majority. It proposed that a second conference be held a year later, at which time a decision would be made on the two issues. It also called for an education campaign to better inform the Indian community about the issues. Resolution 2, introduced by Allan Ahenakew and seconded by Chief W.J. Quewezance, was passed unanimously and provided for the appointment of a committee to advise the Committee on Indian Affairs on the date, organization, and agenda of the 1959 conference, as well as on the organization of the educational campaign. This advisory committee, composed of one representative from each of the nine Indian agencies, was duly elected by conference delegates meeting separately on an agency basis.

With the franchise and liquor issues laid to rest for the time being, conference delegates turned their hand to another pressing problem: the creation of a new Indian organization.[147] Among other things, the protracted conflict between the Union of Saskatchewan Indians, led by John Tootoosis, and the Queen Victoria Treaty Protection Association, headed by William Joseph, had occasioned considerable dissatisfaction with the existing situation. The QVTPA, it will be recalled, was opposed to citizenship and had greatly criticized the union for its supposed close connection with the CCF, as well as for its unwillingness or inability to protect treaty rights. According to Stan Cuthand, who attended the 1958 meeting, there was a growing feeling that the creation of a new, all-inclusive organization might provide a fresh start and allay some of the problems.[148] At the meeting, Tootoosis and Joseph were persuaded to put aside their differences, and both agreed to the need for a new association, to be known as the United Federation of Saskatchewan Indians, later shortened to the Federation of Saskatchewan Indians (FSI). After 'spirited debate,' delegates sanctioned the new federation as the only organization to speak for all Saskatchewan Indians, although this, of course, did not mean the end of the QVTPA and other local associations. The federation was based on an organization through which provincial and regional executives were derived from local band councils in each of the nine agencies. The provisional executive committee of the federation was identical to the membership of the advisory committee to the CIA and included David Knight (chair; Duck Lake), John Tootoosis (Battleford), Absalom Halkett (Carleton; Reverend Stan Cuthand, substitute), Joe Williams (Crooked Lake), David Greyeyes (Shellbrook), John Gambler (File Hills), Louis Quewezance (Pelly), John Skeboss (Touchwood), and Ernest Dillon (Meadow Lake).

The overlap in membership between the advisory committee and the executive committee of FSI proved to be unfortunate because it tended to identify the new federation with the government's agenda. The executive itself was determined to maintain an independent position, but the fact remained that, as in the case of the USI, the federation was dependent on government grants to finance many of its activities. At Sturdy's request, for example, cabinet authorized a $1,000 expenditure to permit the federation's executive to attend business meetings and visit reserves to discuss the franchise and related matters.[149] It was difficult, if not impossible, to avoid the perception that the advisory committee was as much a government agency as it was the executive of a provincial Indian organization, and the perception was bound to have long-term consequences.

In reality, the executive was anything but of one mind on the citizenship issues and was torn by the same kind of doubts and misinformation that plagued the general membership. In June 1959, the FSI executive drew up a list of questions about the vote and changes to the liquor laws and asked that the cabinet provide the answers. The nature of the queries was a clear indication that even the Indian leadership in the province was not completely conversant with either the ramifications of citizenship or the political process in place. Not surprisingly, many of the questions were addressed to whether or not specific rights would be lost as a consequence of voting. But others asked what the word 'vote' meant; whether there was a penalty for not voting; whether the franchise also meant the right to vote in federal elections; and why the government wanted Indians to vote.[150] It was also evident from one question that the executive was under the mistaken impression that at the 1958 conference in Valley Centre 'it was the unanimous decision to defeat the granting of the franchise and liquor privileges.'[151] Undoubtedly, the uncertainties were a product of the legalistic and technical nature of the issues at hand, but they may also have reflected the extent to which the citizenship agenda was being driven not by Indian politicians and interests but by a provincial government increasingly bent on manipulating events to satisfy its own concerns.

This was markedly evident at the second Indian conference, held in the fall of 1959. The gathering was sponsored by the provincial government but billed in the press as the second annual meeting of the FSI. According to an account by Ray Woollam, who at the time was a provincial adult-education consultant, the government did not want the vote and alcohol questions presented on the floor of the conference because, realizing the insuperable opposition to the measures, it feared the measures would be voted down.[152] Consequently, only near the end of the conference and after almost seventy resolutions had already been dealt with, a rather strange motion deflecting the whole question of the vote and ignoring the more troublesome issue of alcohol was introduced:

> WHEREAS in a political democracy the vote is a right and not a privilege and
> WHEREAS some Indians want the provincial vote and others do not want the vote
> THEREFORE BE IT RESOLVED THAT the Federation of Saskatchewan Indians in Conference assembled be not required to petition the Provincial Government on this question.[153]

Evidently, this carefully worded resolution was meant to focus attention on the franchise issue only, neatly sidestepping the liquor debate. According to Ray Woollam, it was also designed to take the initiative away from Indians and place the decision back in the hands of cabinet.[154]

There appear to have been two reasons why this strategy was adopted. First, it seems certain that, under pressure from advisors and cabinet, Douglas was forced to renege on his promise that no steps would be taken by the government unless Indians agreed to the measures. The resolution, in effect, absolved him of that promise. By this time, pressure was mounting in Ottawa to extend the federal franchise to Indians and provincial politicians did not want to be left behind on the issue. Two years earlier, Frank Howard (CCF, Skeena) had introduced a private member's bill calling for the extension of the federal franchise to Indians.[155] In 1958, the bill was set aside on second reading, but the cause it embraced was quickly resurrected in 1959 when it was learned that the Diefenbaker government intended to introduce a Canadian Bill of Rights. As a matter of course, such an act would necessitate the granting of the Indian franchise at the federal level. This, combined with voting initiatives in other provinces, made it politically untenable to provincial politicians that Saskatchewan, as the only province in Canada with a Bill of Rights, should continue to countenance a disfranchised Indian community.

The second factor may have been an attempt to paper over existing divisions in the fledgling FSI. Ray Woollam was of the opinion that the very survival of the federation was at stake. As he explained to John Sturdy and the premier in a confidential memorandum,

> I sense that the future of the F.S.I. hinges on its relationship to these issues. So long as the organization is compelled to have either a positive or negative viewpoint in respect to the vote, it will be a schizoid organization. While the issue hangs in abeyance it creates a cloud of anxiety over the group ... I think it is only when the burden of these issues is removed that the organization will become unified and happy.[156]

Seen in this light, the resolution introduced at the conference was an attempt to prevent the destruction of the new federation. As in the case of the USI before it, the FSI was an important component of the CCF's Indian policy because, without it, the government lacked a would-be partner capable of representing Indian opinion and legitimizing government reforms.

As it turned out, the government's strategy at the 1959 conference backfired, in that delegates almost unanimously voted against the resolution. Ray Woollam placed the blame squarely on Douglas for promising in 1958 that Indian consent would be necessary before the government would act and then ducking the issue in 1959. Progressive chiefs in favour of citizenship, said Woollam, voted against the resolution 'because they had waited all year, on the strength of Mr. Douglas's promise, for the opportunity to face up to these issues at the 1959 Conference.'[157] At the same time, the reactionary chiefs, primarily identified by Woollam as members of the QVTPA, were opposed to any initiative that could be interpreted as an attack on treaty rights.[158] Likewise, those who were not in either of these two camps voted against the resolution simply because they did not understand it.[159]

The fiasco also deepened divisions in the Indian community. Many young chiefs at the conference expressed the opinion that the whole question had been handled 'politically.'[160] They saw it as an attempt by the government to sidestep the issue, given the forthcoming provincial election, and as a ploy to prop up the solidarity of the FSI. The perceived connection between the government and the FSI, as in the past, once more proved to be a political liability, in that many of the young chiefs now threatened to pull out of the federation.[161] The most organized reaction came after the conference from a new quarter, a group from the File Hills-Qu'Appelle Agency and known as the Qu'Appelle Indian Advisory Council of Chiefs Independent. They were solidly opposed to the FSI and refused to become members; they were also against the franchise and ultimately hired lawyers to petition both the provincial and federal governments on behalf of their cause.[162] Although the group was relatively small in number, it was taken seriously by Woollam and others because of the possibility that it might take on a provincewide stature by making common cause with the QVTPA.[163] The latter held a meeting on Little Pine and Poundmaker Reserves to denounce the franchise and liquor reform, and they threatened to tear down polling booths if they were set up on their reserves.[164] Their protests, however, never extended much beyond the Battleford area and there is no indication that QVTPA ever joined forces with the Qu'Appelle group.

Indian opposition notwithstanding, citizenship now became inevitable. Resolutions passed at CCF provincial conventions made it obvious that the rank and file of the party supported the Indian vote. But the defining moment came at the 1959 Provincial Council Meeting where the issue was debated by the party for the last time. Although some MLAs, particularly those with large Indian populations in their constituencies, were clearly fearful that they might lose their seats if Indians were franchised, the majority cast their vote in favour of amending the Elections Act to include Indians. Douglas could no longer delay. Early in the new year, he confided to Dan Kennedy that the time was near: 'we can no longer delay taking this step and I hope that those who are fearful of its consequences will have their fears allayed in due course.'[165] A month later, in February 1960, he announced in the Assembly that, despite his earlier promises to the contrary, his government would proceed on the matter without Indian consent; in turn, the provincial Elections Act was amended in the Assembly, thereby extending the franchise to all Saskatchewan Indians of majority age. On 8 June 1960, Indians in Saskatchewan made history by going to the provincial polls for the first time.[166]

The premier, however, hesitated on the liquor question. Changes to the Liquor Act enabling the government to grant drinking rights to off-reserve Indians had actually been passed in the provincial legislature in 1959.[167] But the government held up implementation, failing to petition the federal government to issue the necessary proclamation under the Indian Act. Ray Woollam, now executive director of the Committee on Minority Groups, was completely dismayed at the delay and vented his anger in a memorandum to John Sturdy, with a copy addressed to the premier.[168] He pointed to a number of examples where the existing situation, rather than integrating Indians, tended to victimize and marginalize them. He argued that whites often would not socialize with Indians because they feared repercussions from the law when alcohol was present; and he cited the example of an Indian matron who, residing in the La Ronge hospital, was dismissed from her position on staff because she consumed alcohol in her own quarters. He also underscored the political dangers inherent in the situation, especially the fact that the Liberal Party was promising liquor reform and that the issue was still causing problems for the FSI. And, with a logic rooted in liberal democratic understanding, he appealed to principle:

> If our Provincial Government policy is to be shaped into the spirit of integration or the spirit of our Provincial Bill of Rights, it is difficult for me to understand why this situation must continue. It seems to me as simple as the fact that we have no justification for any discriminatory legislation which can be changed. The problem is one that is exactly parallel to the problem of the vote and I cannot see any simple rationale which might justify different approaches to these two issues. The real issue in each case is one of 'symbols of freedom.'[169]

Woollam's memorandum, in fact, was indicative of the general climate of opinion in administrative and government circles and it was only a matter of time until the premier himself fell into line. By the late spring of 1960, Douglas had set aside his own personal reservations on the matter and in June the province petitioned the federal government for the necessary proclamation.[170] On 27 July 1960, the federal proclamation giving Saskatchewan Indians liquor rights came into effect. Thereafter, Indians, like anyone else, were free to purchase and consume alcohol, although in the latter instance they could not do so on a reserve unless that reserve had been declared 'wet' as the result of a referendum.[171]

Voting and drink reform, of course, did not revolutionize the lives of Indians. The FSI leadership made no attempt to have the franchise repealed and many, including John Tootoosis, were simply happy to have the issue behind them. By the same token, the rank and file seemingly acquiesced to the changes with either quiet indifference or passive acceptance. While some communities now became the subject of intense lobbying during elections, Indian participation in the larger political process remained only marginal and seldom altered the rhythm of reserve life.

By the same token, the new liquor laws did not significantly modify the pattern of alcohol use, although the provision for reserve referenda did serve to localize and intensify the drink issue in reserve communities across the province.[172] While provincial politicians were quick to admit that the new reforms did not, in themselves, fully integrate Indians into the wider society, they professed to see these measures as an important step in that direction. And, in a fundamental way, the reforms had the effect of capping the citizenship debate during the Douglas years.

5

The Saskatchewan Far North:
The Last Frontier

As an agrarian-based party, the CCF not surprisingly riveted its attention on developments in the southern portion of the province where most people lived. This did not mean, however, that Douglas and his colleagues were blind to the problems and possibilities offered by the province's northland. In point of fact, the North figured prominently in the plans of the CCF almost from the first day it took office. On one level, the far North represented an insuperable obstacle to the kind of rational planning and management in which social democrats took so much pride, at least in theory. On another level, the North was central to a cherished and fundamental goal of the CCF, namely the exploitation of natural resources as a means of financing social reform. Douglas premised his notion of social regeneration, especially the integration of the underprivileged into society, on a developmental model in which the exploitation of natural resources would produce the wealth necessary for modernization and public services. The idea was to expand and diversify the province's economic base, to increase the provincial income, and to spend the resulting tax dollars and royalties on roads, schools, and social programs.[1] Within that context, the developmental potential of the North was not without import in the strategic planning of the CCF government.

Saskatchewan's distant northland comprised some 100,000 square miles stretching from Prince Albert to the Northwest Territories. Ecologically, the region was defined by a narrow forest belt of mixed coniferous and deciduous trees, flanked on the north by a vast area of rocky Precambrian shield. By the time the CCF came to power, the North was inhabited by a sparse population of only 10,000 people, more or less evenly divided between whites, Métis, and Indians.[2] Of the 3,000 white people, about 2,500 were concentrated in the three white mining communities of Goldfields, Creighton, and Island Falls.[3] This meant that outside the mining towns, Natives constituted close to 94 percent of the northern total. Although technically divisible into Cree, Chipewyans, Métis, and

Map 2 Northern Saskatchewan

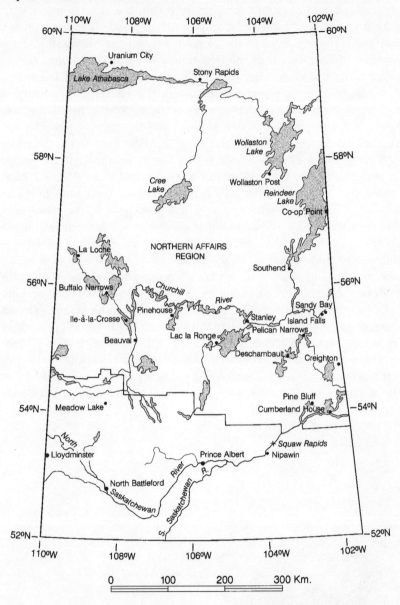

non-status Indians, the Native population was culturally similar and dispersed among thirty or so small communities and isolated cabins.[4] In reality, the North was a veritable wilderness of lakes, rivers, muskeg, and bush, inhabited by a mere sprinkling of people comprising barely 2 percent of the total population of the province.[5] Systematically ignored by past governments, the North was bereft of even the most basic public services and amenities and subsisted in isolation and economic stagnation. It was, in fact, a classical example of third-world underdevelopment.

Administratively, most of the North fell under the jurisdiction of the Northern Affairs Region of the Department of Natural Resources (DNR), a fact in itself underscoring the developmental potential of the North. Although other government departments such as education, cooperatives, and social services would deliver services in the North, the DNR was to be the main instrument of development and the clearinghouse for service delivery in the North. Douglas placed the DNR portfolio in the hands of the irascible Joe Phelps, described by the premier as 'a steam engine in pants.'[6] Prior to the 1944 election, Phelps had chaired a CCF committee on natural resources, which had proposed 'the complete socialization' of all natural resources, and, when elevated to the minister of natural resources, he found himself in control of economic development. Phelps was a no-nonsense man of action with an ingrained hostility to monopolies and special privilege. In cabinet he was known as a radical and, as a minister, his methods were often unorthodox. Phelps ruled the DNR by the seat of his pants, acting as his own deputy minister and disregarding bureaucratic procedure.[7] In some cases, he wrote personal cheques for projects and then had the DNR transfer funds to his account; in others, his cabinet colleagues learned of DNR development projects only after they had already been initiated.[8] His brashness and unbending attitude sometimes made Douglas and the other ministers 'uneasy,' to say the least; nevertheless, Phelps was also widely respected in certain circles,

Portrait of Joseph Lee Phelps, ca. 1948. (Saskatchewan Archives Board R-A10,893)

particularly by the small group of committed Marxists he attracted to senior positions in the northern administration. Included in that group was Allan Quandt, the northern administrator, as well as Jim Brady and Malcolm Norris. The latter two were Métis who had been instrumental in organizing the Indian Association of Alberta and who were attracted to Saskatchewan because of the socialist promises of the CCF government.[9] Phelps also enjoyed the respect and support of the premier. On taking office, Douglas sensed that the province was tired of being the poor sister of the prairie provinces and he promised to take action. That he chose Phelps to head the DNR was a measure of both the confidence he had in Phelps and the importance he attached to resource development.

Within a short time of taking office, Phelps and Douglas made airplane tours of the North to see firsthand what they were up against. They were appalled by what they found. The fur and fish industries, the mainstay of the Native economy, were in a state of severe decline and stagnation, resulting in massive underemployment, poverty, and related social problems. Barely 50 percent of school-age children were in schools; the infant mortality rate was far above the national average; although there was a hospital at Ile-à-la-Crosse and a nursing station at Cumberland House, medical services were not available for most of the region; and life expectancy was little more than thirty years.[10] Symptomatic of the alarming degree of underdevelopment generally was the state of Lac La Ronge, a main administrative centre in the region. Unlike most other places, it had a school, two stores, an Anglican Church mission, a DNR officer, an RCMP officer, and a population of about twenty-four families. But it had

Jim Brady, a staker for Pre-Cam Explorations and Development Ltd., making claim post, July 1957. (Saskatchewan Archives Board R-A13459-3)

Malcolm Norris (seated on table), of the Department of Mineral Resources, lecturing to a class at the DMR Prospectors School in La Ronge, May 1956. (Saskatchewan Archives Board R-B5989-3)

no all-weather road access of any sort, no health care of any description, no access to a high school, and no filleting plant. And, as if to punctuate its isolation and improbable future, its only airfield was in a state of complete disrepair.[11] The airstrip had been abandoned in 1929 when the province took over control of its natural resources from the federal government. For a ten-year period, a guard had been placed on the premises to protect the equipment, stores, and stockpile of gasoline. But then the airfield was simply forsaken. By the time Phelps and Douglas arrived, the airstrip was seemingly still being used, but it was in a dilapidated condition, with barrels of gas belonging to the federal government strewn around the property and hidden in the adjacent woods.

Upon their return to Regina, both the minister and the premier issued a number of policy statements promising a 'new deal' for the North.[12] Later, in a radio address, Douglas insisted that Saskatchewan's northland was 'Canada's last frontier,' destined for extensive development.[13] The reference, of course, implied an entirely new emphasis not only on rejuvenating old economies but also on exploiting virgin resources in the North, including the mining of uranium. As he made explicit in 1948:

The next four or five years will see tremendous development in northern Saskatchewan. Everyone knows that very valuable deposits of uranium have been found at various points in the north. Standing as we do on the threshold of the atomic age, uranium is of tremendous importance to our industrial development. At the present time Saskatchewan has probably the best uranium prospects in North America. This could be our golden opportunity if we handle it properly.[14]

The concept of 'last frontier' was fundamental to Douglas's development model for the North, but from a policy perspective it meant more than economic development or development for its own sake.

In the first place, development of the last frontier was predicated on meaningful conservation through which sustainable yield was to be accomplished. Development was not rationalized as a purely socialist experiment, although the extent and role of private capital in the North was never clearly articulated. What was made explicit was that government regulation, in the interest of conservation, would be ever-present. Both Phelps and Douglas publicly condemned the thirty-five-year rule of the Liberals, during which, they insisted, individuals and corporations had been allowed to ravage the landscape and plunder natural resources for their own selfish ends. The premier pointed to the lumber industry north of Prince Albert where a few corporations had been allowed to '"cut out and get out," leaving our people in a veritable wilderness without any means of support.'[15] The only solution, he said, was to make sure that conservation was superimposed on development through government regulation. As Phelps explained, 'the resources of Saskatchewan were placed here by the Creator' and not 'for either the benefit of a few, or solely for one generation.'[16] It was partly out of deference to the need for conservation that, during the first great reform session of the Assembly between 1944 and 1948, the CCF amended the Natural Resources Act to provide tighter control over development.

Secondly, subsumed in the concept of last frontier was the clear understanding that development of the resources could not be dissociated from the development of the people who used them because of the importance of natural resources to the economy of northern people. The DNR was mandated not only as a manager of the northern economy but also as a manager of the people who inhabited the land. At one point, Phelps actually referred to himself as the minister of 'human' resources.[17] The Natural Resources Act, as amended in 1944, gave the government unprecedented rights to intervene in economic development, and this was defended in the Assembly on the basis of social need and the rights of society over those of the individual. Driven by the tenets of moral indignation, social gospel, and egalitarianism, the ideology of 'humanity first,' proudly proclaimed by Phelps as the 'watchword' of the CCF,[18] predetermined that the government would attempt to ameliorate the conditions of northern Natives. Within that context, the DNR was fashioned as an engine of social reform.

Finally, Douglas's notion of the last frontier was laced with ethno-centrism and paternalism. Far from walking in the Indian moccasins of northern people, the CCF perceived the North as a remote hinterland in need of effective colonization; hence, the solutions it imposed there were little more than reflections of the values and agenda of southern society.[19] CCF reformism was rooted in the notion of massive interven-tion in the interest of economic and social engineering and, by defini-tion, this spoke to the need for a heavy management hand. Even in the late 1950s, when policymakers placed new emphasis on the self-help philosophy, closely associated with the concepts of community develop-ment and cooperative organization, government paternalism and control continued.[20] In the same way that the CCF dominated development in the Métis colonies of the South and intruded into the political activities and organizations of Indians, Douglas and his ministers were quite pre-pared to influence – and even dominate – the lives of northern residents, in theory to save them from themselves. This meant that throughout the Douglas era, control was carefully maintained in Regina.

Native Economy

The heart of the so-called 'Native economy' was the fur industry, with Indians and Métis constituting more than 96 percent of the trappers by the late 1950s.[21] In the past, the industry had been plagued by a series of structural problems that had caused declining incomes and a severe deple-tion of fur stocks. These problems had been endemic to fur production for decades and had brought the industry to the brink of disaster.

Traditionally, the trapper had been victimized by fluctuating fur prices determined on the world market, by the natural cycles in fur-bearing animals, by the excessive profit margins extracted by the trading com-panies, and by the ability of the fur companies, particularly the Hudson's Bay Company, to manipulate the terms and conditions under which credit was given to the trapper. To make matters worse, the lack of government regulation had led to horrendous overtrapping, to the extent that some species – such as the beaver – were close to extinction in most parts of the North.[22] A large part of the problem had been a massive immigration of white trappers from the South during the Depression. Some were muskrat trappers who moved from south to north each year as the season opened in one area after the other; others, economic refugees attempt-ing to 'live off the land' in response to widespread unemployment in the South, often stayed on and became permanent residents.[23] These immigrants, competing with long-time residents for existing fur stocks, severely threatened the ability of animal life to replenish itself. And to exacerbate an already dangerous situation, overtrapping was accelerated by a lease system that did nothing to encourage conservation. To curb the wanton activities of freelance trappers, a Liberal provincial government had introduced a system through which individual trappers were given exclusive harvesting rights to certain areas during unregulated 'open' seasons. Regrettably, this encouraged an orgy of trapping during the open season and massive unemployment during the closed season.[24]

In response to these problems, in 1944 the CCF set up the Saskatchewan Fur Marketing Service (SFMS). The SFMS was a crown corporation that acted as a commission service for trappers. It was designed to increase fur prices and enforce defined quotas on certain species as a measure of conservation. Although most furs could be sold to whatever agency the trapper chose, beaver and muskrat pelts by law had to be marketed through the SFMS. The compulsory nature of the program was meant to enforce quotas on the number of pelts taken in order to regenerate the beaver and muskrat populations and to ensure that the public treasury received a fair share of the profits to fund its conservation program.[25] But this proved to be extremely unpopular for two reasons. The SFMS took 10 percent of the profits to finance its operation, and this was greatly resented by local trappers. But more than that, the forced marketing of beaver and muskrats destroyed the trapper's access to credit from private companies, which traditionally had been the means of financing trapping activities. The SFMS gave the trapper an initial payout for his or her pelts and a final payment once the actual price of the furs had been determined by auction; however, there was no provision for pre-trapping credit because the SFMS had neither the resources nor the administrative network to accommodate such a scheme.[26] At the same time, the Hudson's Bay Company and other firms were understandably reluctant to extend credit because beaver and muskrat pelts could no longer be traded through their own marketing systems. There was also the added problem that, unlike in the past, companies no longer had the leverage to make sure that the trapper repaid the loan once his furs had been marketed. As a consequence, the trapper often lacked the means to finance his annual operations, a problem compounded by escalating costs for equipment and provisions in the postwar period. The compulsory aspect of the SFMS ultimately proved so unpopular that, in 1956, the government abandoned it altogether, thereafter allowing trappers to sell furs of every description to the private companies as well.[27]

As important as the SFMS was in reinforcing the conservation program, in its own right it did not represent a major solution to the problems of the North. By design it was never meant to apply exclusively or even primarily to the North, nor after 1956 was it widely used by northern trappers.[28] From its inception it provided a service for trappers, fur ranchers, and dealers in all parts of Saskatchewan and even for shippers outside the province. A large percentage of the furs – auctioned in Regina eight times a year – came from southern and central Saskatchewan. Northern trappers showed a definite aversion to the SFMS, and after 1956 relied heavily on the private marketing systems. As one Northern Affairs Branch report explained, 'only a very small percentage of trappers in the North market their fur through the Saskatchewan Marketing Service. This is especially true of the native trappers who are largely dependent on their local credit.'[29] Certainly northern trappers did benefit from the SFMS in that the existence of the crown corporation reduced the degree of monopoly in the fur business and caused a modest increase in fur prices, but northern trappers were not always aware of these advantages.

Far more important than its marketing service, though not unrelated to it, was the government's Northern Fur Conservation Program (NFCP). The NFCP, heralded by Joe Phelps as 'a bill of rights for the people of northern Saskatchewan,'[30] was the result of a two-year wildlife study initiated in 1944 by a committee of the Department of Natural Resources. It was based on a joint agreement signed by the federal and provincial governments in July 1946. It called for the dominion to pay 60 percent of the costs of the program in recognition of its responsibility for Indians in the area, the remainder being borne by the province.[31] The main feature of the agreement was the establishment of a huge conservation reserve north of the 53rd parallel, roughly corresponding to the Northern Affairs Region of the DNR. In turn, the reserve was divided into conservation areas or 'fur blocks' trapped exclusively by local residents. To be included in the program, a trapper had to be sixteen years old and a British subject or a female who supported a family. Although there was an attempt to allot traplines to those who had previously occupied them, Natives per se were not given a preference over whites. Each block was administered by a five-person local trappers' council, which had to include both Indian and Métis representatives from the local area and two elected members. Each council, in cooperation with a field officer from the DNR, was responsible for establishing and enforcing the conservation quotas for beaver and muskrat and making sure that all trappers in the block were treated fairly.

As a solution to problems in the northern fur industry, the NFCP offered a number of advantages. First, it was based on a new infusion of money to support the northern trapping industry. The dominion-provincial agreement called for an expenditure of up to $50,000 a year for development of the fur industry over the next ten years.[32] In addition, funding was made available for special projects, such as wildlife studies, the clearing of portages, and building dams to raise and maintain water levels in support of muskrat production.[33] Second, northern trappers were guaranteed a degree of lease tenure and continuous harvesting. To stop itinerant trappers from coming in and skimming off the cream of the crop and then moving on, licences were granted only to those who had been resident in the district for a twelve-month period.[34] At the same time, regulations placed restrictions on the excessive harvesting of wildlife. The taking of most furs during open season was not subject to quotas per se, but regulations required that there must always be enough animals left alive to ensure adequate propagation of the species; and in the case of beaver and muskrats, trapping was permitted on a community basis only, each trapper being allowed to trap a fair quota of the estimated number of animals. The net effect was to ensure a more stable income for legitimate resident trappers, in that the supply of furs was less vulnerable to wanton destruction, especially by transient trappers. Third, strategic restocking was a central feature of the program, at least during the early years. In a two-year period alone, some 1,127 beaver were live-trapped in the South and flown North – giving some northern Natives their first glimpse of live beaver.[35] The success of the transplant program was registered in burgeoning harvests and, in part, explains why in 1956 the government felt justified in dropping the compulsory part of its fur marking service, arguing that beaver conservation in particular was no longer as necessary.[36]

Next in importance to furs in the Native economy was the commercial fishing industry, most of which was centred in the North. Furs and fish, in fact, were intimately interrelated, in that those who engaged in

Oscar Stromberg heading home with trapped beaver and examining a mink den beside Torch River, 1959. (Saskatchewan Archives Board RB-4753-2)

fishing were also usually trappers. For Natives, commercial fishing was significant because it was one of only a few industries in the North that had the potential to employ large numbers. However, not unlike trapping, the fishing industry in the North had a checkered past and was plagued by a host of structural problems. As a result, the industry not only lacked competitiveness but also did little initially to incorporate Natives either as entrepreneurs or workers.

Placed in historical perspective, commercial fishing was a relatively new industry in the North. Fishing operations at Big River date back to 1911; and at Peter Pond, Ile-à-la-Crosse, and Churchill Lakes to the 1920s.[37] By the beginning of the Second World War, the industry had spread to a number of lakes in the Northern Affairs Region, including La Ronge, Pinehouse, Lake Athabaska, Beaver Lake, and Reindeer Lake.[38] However, apart from a few communities – most notably Beaval, Ile-à-la-Crosse, and Buffalo Narrows on the east side of the province – commercial fishing at the time was not of primary importance and overall meant little to the northern economy. The industry generated little income, especially for Natives, and contributed little to provincial coffers. In the early stages, it was also a business dominated by white people. Most were either farmers, principally from settlements on the fringe of the North, who had turned to fishing in winter to supplement their income, or often Scandinavians who had settled in the North and pioneered the fishing operation in a number of communities.[39] In many cases, they were also non-residents from Manitoba or Alberta. However, in the postwar period this trend was effectively reversed when the CCF instituted regulations limiting commercial fishing to bona fide northern residents. In practice, this did not entirely eliminate either southern or extraprovincial inter- lopers, but the regulations did ensure that the vast majority of fishers – as much as 94 percent by the late 1950s – were actually northerners, most of whom were Indian or Metis.[40]

Fishing operations had expanded greatly during the war years, mainly as a consequence of rocketing prices. The ravenous wartime demand for food from whatever source, coupled with the destruction of the Great Lakes fishing industry as a result of lamprey infestation, proved to be a tremendous incentive to more intensive and extensive fishing operations in the Saskatchewan North. The industry expanded to new lakes and greatly increased production: pickerel by 33 percent, whitefish by 58 per- cent, and trout by 73 percent.[41] By 1943, Saskatchewan had become Canada's leading producer of whitefish and was supplying close to a third of all the trout.[42] Although some of this added production was drawn from lakes in the fringe areas, such as Prince Albert and Meadow Lake, most came from the North where, at the peak of the wartime boom in 1944, some 140 lakes were open to commercial fishing.[43]

Soon after the CCF came to power, the wartime boom subsided. In the minds of Douglas and his colleagues, the fishing industry held out the promise of substantial resource development as a solution to the problems of the North, especially in the Native community. At the same time, it was painfully evident that the conditions that had given rise to the expansion of the industry during the war had done nothing to solve the structural obstacles that made the industry uncompetitive during peacetime. In fact, the war years had exacerbated the situation because the boom had produced an expansion in the industry that had simply masked over the reality that, under normal circumstances, it cost more to produce fish in Saskatchewan than in Manitoba or the Great Lakes. That, of course, threatened the industry's viability in national and international markets once the artificial stimulus of the war had been removed.

One problem was the scattered and isolated nature of operations. In Manitoba, three-quarters of the commercial fishing took place on large lakes, particularly Lake Winnipeg, and there the average annual production was in the neighborhood of 15,000,000 pounds.[44] By contrast, Saskatchewan production was scattered over more than 100 lakes, all of which were inaccessible by roads and none of which equaled the Manitoban annual poundage. The most productive lake was Reindeer, which yielded 1,000,000 pounds; only eleven lakes topped 150,000 pounds, and most were limited to considerably less than that in any one year.[45] The single largest cost was transportation to a southern railhead, mirroring the fact that in 1945 no road went North. Planes were sometimes used but costs were normally prohibitive, so the normal means of transportation was tractor trains, hauling fish some 150 miles from places like Reindeer Lake.

Geography and climate created other problems. Because fish were taken mainly in winter, they were often frozen before proper cleaning, and hence were marketed in an ill-prepared state and received low prices. The marketing of fresh fish, which commanded the highest prices, was nearly impossible in light of the long distances and transportation problems. And because of the small size of the Saskatchewan lakes, economies of scale and the application of new technology were not always possible, especially in comparison to the large and modern production process found on Lake Winnipeg or on the British Columbia coast.

To make matters worse, whitefish from Saskatchewan's North were frequently infested with a parasite technically known as triaenophorus crassus. Although harmless, the parasite greatly detracted from the appearance of the fish, and this proved especially problematic in exporting whitefish, particularly to the United States where the product was in great demand. As early as 1930, American inspectors routinely turned back fish lots found to display any degree of parasitic infestation. This meant that large volumes of whitefish, as much as three-quarters of a million pounds in some years, had to be sold off in the Canadian market at bargain-basement prices.[46]

The nature and ramifications of these problems were made the subject of a Royal Commission established by the Douglas government in 1946.[47] But even before then, the CCF had resolved to make the northern fisheries a source of income for northern residents and, to that end, had made a deliberate decision to foster the industry. Although the government's intervention did not always produce the kind of results that were expected, it was dramatic, if not revolutionary, in both its intent and impact. Of all the factors shaping the fishing industry over the next fifteen years, government was an ever-present and determining force.

Among the earliest and most effective reforms was an attempt to deal with the problem of American border rejections. Only months before the CCF took office, the federal government had passed the Whitefish Inspection Act resulting in the closure of a number of lakes in the Prairie provinces because of the substandard quality of their fish.[48] In response, the Douglas government not only honoured federal regulations but also played a pioneering role in establishing an internal system of quality control. A main feature, carried out at considerable cost and time to the province, was the testing and classification of literally hundreds of lakes. Under the new scheme, lakes were designated either 'A' or 'B' according to the degree of parasitic presence. The export of whole whitefish was permitted from A lakes only, where infestation was low; for B lakes, where parasites were most active, whitefish by law had to be processed before marketing, and this meant candling (removing parasitic cysts) and filleting. Although it did not completely eliminate border rejections, the measure was important in making Saskatchewan fish competitive in the American market, especially in comparison to provinces like Manitoba where border rejections ran as high as 20 percent by the late 1950s.[49] It also put the province in a favourable position when the federal government, in the early 1960s, moved to compulsory certification of export whitefish.[50]

In keeping with the new regulation system, the government provided and encouraged investment in filleting plants in the North. By the late 1940s, private business had built plants at Dore, Big River, and Buffalo Narrows, while the province had completed plants at La Ronge, Beaver Lake, and Deschambault Lake. By the time Douglas left the province, an additional five plants had been constructed, four of which were government owned. All government plants met the dominion's stringent inspection criteria and qualified for the status of 'Canada approved.'[51] Filleting plants were crucial in overcoming the problems associated with B lakes, but they also helped reduce transportation costs. Premium prices

Old Sask Fish Board Plant, Deschambeault Lake. (Glenbow Archives PA-2218-465)

were paid for round dressed fish (cleaned whole fish), but filleting was profitable where the quality of the fish was low or transportation costs high. Filleting reduced losses from spoilage, the produce could be more easily stored, and the marketing could be spread out over the year, thereby stabilizing returns. And where air transportation was necessary, such as from Cree or Wollaston lakes, the reduced volume saved money.[52]

Transportation nevertheless remained a central problem, one roundly condemned by the Royal Commission on fishing, and to offset its effects the Douglas government also invested in infrastructure. A landmark development was the construction of all-weather roads: in 1947, a highway was completed between Prince Albert and La Ronge; between 1955 and 1957, a road was cut through forest and rock to Buffalo Narrows, thereby linking the major fishing areas of Beauval, Ile-à-la-Crosse, and Buffalo Narrows on the east side; and in 1958, the La Ronge road was extended to Neneiben Lake. Although air transportation remained important, especially in the fresh fish operation, the construction of highways was important in reducing costs associated with getting fish to road and railheads for transshipment to market. Transportation facilities also nurtured a transition from winter fishing, which had been characteristic prior to 1944, to a wholly new emphasis on summertime commercial fishing.[53] This was advantageous to the more than 600 trapper-fishers because the changeover permitted two seasons of employment.[54] In addition, spoilage from B lake production, as a result of losses when inadvertently frozen fish were thawed for filleting, was greatly reduced.[55]

To further rationalize the marketing process, the government in 1945 set up the Saskatchewan Fish Marketing Board (SFMB). The SFMB was a subsidiary of a crown corporation known as Saskatchewan Fish Products, which oversaw all processing and marketing operations under the management of a board of directors composed of Phelps and managers of the filleting plants.[56] In the past, private fish dealers had been reluctant to push their operations into the more isolated lakes and often only purchased fish in accessible areas during high season. The situation smacked of abuse because there was no competitive buying of fish and usually fishers had no choice but to purchase their supplies from the same dealers at monopoly prices. The systematic purchase of fish through a government marketing agency, operating much like the wheat board, was meant to obviate these problems in so far as the board not only bought fish but also sold needed supplies in remote areas and extended limited credit for equipment and other necessities.[57] In addition to promoting fish products both in the Canadian and American markets, the board attempted to stabilize income. The board set advance prices, which were paid when the fish were delivered to the board, and at the end of the season the balance owing, minus the expenses, initial payment, and fisheries development fees, was paid to individual fishers in proportion to their contribution.[58]

Despite the advantages it offered, the Fish Marketing Board was less than successful. In fact, notwithstanding CCF disclaimers to the contrary, it became one of the most hated features of government policy in the North. Part of the problem was that the board had been foisted onto the North in the expectation that it would lead to an increase in incomes, and when this failed to materialize owing to the persistence of structural problems in the industry, disappointment turned to anger. Also at issue was the heavy management hand of the government. Phelps insisted that the government was committed to co-op development in the North and among other things he promised that, as soon as fishers indicated their desire to take over the operation of filleting plants on a co-op basis, the government would turn them over.[59] The SFMB, however, seemed to fly in the face of that commitment. As a crown corporation, it precluded local participation in the policy direction and management of marketing and reinforced the kind of government paternalism that had always been evident in the North. Rather than fostering the development of local management skills or returning profits to northern fishing associations, the corporate structure of the SFMB promised only indirect benefits. As the minister of the DNR explained, surpluses in buying and marketing fish would accrue to general revenues and be returned to fishers indirectly through social welfare and industry improvement, not through higher prices.[60] Finally, and undoubtedly most important in explaining the antipathy of northern fisheries people, the compulsory nature of marketing ran against the grain of northern laissez-faire sentiment. In order to ensure that government plants, warehouses, and freezing equipment were economically feasible, the government required that all fish taken within a seventy-five-mile radius of its main plants at Beaver Lake, La Ronge, and Meadow Lake had to be marketed through the SFMB.[61] As in the case of the Saskatchewan Fur Marketing Service, the benefits in government marketing of fish were not always self-evident, especially when they did not translate into higher prices; hence, there was little to offset the feeling that forced marketing was little more than an unwarranted and manipulative intrusion into the lives of northern fishers.

In the end, opposition to the Fish Marketing Board proved decisive in forcing the government to modify its policy. In 1949, the board was replaced by the Fish Marketing Service (FMS), once more a crown corporation headquartered in Prince Albert, but organized on different principles. The FMS, although it operated much like the old board, was unlike its predecessor in three important respects. First, the service was not based on compulsory marketing, but rather operated only as a commission service for those in the fish industry who wanted to market through the crown corporation.[62] It was only at the request of local fishers, based on majority vote, that the service would buy and market fish. Second, in 1949 the FMS adopted a 'floor price plan,' which, in effect, established a minimum price for fish in any one year. The plan, designed principally for outlying and marginal areas where transportation costs were high, was an acknowledgment that the government would use public funds to support fish prices and was tantamount to implying some sort of minimum income for fisheries workers.[63] Those who joined the service could not then sell their produce to private dealers because there would be a tendency to market fish through private companies when the price was high and through the FMS when prices were low, thereby inflicting heavy losses on the government agency. Third, the creation of the service was based – at least in theory – on a renewed acknowledgment by the CCF that cooperative organization of the fishing industry was still a major goal. There was a provision in the act creating the FMS that said that when three-quarters of the fishers in co-ops requested it, the marketing agency would be turned over to them. But as the director of the Northern Affairs Branch of DNR acknowledged, this was an entirely unreasonable condition given that 'even the most highly co-operative countries in the world have much less than 75 percent of the producers organized.'[64] In his opinion, it was akin to placing the whole co-op issue in 'a sort of never-never-land.'[65] Nevertheless, two years later, Douglas reiterated the commitment in a radio broadcast, reassuring fishers that they would have complete control over marketing 'as quickly as they are ready for it.'[66]

The government's commitment to the cooperative organization of fishing had a hollow ring to it, in that throughout most of the Douglas years the time never seemed right to turn marketing over to local control. It is difficult to escape the conclusion that the government distrusted the competence and business acumen of northern fishers who, for the most part, were woefully undereducated and largely disorganized. The first northern fish cooperatives had been set up in 1950 at Reindeer Lake, Cumberland House, and Beaver Lake, but within a few years the latter had collapsed. In the late 1950s, a half dozen other co-ops also came into being in the northern region, but despite the best efforts of the Department of Co-operatives to organize the northland fisheries, there was little success. In 1956, a special cabinet committee on the fisheries reported that 45 percent of the fishers were co-op members and that 36 percent of the annual provincial production of fish was handled through local co-op organizations; but, as the committee also pointed out, these same co-ops were largely 'devoid of function and in the main exist[ed] in name only.'[67] Douglas tended to blame fishers, particularly Native fishers, for the lack of cooperative development, insisting that organizing Natives was 'up hill work because they are not familiar with the co-operative movement.'[68] But other, more important factors were also at play. Part of the problem was that, with the government's processing and marketing infrastructure already in place, there was little room left for the activities of local associations. Undoubtedly, the government's crown-corporation approach to marketing was also a factor because it enhanced the tendency toward paternalism and control from the top down, effectively discouraging local initiative and input.

By the mid-1950s, the Saskatchewan Fish Marketing Service had become the lightning rod for seething discontent throughout the fishing industry. A major part of the problem, apart from the heavy hand of government, was the confusion and inefficiency associated with the operation of the FMS. This was largely a product of the confused and inconsistent working relationship between the FMS, the DNR, and the Department of Co-operatives.[69] In response to the confusion, in 1957 a cabinet committee on fisheries policy recommended that fish marketing be organized as a cooperative; a year later, the cabinet committee on Northern Affairs made the same recommendation.[70] In turn, cabinet endorsed the recommendation and this put an end to the FMS. In its place, the government now set up the Co-operative Fisheries Ltd., theoretically creating a new cooperative marketing agency in fulfilment of Douglas's long-standing promise to do so.[71]

In actual fact – and reflecting the government's conservatism on the issue – Co-operative Fisheries did little to place power in the hands of local organizations. Cabinet committees had consistently reported that, while the move to a cooperative 'form' of organization might solve some of the problems in the fishing industry, actual control by local people would take place only over a ten-year transition period, allowing for the sufficient education and training of northern participants.[72] Rather than being owned and run by member associations, Co-operative Fisheries permitted some local input and investment, but was capitalized mainly by government money and its policy was determined by a government-appointed board of directors. The board, in fact, was made up of members from the southern administrative establishment, including the minister of the DNR, the director of Northern Affairs, the director of Saskatchewan Federated Co-operatives, as well as officials from the Saskatchewan Wheat Pool, the Co-operative Life Insurance Company, and the Saskatchewan Credit Union Society.[73] Indeed, the only representative of local interests on the board was B. Larsen, president of the Reindeer Lake Fishermen's Co-operatives.[74] Co-operative Fisheries Ltd. was, in fact, a pale shadow of what a central cooperative was supposed to be.

While hunting and fishing were deemed the twin pillars of the Native economy, the Douglas government sought to develop other industries as well. These other forms of development were important in their own right, but they did not impact on Native society in any major way. Mining was a case in point. The development of sub-surface resources, particularly uranium, had the potential to outstrip all other forms of wealth in the North, but it was almost exclusively a white man's domain. Although some Indians and Métis were trained as prospectors, Native people without exception did not work in the mines, nor did they sell produce or goods to the exclusive white mining community cloistered in fenced enclaves.[75] By the same token, lumbering brought few benefits to Natives. It is true that the forest industry was a major target of CCF reform, establishing, among other things, conservation and reforestation programs, compulsory marketing through a government Timber Board, and a new schedule of royalties on timber berths.[76] But the forest belt itself was largely peripheral to the Northern Affairs Region and almost all of the operators were non-Native. Employment in the industry was only seasonal, lasting from one to three months during the winter, and although some Native labour was employed, the majority of workers were 'outsiders,' mostly white farmers from the South.[77] Even the CCF's new emphasis on fire prevention did little to provide meaningful employment for Natives. Although an ever-increasing number of Métis and Indians became firefighters, recruited from Indian reserves such as the one at Montreal Lake, their involvement was more often a subject of complaint than a matter of gainful employment. The work was highly dangerous and the wage returns pitifully small;[78] consequently, Native participation was reluctant at best and often came about only as a result of forced conscription, allowable by law during emergencies.[79] As a result, firefighting was never more than a marginal activity and did nothing to alter Native employment patterns.

The same could be said about the farm industry. Although the far North was a land of rock, muskeg, and trees, it was not beyond the pale of cultivation in particular areas. Whereas most settlements in the North had grown vegetables for home consumption, the missions at Beauval and Ile-à-la-Crosse had raised livestock and produced fruit and vegetables, some of which was sold commercially.[80] The main commercial development, however, was at Cumberland House on Big Stone Island where an experimental farm had operated since 1935. The original operation, managed by a Mr. Harvey and Mr. Howell, was equipped and housed by the DNR and employed local Native labour.[81] During the early 1940s, the farm boasted some 300 to 400 head of cattle. The successor to the so-called Harvey farm was a DNR model farm, designed to employ and train local Métis labour in agribusiness and to produce low-cost food. In addition to Cumberland House, there was also some potential for agricultural development in the Buffalo region, on the west side; there, the area fell within the grey forest soil zone and, precisely because it was not attractive to white farmers, it did represent an opportunity for Native farmers.[82] By far the greatest potential for agriculture, however, was the Saskatchewan River delta, a half-million acres of land stretching between Squaw Rapids and The Pas.

Despite its potential, agriculture nevertheless contributed little to the Native economy and CCF reforms did not change this. During the Douglas years, an attempt was made to expand both domestic and commercial production, but the effort was far short of the task. A major problem was that in order to transform the Saskatchewan delta into a commercial development analogous to agriculture in the South, the area had to be subjected to massive drainage and irrigation. During the Douglas era, a start was made on the Squaw Rapids Dam and on reclamation work in the Pasquia area near The Pas but, in the end, only a small portion of land was put into production during the Douglas years.[83] Another problem was that Natives were not attracted to either livestock or agriculture; they lacked experience and the potential for commercial development was poor, while, at the same time, government programs offered little incentive. Indicative was the fact that in any one year there was only one agricultural extension worker for the entire northern area; moreover, although the Douglas government did introduce a loan program to help finance the purchase of livestock and machinery, loans were small, only five were available in any one year, and there was almost no follow-up supervision once the loan had been granted.[84] Even the government's central farm at Cumberland House did almost nothing to integrate Métis labour into the farm economy. While it did employ Native labour, the farm was managed by white farmers and bureaucrats more interested in the economy of production than in training a Native farm community.[85] Thus, agrarian reform under the CCF went largely unnoticed in northern Native society.

Similarly, the building of a road system in the North produced ancillary developments, none of which represented major economic benefits for Natives. Tourism, for example, was initially touted as an important asset to the Native economy, but, as it turned out, its application in the North was limited and specific to certain areas. Not all northern communities were accessible by road and few offered the kind of fishing that anglers found attractive. The exception was the La Ronge area where guiding provided some employment. During the peak months of June and September and intermittently during the summer, twenty-five to thirty Natives in La Ronge were employed regularly as guides, and during peak periods they were joined by perhaps an additional forty Natives working as guides while the demand lasted.[86] Natives also found minor and limited employment in other areas of the La Ronge service industry. Even so, the advent of the northern tourist industry did nothing to integrate Natives into the northern economy. It has been estimated that, by the late 1950s, the tourist industry in La Ronge was worth half a million dollars, only 10 percent of which found its way into Native hands. Most of the money went to the small group of whites, sometimes newcomers to the North, who had access to the necessary capital. It was they who operated and staffed the cafes, garages, outfitting businesses, and supply stores, some of which were strategically situated in Prince Albert at the gateway to the North.[87]

Northern Social Reform

While the Douglas government saw economic reform as an important panacea for northern problems, it also realized that commercial and

View of La Ronge, 1954. (Glenbow Archives PA-2218-711)

industrial development would be meaningless unless accompanied by social change. If northerners, and particularly northern Natives, were to participate in society on an equal basis, they would have to receive the kind of social benefits southerners increasingly took for granted. The CCF fully endorsed the premise that, whether in the South or the North, the rehabilitation of underprivileged groups was the responsibility of the public sector. As Douglas put it: 'So long as any person or group of people in this province is underprivileged, the social and economic democracy to which this Government is pledged cannot be realized.'[88] As in the South, the notion of 'humanity first' was to be the guiding principle for northern social development and, at the very least, this meant an adequate health-care system and the schooling of the unschooled.[89]

One landmark development was the creation of a northern hospitalization scheme. Initially, northerners were excluded from the provincial hospitalization plan simply because there were neither public medical facilities in the North nor any administrative structure through which hospitalization premiums could be collected. However, in 1946 the province established a subsidized Air Ambulance Service through which patients could be airlifted to hospital for a fee of only $25.00 per trip,[90] and by 1950 the government had constructed four outpost hospitals in strategically located centres in the North.[91] This basically meant that medical services could be delivered to most centres in the North, and so in 1948 the North was integrated into the provincial hospital plan, with the premiums being collected by DNR officials and Hudson's Bay Company factors.[92] Health reform was of momentous importance because, although nutritional and hygiene surveys in the late 1950s continued to confirm the tremendous disparity between northern and southern health standards,[93] CCF reforms went a long way in reversing appalling health trends in the North. Overall, the new health-care system contributed greatly to a declining mortality rate for northern residents.

Far more challenging was the obvious need for public schooling. Since the 1840s, education in the North had been targeted at the Indian population only and organized mainly under the tutelage of church missions, often supported by the Hudson's Bay Company.[94] Church of England missions had followed the Churchill River trade route and had had a strong presence in places like Cumberland House, La Ronge, Stanley Mission, and Montreal Lake. By comparison, Catholic missions, organized principally by the Oblate fathers and Grey Nuns, had had a more visible presence in the western portion of the North, at places such as Ile-à-la-Crosse. But even in their heyday, mission schools had been greatly criticized for schooling too few children and providing an education at cross-purposes with social integration. Denominational education, said critics, was more often aimed at saving souls than in preparing students for survival in a secular society, and whatever contribution the HBC had made to education in the past had been limited to narrow economic ends, namely the public-relations value of its support and the training of a disciplined labour force for service in the company.[95] Indicative of the general neglect of northern education was the situation in La Loche on the eve of the Second World War: the settlement had 107 school-aged children, only 13 of whom attended school; of these, 11 Indian children were enrolled in a residential school in Beauval and 2 Métis youngsters went to a mission school in Ile-à-la-Crosse.[96] When the CCF came to power in 1944, officials found that less than half the school-aged population of the North was attending school. Even then, what schools existed were little more than a cacophony of unregulated facilities, including Indian day-schools, private day-schools, Indian residential schools, private boarding schools, and community day-schools. Indeed, throughout the entire northland, only two public schools were organized under the province's School Act.[97]

One of the first things the Douglas government did was appoint C.H. Piercy, superintendent of schools for Kinistino, to examine and make recommendations on the northern school situation. The so-called Piercy Report represented a blistering condemnation of northern education as an affront to the principles of social equality. Its main recommendation was that the province take full responsibility for creating a northern school system, one 'which would bring equal opportunity to every child,' and one that would be guaranteed by provincial grants where local resources were limited.[98] The Piercy Report was eagerly embraced by the Douglas government because, among other things, it honoured the principle of universal childhood education. Schooling the unschooled, irrespective of residence, was a declared aim of the CCF, and as the Reverend G. Laviolette explained in 1944, 'The goal of the new provincial government is to see that every last child goes to school; regardless of where the child may live, the Department of Education is determined that no one is to be overlooked any longer.'[99]

School reform was of fundamental importance to the CCF because it served wider social purposes. As in the South, the school was seen as the instrument of equalitarianism through which Natives and non-Natives alike would become more productive and better integrated into provincial society. As set out in a Department of Education handbook for teachers, the first objective of northern education was to provide a schooling through which children would become 'more useful, happier, and better-integrated citizens.'[100] As in the South also, the school was to be instrumental in generating a healthy sense of community. As the school administrator for the North explained in 1948,

The advantages of the day school are becoming apparent for the children remain at home and thus the influence of the school particularly in health habits and citizenship is extended throughout the community. With the school and teacher in the settlement, education through night classes can be extended to the parents and other adults. The school becomes a community hall, [and] community spirit and pride are developed by the residents. Play and recreation through teacher leadership prove important factors in welding the community together, in developing interest in community life and in providing wholesome outlets for surplus energy.[101]

Thus, in CCF thinking, the importance of schools transcended the narrow purpose of a child becoming literate. A provincial education system for the North would be the means to social regeneration at the local level; for that reason, education reform was integral to government attempts to restructure northern society.

The Northern Areas Branch (NAB) of the Department of Education was established by Order in Council in 1945. The administrator of the branch, an office held by none other than C.H. Piercy himself, was invested with wide-ranging responsibilities and power. Piercy, in fact, was principal, supervisor, superintendent, chief executive officer, and school board all rolled into one, although for the purposes of teacher recruitment and related matters, he was assisted by a Northern Education Committee.[102] The latter was an advisory committee appointed by the minister and composed of senior civil servants. The NAB was essentially departmental, in that it was based on educational standardization, derived mainly if not exclusively from southern educational norms. It was also an expression of colonialism in so far as the power and application of policy were centralized in Piercy, the representative of southern educational authority.[103]

A main aim of the CCF was to school northern children as quickly as possible and so, not surprisingly, success was measured largely in terms of new school buildings and the number of children 'netted,' as the administrator of the NAB put it.[104] During the late 1940s, the government invested heavily in northern education, even to the extent that for a short time, per capita expenditures for northern education actually exceeded that for the South.[105] The province took over a few mission schools and remodeled and enlarged old schools, but most of the money went to building new schools in strategic locations. By 1951, the North boasted fourteen new school buildings and through the 1950s another four were built.[106] In addition to these provincial schools, the CCF initiated negotiations with the federal government aimed at creating jointly operated federal-provincial schools for both Indians and Métis living in remote areas of the province. Of particular concern to the province was the more than 1,000 treaty children in isolated areas who had no access to formal education. R.A. Hoey, director of the Indian Affairs Branch, was supportive of the notion of joint federal-provincial schools and in the 1950 revision of the Indian Act he included provision for agreements with provincial departments of education through which joint schools in remote areas, incorporating both Indian and Métis students, could be operated. The first such school, built on a cost-sharing basis between the two levels of government, came into being in 1952 and was followed by others of its kind, although not at a pace favoured by the province.[107] To reinforce the building program, the province also instituted a provision making the family allowance contingent upon school attendance. Because of the high rates of poverty and unemployment in the North, parents relied heavily on various forms of social assistance, so the threat of withholding a major source of income was a powerful incentive for parents to school their children and honour truancy regulations.

The building program, reinforced by coerced attendance, had the desired effect. By the early 1950s, the school population of the North had doubled, and by the time Douglas had left the province, most children in the North, including those of Native ancestry, had access to some form of primary education.[108] Not every centre in the North had a school, but where there were no facilities, children were often housed in outside communities, their parents receiving boarding allowances to offset the added costs of having their children live away from home.[109] While there were flaws in the system, not the least of which was the uneven quality of education received by Natives and non-Natives, CCF education reforms in the North brought the province much closer to the ideal of universal childhood education.

Flaws in Provincial Policy
The CCF imposed on the North a government presence that was truly unprecedented in both intensity and scope. For the first time, northerners were continually reminded that they were part of a larger provincial society and that the host of bureaucrats and administrators who had descended on them were there to transform and modernize their existence. The results of CCF reform, however, were not always what had been anticipated and, in some instances, proved devastating to the Native community. It can be argued that meaningful reform in the North required far greater resources and time than the CCF could afford; it can also be said that the government could not be blamed for the unwillingness of private capital to invest in the North. But this is far from the whole explanation of what went wrong. In effect, the CCF introduced reform on a piecemeal basis without any overarching vision of how its various policies could be melded into a coherent whole. Individually,

programs were purposeful and inherently rational, but as a collectivity they were not addressed to an integrated and overriding purpose, often resulting in inconsistency and contradictions. Government reforms, with some precision, began to break down the old way of life but without effectively integrating northerners into provincial society. And when the failure became obvious, the administration simply papered over the problems with policies that were meant to relieve government of its responsibilities in the North.

At the most fundamental level, the administration of CCF policy was plagued by lack of coordination and control. The Northern Affairs Branch of the DNR had been created to get around this problem, in that it assumed responsibilities that normally would have come under various other departments. The problem, nevertheless, persisted. The Indian Affairs Branch was primarily responsible for some 4,000 Indians within the Northern Affairs Region, and although the federal and provincial governments were moving toward increased cooperation and joint projects, the effective coordination of programs was tentative at best and often disturbed by feuds between Ottawa and Regina.[110] At the same time, there were no fewer than six provincial departments that delivered services to the North, independent of the activities and priorities of the Northern Affairs Branch. These included the Departments of Education, Social Welfare, Public Health, Co-operatives, Mineral Resources, and Municipal Affairs. Although the Northern Affairs Branch acted in an advisory capacity to these departments, it could not dictate policy nor determine the everyday activities of these and other agencies. As a consequence, despite the mandate given to the Northern Affairs Branch to manage the North, key decisions and policies not infrequently were determined by other departments, resulting in considerable friction and acrimony.[111] To solve the problem, an interdepartmental coordinating committee was set up in the late 1940s, but as a Budget Bureau study of the DNR concluded in 1951, the committee 'has almost ceased to function and has become quite ineffective.'[112] In 1953, this committee was formally replaced by a Northern Advisory Committee, and still later by a cabinet committee on the North, but this did little to solve the problems of divided jurisdictions and confusion.[113]

The absence of coherent policy was illustrated in educational goals. On the one hand, the Northern Areas Branch of the Department of Education created a school system based on provincewide standards of education. This basically meant an attack on illiteracy through formal education following a curriculum that had been fashioned in the South to meet the needs of southern urban society.[114] On the other hand, CCF economic strategies inferred that northern people, particularly Native people, would make a living by trapping, fishing, and guiding. That being the case, a formal academic education was largely irrelevant to the life skills that needed to be imparted and clearly operated at cross purposes with the bush economy. Because mothers' allowances were contingent upon school attendance, mothers and their children had no choice but to leave the trapline and fish camp and take up ongoing residence in settlements that had access to schools. Cut off from the field education of the bush economy, children were now schooled in preparation for the kind of jobs that might be found in the South but that simply failed to materialize in the North.

Even in its most optimistic form, the CCF's northern strategy never envisaged a commercial and industrial development analogous to that of the South. On the contrary, the goal was to raise living standards by restructuring the old economy in such a way as to increase and stabilize the prices for fish and fur, as well as to enhance the service industry as a by-product of new tourism. However, the goal was not realized because it was confounded by seemingly insuperable problems that kept income levels low. By simply 'tinkering' with the existing economy, the CCF failed to notice, or blindly ignored, the inherent weaknesses and limitations of northern industry. Central to that fact was the reality that both furs and fish were dependent on external markets where prices were determined independent of the best efforts of government. In the fur industry, for example, CCF reforms were instrumental in greatly increasing fur stocks and production, and yet at the same time, external market conditions dictated a more or less continuous decline in prices. By the early 1960s, fur prices were down 50 percent since the late 1940s, with the dollar value of furs being no greater than that when the CCF had first come to power.[115]

Further exacerbating the problems of prices and income was the surging population growth of the North. During the Depression, the North had only about 5,000 people scattered over a vast region with limited exploitable resources; by the early 1960s, that number had more than doubled to almost 12,000, the main increase being in the Native community.[116] The rate of increase, consistent with that in third-world countries at the time, was nevertheless one of the highest in the world. It was caused by a sharp decline in mortality, especially for children, due to increased access to medical, health, and welfare services, most of which had been introduced by the CCF. It was compounded by the general disinclination of northerners, particularly the Native majority, to out-migrate in search of employment.[117] The inevitable result was a burgeoning population that could not be supported by the limited resources of the North, no matter how the fish and fur industries were restructured.

The consequent pattern was one of unemployment and underemployment, a central characteristic of underdeveloped regions generally and one that marked the Native economy in particular. It is true that for a limited number of Natives, such as those trapping in the remote interior, or those involved in large-scale fishing operations at Reindeer and Wollaston Lakes, the economy worked to their advantage and returned profits similar to those of the South. Yet for the vast majority of Indians and Métis this was not the case. Most were encapsulated in an employment cycle of part-time, casual labour with earnings well below the poverty line. It has been estimated that, by the early 1960s, there were some 2,200 Native men in the labour force of the North and that, of these, fewer than 200 had regular, year-round employment.[118] By far the greater part of the labour force worked on a seasonal and often casual basis as trappers, trappers/fishers, and fishers, while some worked part-time in the service industries in the main centres. Only a small percentage of Native people earned as much as $1,000 a year, and most earned less than half that.[119] The 1961 per capita income at Sandy Bay, for example, was only $600, at Cumberland House $335, and at La Loche a mere $200.[120] The paltry nature of northern incomes was underscored by the fact that in 1959 the annual per capita income provincially was more than $1,200 and nationally (excluding agriculture) over $3,800.[121] For some northerners, wild meat and other bush harvesting undoubtedly supplemented their meager income, but with the shift to village life and the concomitant limitation in mobility, free moose and fish were anything but standard fare. Even where hunting did supplement earnings it could hardly make up the difference in income enjoyed elsewhere. As one writer put it: 'While it is obvious that northern people do live much more cheaply than their fellow citizens to the south, it is chiefly because they live less well.'[122]

The absolute poverty of the North was mirrored by the fact that, by the end of the Douglas era, social assistance in the North had become a major source of income. More than that, it actually outstripped trapping and fishing in dollar value. Transfer payments of every description from both the federal and provincial governments, including family allowances, old age pensions, social aid, and relief, totalled more than a million dollars a year; by comparison, the annual gross returns from furs was $800,000 and for commercial fish only $750,000.[123] For more than half the Indian households in La Ronge, the family allowance and old age pension accounted for anywhere from 20 percent to 78 percent of total income, while at Buffalo Narrows some households had no income whatsoever apart from the family allowance.[124]

All of this was accompanied by an assault on family structure and traditional values. CCF reforms had the effect of centralizing much of the Native community in settlements in order to deliver social benefits. The greatest population pressure was in the so-called larger settlements – those with more than 500 people – where a majority of the Native community now came to reside. Although decidedly small by southern standards, these settlements had doubled and tripled in size over a twenty-year period following the war. More than 5,000 Indians and Métis, representing almost 60 percent of the total Native population, were centralized in eight of these settlements.[125] The change in residential patterns notwithstanding, trapping continued to be the most important source of earned income; however, unlike in the past when it was basically a family enterprise, it now became mainly an adult male activity. In tying the family allowance to school attendance, the government, in effect, required the trapper's family to split up, the father remaining on the trapline for extended periods, the mother and children confining themselves to the settlement. Men found themselves confronted with unfamiliar female tasks, such as cooking and dressing pelts, and suffered a derogation of status commensurate with their inability to make a decent living on the trapline. By comparison, their settlement-bound wives often received larger incomes, mainly in the form of family allowance and welfare payments, and now made family decisions that in the past had been the prerogative of their spouses.[126] Children suffered a similar fate. In light of the disjuncture between what the schools taught and the socioeconomic structure in existence, youngsters were no longer schooled in trapping and tanning hides and, more importantly, no longer respectful of the traditional ways of their parents and grandparents.[127] They were also afflicted by prolonged periods of inactivity and unproductiveness, a result of high truancy rates in school and unemployment in the settlement.[128] In all, the shift in residence patterns produced a painful reordering of traditional roles and status and, as might be expected, sowed the seeds of family violence and other forms of social pathology.

The problems associated with CCF reforms were compounded by a growing disenchantment with the North in Regina. It was during the first frenzied sitting of the Assembly that the CCF introduced many of its reforms, but when it became evident that northerners themselves were less than enamoured with government policies, reform enthusiasm was tempered with self-doubt and inertia. The acid test was the election of 1948, the first since the party's ascent to power. The CCF was easily returned to office, capturing 48 percent of the provincial popular vote in comparison to the Liberal's 37 percent,[129] but the results in the North could only be interpreted as a blistering rejection of CCF northern resource policy. This was especially so given that Walter Tucker and his Liberals had made northern development an issue both in the legislature and during the election campaign.[130] The two constituencies in the far North, Cumberland and Athabaska, encompassed a third of the entire Saskatchewan land mass and represented the bellwether of northern sentiment. Four years earlier, the former constituency had returned a CCF candidate and the latter a Liberal, but in this election one went Liberal and the other Independent by sizable majorities.[131] To make matters worse, Joe Phelps himself went down to defeat, and in the six northern constituencies on the southern fringe of Cumberland and Athabaska, the CCF saw its popular vote drop by a small margin and lost two seats to the Liberals.[132] The *Commonwealth*, the CCF's party journal, was able to take some comfort that 'C.C.F. timber, fish and fur policies in the North had not brought about the wholesale conversion to Liberalism the Grit campaigners had forecast.'[133] Likewise, acting on behalf of the new ministry, J.H. Brockelbank (Phelps's successor) tried to put the best face on the situation. In the legislature, he insisted that 'the results in the North had shown no consistent vote either for or against government resources policy.'[134] But inside government, politicians and administrators alike, if not shaken by the experience, were certainly troubled and disillusioned by the outcome.

The aftermath of the election has been variously described as a 'period of bog down,'[135] and as policy 'stagnation,'[136] particularly where the North was concerned. Although these epitaphs are not entirely justified, they do point to the reality that northern policy in the 1950s was characterized by self-doubt, growing cynicism, and ultimately retreat. Field officers of the DNR began to doubt the efficacy and wisdom of the measures taken to deal with the so-called Native problem, particularly when they witnessed firsthand the ill effects of government policy and bore the brunt of Native antipathy. Similarly, a government-sponsored study conducted by anthropologist Vic Valentine in the early 1950s raised serious questions about what the CCF was doing in the North. In addition to condemning government officials for being insensitive to the cultural needs of Native people, Valentine in effect slammed government for severely undercutting the traditional Native way of life and merely replacing it with welfare.[137] By 1952, even DNR officials were openly questioning government policy. A.L. Davidson, the DNR planning officer, was perturbed over the inconsistency of policies, some addressed to assimilation of the Natives and others to segregation, and in a memo to his superior he said so.[138] In the end, cabinet confirmed that the overall goal of policy was the integration of northern Natives, but Davidson's concerns nevertheless were indicative of the continuing lack of direction and purpose behind northern reform. Indeed, even Brockelbank, the minister of the DNR, had major reservations and in a covering memorandum to an Advisory Committee report on northern Métis, he admitted: 'I can't help but feel that at times we have inaugurated schemes in the North which have not given due regard to the ultimate end to which the Métis ought to be moving.'[139]

As telling as these administrative concerns were, even more important in explaining the growing pessimism over northern reform was the irresistible perception that the Native economy was a lost cause. Understandably, few people in government were willing to draw such a conclusion because it made a mockery of everything the CCF had been attempting to do in the North. But it was a view that lurked in the background throughout the early 1950s and one that was clearly articulated by 1958. In that year, the director of research and planning in the DNR, M. Miller, drew up a report that unequivocally condemned the development potential of the Native economy. He argued that the only hope of industrial development in the North was the exploitation of mineral resources and that that was entirely dependent on market forces, not on the efforts of local government:

> It is essential that we keep in mind that talk of the rich resources of the north and the resultant economic development hinges solely on the possibilities of mineral exploitation. The 'under-ground' resources – uranium, base and ferrous metals, and even oil and gas – are the only source from whence will come the rich materials for industry on any large scale and, by the nature of things economic, 'outside' forces, both continental and international, will determine the rate of development of Canada's north.[140]

By comparison, he insisted that the exploitation of 'above ground' resources – the renewable resources of fish, fur, and forest – was 'a marginal operation at best.'[141] He pointed to the dismal income generated by the fur and fish industries on which Native people were dependent, adding that

> If the resource base will not support the growing population even at a 'subsistence' level which is already culturally set at an extremely low level, add the fact that a profound cultural change is going on which disdains the pursuit of the old economic ways with its rigors and instabilities and the outlook for income from these resources is dismal indeed.[142]

To make matters worse, he also noted that whatever development might take place in mineral exploitation would be carried out without any involvement or benefits accruing to Native society.[143] Confirming Miller's conclusions was a report prepared in the same year for a Northern Development Conference. It likewise observed that mining production now outstripped all other sources in value of output, but that 'for the indigenous people, fish and fur remain the major source of income and food and seem destined to play a significant albeit declining role in their lives for the foreseeable future.'[144] Taken together, these reports expressed an undisguised pessimism concerning the Native economy and very much questioned, if not repudiated, the main thrust of CCF reforms in the North.

In light of the growing unease and cynicism concerning northern problems, a new orthodoxy in government policy was gradually enunciated – the importance of mutual self-help. Late in 1954, the government held a conference of northern policy analysts and administrators to 'discuss and analyze the social and economic position of Northern Saskatchewan indigenous folk and to examine government activities in relation to this situation.'[145] At the conference, participants agreed that nothing could be gained by continuing government paternalism – 'doing for' the Native – and that the new role of government in the North should be to help the Native help himself. The role of government, it was concluded, was 'To see the development of an economically and socially independent people, cognizant of their changing scene and confident that they are capable of coping with their environment – whatever that environment might be.'[146] The change in emphasis implied a relaxation of control from Regina and a greater commitment to involving northern Natives in government planning. In point of fact, it also called upon Native society to take greater responsibility for solving its own problems.

The notion of mutual self-help and 'bottom up' input into government was anything but new to an administration founded on social democratic rhetoric; what was different was the renewed commitment to the principle in administering northern policies. In 1955, the Northern Advisory Committee – set up two years earlier in order to provide a coordinating forum for government agencies working in the North – submitted a report to cabinet recommending the change in policy. It called upon government to adopt methods through which the Métis of the North would acquire the ability to conduct their own affairs and solve their own problems without excessive reference to government or other agencies. In October of the same year, cabinet gave the recommendation its official stamp of approval, thereby signalling the government's acceptance of the self-help model.[147] Among the changes introduced by government was a demand that government personnel be more culturally sensitive to Native clients, and to that end cross-culture training courses were introduced for administrators and field officers in the DNR.[148] The government also paid lip-service to the new orthodoxy by asserting its renewed commitment to community development, cooperatives, and greater northern control over its own affairs. The commitment sounded fine in theory but, as it turned out, the underlying principles were not always honoured in practice.

The concept of community development embraced the idea that local residents, united with government authorities, would undertake to improve the economic, social, and cultural conditions of the community and, in the process, become integrated into the life of the nation.[149] It implied a process of action and planning for change and emphasized bottom-up participation and decision-making by local residents, rather than having solutions imposed on the community by government. The concept was endorsed by the CCF because it not only fit well with party philosophy but also was thought to be especially appropriate to the underdeveloped state of the North. The idea became one of the main operating principles of the Northern Affairs Branch of the DNR and, among other things, was expressed in the concern that DNR conservation officers work with the people as much as with the resources of the North.[150] The precepts of community development provided the underpinning of various 'people' organizations, including ratepayers associations, co-ops, and fur block councils, but perhaps one of the best examples was the 1959 Pinehouse Housing Project.[151] In this case, the province provided the necessary infrastructure, including the planning sessions, blueprints, a sawmill, credit arrangements, and a supervisor to assist the unskilled builders. But the project rested entirely on the shoulders of the local participants. It was they who did much of the planning and all of the building, and it was they who had to honour repayment from their earnings. Similar housing projects were attempted elsewhere, with government assistance varying from a portable DNR sawmill to a full range of aid such as was seen at Pinehouse. But, because of the considerable expense to government, community development housing projects were not extensive during the CCF period nor did they fundamentally alter the pattern of substandard housing in the North.[152]

As important as community development may have been in administrative rhetoric, the government often ignored the fundamental principles on which the concept rested. For the purposes of public posturing and convenience, the Northern Affairs Branch grouped most of its ongoing projects under the general category of community development. The construction of streets, grants for skating rinks, street lighting – all were described as community development, when in fact they were simply government public works projects.[153] While local people may have wanted the improvements, and were perhaps even consulted about them, the projects were undertaken, financed, and directed by government agencies, with little regard for 'bottom up' planning and input. This meant that projects that, in the truest sense, fell under the category of community development were grossly underfunded. By the late 1950s, moneys officially earmarked for community development averaged about $80,000 per year, but only a little more than half of that was spent on actual community-based projects, such as community halls, vocational training, and the portable sawmill program.[154] A related problem associated with the CCF emphasis on community development was that it camouflaged the need for massive outside investment in infrastructure. Community development in its own right could never be a panacea for the structural problems of the North, and its importance as a guiding principle in the CCF administration served only to obscure the real need for training, education, and the mobilization of capital for new enterprises.[155] Moreover, because community development was predicated on a high degree of cooperation between diverse groups and interests, it proved especially ineffectual in communities where Natives and whites interfaced on a day-to-day basis. In reality, mixed racial communities, such as La Ronge, were often deeply divided along racial and class lines and this, together with the lack of opportunity and upward mobility in the Native community, severely limited even modest cooperation.[156]

A similar story can be told about the government's support of northern cooperatives, a form of community development. In the early 1950s, the introduction of co-ops to the North was still largely in the planning stages. In 1952, a committee comprised of heads of various government departments and agencies operating in the North was set up to examine the ways and means of implementing a co-op program, and this was followed by the first community leadership programs organized by R. Lavoy on behalf of the Department of Co-operation and Co-operative Development (DCCD).[157] Within a year, some 300 northerners were members of some sort of cooperative.[158] But it was only after 1955, in response to cabinet's endorsement of the self-help model, that co-op development in the North took root. Certainly not everyone in the Douglas government was enthusiastic about cooperatives, many in the field and in government preferring centralized control from Regina.[159] Nevertheless, few people openly repudiated the idea if for no other reason than that, at the time, the premier himself was minister of the DCCD and was determined to implement the concept. Indicative of Douglas's commitment was his response to a report from Vic Valentine detailing his efforts in establishing a co-op store at Ile-à-la-Crosse in 1955. The Fort Black Co-operative Store there had been set up despite bitter opposition from local vested interests, particularly the Hudson's Bay Company, and although not the first such store, it is generally credited with being the real beginning of consumer co-ops in the North.[160] Douglas's response to the report was to distribute it to all of his ministers with a covering memo that left little doubt as to the importance he attached to cooperatives:

I am urging all Ministers to read this document because I think it indicates the fact that the methods we have tried have failed to benefit the native population. Mr. Valentine's social experiment in getting natives to form co-operatives could have significant and far reaching implications for the future.

I am particularly anxious to have all Ministers read this document so that they will appreciate the need for having field staff in the North who have a sympathetic appreciation and understanding of the part which the co-operative movement can play in the lives of the peoples of the North.[161]

Certainly not all cooperative development in the North can be attributed exclusively, or even primarily, to government financing and support, especially given the limited budget available for community development generally. Nevertheless, field workers from the DNR and DCCD did play an important role in pushing co-op organization at the local level. Cooperatives of almost every description, including recreation, gardening, housing, wood products, handicrafts, and power co-ops, were in existence by the early 1960s. Among the most important creations were the production co-ops that grew up in the fishing industry.

Also of special import were northern retail stores. From the earliest days, the CCF paid lip-service to the importance of co-op trading posts as an assault on the monopoly enjoyed by the Hudson's Bay Company in northern merchandising. Such stores were difficult to organize, however, and really only got off the ground following the 1955 success story of the Fort Black Co-operative. By the early 1960s, seven of these stores were in operation at places such as Ile-à-la-Crosse, Buffalo Narrows, La Loche, Patuanak, and Churchill and, according to newspaper reports, had reduced costs to local consumers by about a third.[162] In addition to these seven trading posts, the province itself established a network of government-operated stores in the North, first as a division of the Saskatchewan Fish Board and then as a separate entity known as Saskatchewan Government Trading (SGT). Very early on, the CCF decided that in order to reduce consumer costs, particularly in remote areas where the HBC refused to operate stores, it would be necessary for the government to become directly involved in merchandising.[163] To that end, in 1946 the province built a trading post at Wollaston Lake in preparation for the development of a commercial fisheries operation in the area.[164] By 1956, this store had been followed by others at La Ronge, Stanley Mission, Pinehouse, Cumberland House, and Deschambault.[165] Initially, Phelps had suggested that these government stores might be operated as cooperatives, but little serious consideration was given to the idea at the time. As in the case of fisheries development, the network of stores was run under a crown corporation structure. However, following the shift to the self-help model and the growing criticism of crown corporation management in the fishing industry, in 1959 the SGT, along with the Fish Marketing Service, was transformed into a cooperative structure known as Northern Co-operative Trading Services (NCTS). This, together with the privately operated co-ops, meant that by 1961 there were some fourteen cooperative retail outlets in the North, with collective annual sales in excess of a million dollars.

As a form of community development, the cooperative movement suffered from many of the same shortcomings and hardly justified the government's faith in it as a solution to northern problems. On the contrary, it can only be concluded that the entire self-help orthodoxy was really a process of offloading, making northerners responsible for their own salvation at a time when government was neither willing nor able to fund meaningful reform. Cooperatives at best had only a limited capacity to create new forms of capital investment and mobilize local human resources. This was especially so for the North where government and environmental factors tended to distort co-op organization and principles.

In the first place, cooperative organization did not mean the end of paternalism and control from above. Privately operated co-ops were normally capitalized by a combination of local savings and government loans and, in practice, this meant rigorous government supervision of the business, especially its management and accounting practices.[166] The tendency was particularly pronounced in government marketing services. As in the case of Co-operative Fisheries Ltd., the new NCTS was really a hybrid organization, on the one hand boasting the co-op label and some of its forms, but on the other embracing a top-down corporate structure in terms of management, capitalization, and policy.[167] At the same time, the co-op movement had only a limited capacity to effect financial gains either by increased returns for production or by lowering prices for consumer goods. In practice, sales by the average fisher and purchases by the average patron at a co-op store were not large enough to alter significantly the general pattern of income.[168]

Even more important, the cooperative movement did not relate well to the Native community, despite the assumption that it was a form of organization appropriate to traditional Indian values. Not uncommonly, Indians did not take their business to the local co-op, preferring instead to deal with the HBC factor or other traders who, unlike those at the co-op, were often long-time residents who spoke the Indian dialect.[169] Nor did Natives play a significant role in the management of local cooperatives, ostensibly because of their continuing low level of education. Fish marketing, for example, was not an especially profitable enterprise and to show a business return it took a highly skilled and efficient manager to overcome the problems of high transportation costs, scattered settlement, and adverse conditions in the North.[170] Natives seldom had the requisite training and educational background to assume leadership roles in such businesses and there was little in place for educational upgrading. Co-ops themselves were mandated to provide adult education for their membership but, given their limited financial and human resources, they did almost nothing to integrate Natives into positions of responsibility. Nor did formal education in the North make much difference. The new school system suffered from high Native absenteeism, declining provincial funding, and limited goals. That no high school was ever built in the North during the entire Douglas era suggests that little was expected beyond basic literacy and explains why the school system did not act as a vehicle for upward social mobility in Native society.[171] Hence, Native participation in the co-op movement was severely restricted, although there were some exceptions, most notably in the remote retail industry. Of the fourteen co-op stores in existence at the end of the Douglas period, five had Native managers and/or boards of directors, and most employed some unskilled Native labour.[172]

Finally, despite the new freedom promised by the self-help model, the Douglas government proved reluctant to relinquish control from Regina. This was underscored in its obvious preference for crown corporations and its qualified transition to cooperative forms of organization. But the subject that, more than any other, exposed the government's conservatism on the issue was the question concerning a 'single agency' for the North. As noted above, the northern administration contained a small group of socialist radicals, including Quandt, Brady, and Norris. There were those in the group, particularly Brady, who worked closely with local communities and were well aware of the fallacies of government programming. Among other things, the group lobbied hard for a greater degree of self-determination for the North. One of their main goals was the creation of a single agency – perhaps a government department or branch that would coordinate and consolidate service delivery, give some profile in cabinet to northern concerns, and allow northerners greater input in fashioning their own institutions. The group itself increasingly fell into disfavour, especially after Phelps's departure, and many were either fired or resigned.[173] But the idea of a single agency lived on and, among other things, figured as the subject of a submission to cabinet, probably drafted by Jim Brady on behalf of the La Ronge CCF Club in 1960.[174] The idea also had supporters in Regina who saw it as a means to ending the confusion and contradictions in northern program delivery. In 1960, the idea was twice endorsed by meetings of the deputy ministers as well as by the powerful Budget Bureau.[175] But in the end, the concept was rejected for reasons that represent a telling commentary on the government's integrationist predilections concerning both the North and Native people generally.

The most thoroughgoing discussion of the single agency concept occurred at a 1961 meeting of the provincial Committee on Minority Groups. This committee, it will be recalled, was chaired by the premier and functioned as a kind of clearinghouse for Native issues of the day. The focus of the discussion was a thirty-page document, 'Some Proposals Concerning Provincial Government Organization and People of Indian Ancestry,' drafted for the premier by Ray Woollam, the executive director of the CMG. The document represented a complete repudiation of the single agency idea, and to that end Woollam mobilized an array of arguments meant to show that such an idea had failed elsewhere and that it would be both costly and inefficient. The main thesis was that a single agency would destroy the government's cherished goal of integrating both northern and Native people into the provincial body politic. According to the preamble, 'It is the contention of these pages that the "Northern question" and the "Indian and Métis" question have much in common – that the province is not so much dealing with an "underprivileged region" as it is with an "underprivileged group."'[176] What Woollam meant by this was that the North should not be treated as a separate solitude, with its own distinctive character and unique set of problems. On the contrary, he insisted that the problems confronting northern Natives were essentially the same as those of southern Natives – their common ethnicity being conditioned by their shared underprivileged state. He anticipated the day when all Indian affairs in Canada would be handed over to the provinces, with Indians and Métis alike coming under provincial jurisdiction and with the Federation of Saskatchewan Indians representing not only Indians but also the Métis.[177] The ultimate goal of government, he contended, was not to recognize two separate social and geographic realities, as implied by the single agency precept. Rather, the central purpose in delivering special programs to underprivileged groups should be the preparation of those groups for eventual integration into normal service delivery. As he put it, '"Special programs" to these minority groups must be limited to those which are required to bridge the gap between present unreadiness and a potential readiness to accept the normal services offered by provincial departments. These programs would be devised to *fulfill rather than displace* normal functional services.'[178] Hence, Woollam's report recommended that cabinet 'clearly abandon' any consideration of a single agency and that the DNR Northern Administration continue to administer northern programs.

Woollam's report proved decisive both in the committee and in cabinet. By this time, the Douglas government had been in power for more than sixteen years and it seems likely that it was suffering from a certain degree of complacency, if not inertia. Also important was the perceived cost associated with the structural reorganization that a single agency would occasion. But probably the most important factor was the intimated loss of power in Regina. The integration of both the North and Natives into provincial society, at its most fundamental level, was premised on the need for a singular and centralized authority that could fashion and shape provincial development for the benefit of all. Among the avowed opponents of a single agency was Douglas himself and, as he explained, he rejected it because it implied 'two governments in the province.'[179] By inference, he was saying that power would remain in Regina and that the North would continue in its neo-colonial relationship with the South. Indeed, that would remain the position of the CCF right up to the election of 1971 when, in an appeal to northern voters, the party finally committed itself to the creation of a provincial Department of Northern Affairs.

It seems clear that, in intervening in the North, the CCF fell victim to the 'myth' of the northern frontier. Like most southerners, the party and government initially believed that the North was a hinterland of endless natural resources. It was a place, they thought, where Natives could easily make a living from the land, if the government would provide the infrastructure of a modern society. Such a structure would tie the North to southern markets and influence and create a literate and employed Native labour force. But when the CCF's vision of the last frontier proved illusory – when hunting and fishing proved only marginal and transitory in comparison to mining, and when Native prosperity failed to materialize – the Douglas government retreated. The self-help model represented a tacit acknowledgment that the CCF lacked the political will, and perhaps capacity, to solve the problems that made prosperity in the North so elusive. In effect, it was an offloading process through which the CCF made northerners responsible for their own redemption, all the while ensuring that the levers of power remained in Regina.

6
Opposition to Native Reform

Unlike any other government before it, the CCF embraced an ideology and rhetoric that promised to turn society upside down and root out the vested interests inherent in the status quo. In practice, CCF reformism proved to be a far cry from the revolutionary changes promised in the Regina Manifesto and other socialist pronouncements. The fact that the party in general and Douglas in particular self-identified as social democrats, rather than as democratic socialists, was itself a clear indication of the limits to CCF reform. Nevertheless, the CCF's commitment to social equality and justice – to 'humanity first' – was neither bombast nor bravado. The Douglas government was determined to integrate disadvantaged and dispossessed people into the existing social order through which long-standing inequities would be ameliorated. Whether it was the development of co-ops so that small farmers could compete with eastern monopolists, or the creation of a public health system in opposition to the personal interests of the doctors, postwar Saskatchewan was subjected to unprecedented change. As might be expected, Douglas's reforms infuriated the vested interests that had profited both socially and economically under the old order; but, in some cases, these reforms also alienated those who were dismayed by the ineffectual, and sometimes destructive, nature of the changes introduced. In both cases, they provoked an opposition to reform that often qualified, if not undermined, the best efforts of the CCF.

This was especially so of the opposition to Native reform. On the surface, it would seem there were few vested interests associated with the existence of either the Métis or the Indians, especially given the marginalized role of Natives in the provincial economy. But, in actual fact, there was a vast array of special interests who profited in some way or other by leaving the Native situation unreformed. This was true of the southern farmer or small contractor who was able to exploit the labour power of migrant Métis during the summer months, the civil servant reluctant to abandon old habits to meet the special needs of Natives, the independent fur trader or fish buyer who sold goods to northern Natives at exorbitant prices, and the racists who promoted their own social standing by discriminating against the dispossessed. Then, of course, there was the powerful triumvirate that historically had dominated the northern part of the province: the Liberal Party, the Hudson's Bay Company, and church missions.[1] Prior to the CCF, the three had acted in concert in securing Indian votes, furs, and souls, and, collectively, they represented a dominating and controlling interest diametrically opposed to government intervention in the North.

Finally, there was the opposition of Native people themselves. As has been shown in the case of Métis colonies in the South and government marketing services in the North, reforms were not always in 'sync' with what Natives wanted and in some cases were at complete variance with their wishes. Native people did not accept such reform passively or without protest, as the CCF soon came to realize. But the articulation of their concerns was seldom expressed in the public press or in the legislature simply because they lacked access to the instruments of power. Even in the delivery of public services, their voices were often filtered through layers of bureaucracy geared to 'doing for the Native,' rather than listening to the concerns of the local community. Nevertheless, they did protest through those avenues available to them. In the 1950s, employable adults fled the Métis colonies in search of wage labour in the city, while those who had been transplanted to Green Lake often made their way back to the South. In the North, Native trappers and fishers continued to do business as usual, working through old trade networks, including that of the Hudson's Bay Company. Some bureaucrats attributed these practices to the unprogressive, even defective, character of Native people but, in truth, they expressed opposition to policies that did not serve the wishes of those targeted for reform. Native opposition, in fact, represented an indictment of the very notion that the CCF was walking in Indian moccasins.

To make a complete catalogue of the groups threatened by CCF reform would be neither profitable nor practicable. A few examples, however, will lend insight into the existence and entrenched nature of the opposition and, by implication, into the problems faced by the Douglas regime. Like all governments, the CCF lacked the political mandate and social sanction to carry out whatever changes it wanted, and, as in the case of other governments also, the limits of its reform agenda were defined by the need to accommodate entrenched interests, especially those with economic or social authority.

Roman Catholic Church

A case in point was the Catholic Church. Historically, Catholics were not alone in decrying attacks on denominational privilege, including state support of mission schools. The United, Presbyterian, and especially the Anglican Churches had invested heavily in missions for Indian people in the West and, like their Catholic brethren, were reluctant to give up control to the state. However, both by tradition and commitment, the Protestant denominations more readily accepted a division between the sacred and the secular because it served their interests. Frequently, state control was synonymous with being Protestant, personified by Douglas himself as a Baptist minister, while even the notion of 'Canadian' in secular circles was often defined as white, Anglo-Saxon, and Protestant.[2] Hence, while Protestant missions had played an important role in con- verting, hospitalizing, and schooling Indians in the absence of both federal and provincial services, they also acknowledged the legitimacy and inevitability of non-denominational institutions, particularly public education. The fact that, historically, the vast majority of Indian Affairs appointees had been Protestant also smoothed the transition to greater government control in Indian matters.[3] By contrast, Catholic leadership clung to the notion that secular society was often composed of godless institutions destined for moral decay. While fully acknowledging the authority of the secular state, Catholics aimed at a Christian society firmly resting on religious precepts, and by inference, this meant that the educa- tion of the young was deemed useless unless grounded in religious under- standing. In a political context, Catholic leaders believed that the main threat to Christian society was the far Left, with communists worship- ping statism and secularism as false idols.[4] Even if the CCF disavowed communist connections, its abiding faith in the ability of the state to transform society automatically made it suspect in the eyes of many Catholics.

The Catholic hierarchy itself was not officially opposed to the CCF. As early as 1943, a conference of bishops and archbishops, meeting in Quebec City and constituting the Roman Catholic Church in Canada, issued a statement condemning communism 'as degrading to the human person.'[5] At the same time, the conference insisted that 'the faithful are free to support any political party upholding the basic Christian tradi- tions of Canada and favoring needed reforms in the social and economic order.'[6] Even more important, an accompanying statement by the Catholic registrar acknowledged the CCF as an acceptable alternative to the extreme Left. Depicting the CCF as a 'sincere and effective opponent of communism,' the registrar applauded the fact 'that there is such a party as the CCF to attract those voters who, as recent elections have shown, are dissatisfied with the older parties and who, in the absence of the CCF, might give their support to the Communists disguised as a labor party.'[7] These statements, although not recommending the CCF to Catholic con- stituents, represented an official pronouncement that the CCF constituted a legitimate political party and could be supported by Catholics as a matter of personal conscience.

Nevertheless, the CCF accession to power sent a ripple of fear throughout the Catholic Church in Saskatchewan. The church had been one of the earliest to evangelize the Indian communities of the Northwest Territories, and after the establishment of reserves, its work there had continued unabated. Technically, Indian education was the responsibility of the Department of Indian Affairs because, constitutionally, Indians were a federal responsibility and Indian education was a treaty right. But in practice, the DIA had relied heavily on missionaries to organize and staff Indian schools both on southern reserves and in northern missions. Missionaries, both Catholic and Protestant, represented a cadre of experienced personnel and offered the added advantage of being financially supported by their mission societies. For its part, the DIA assumed some management responsibilities and provided per capita funding to the schools, but otherwise it left the churches alone to stake out their claim to Indian souls. The result was a fierce interdenominational competition, virtually dividing the Indian community into rival spheres of religious influence. By the end of the Second World War, no fewer than 95 percent of the entire Indian population of Saskatchewan was nominally Christian, and of this, Indian membership in the Catholic Church was greater than that of all the Protestant denominations combined.[8] Consequently, to the extent that the CCF's election presaged an attack on denominational privilege, the Catholic Church stood to be the big loser.

Resistance to CCF policies was animated by a number of concerns. Local priests were ever vigilant about the evils of socialism and were not diffident in communicating that message to their parishioners during Sunday sermons. The opposition of the Catholic priest in Duck Lake to the Union of Saskatchewan Indians because of its association with the CCF was a case in point, referred to earlier. Even among those who were quite prepared to work with the CCF, opposition to particular aspects of government policy was evident. Welfare delivery to the Métis colonies in the South, for example, was one subject that sometimes generated considerable concern among the local Catholic leadership. Indicative was a 1956 meeting in Lestock attended by local priests and two representatives from Catholic Social Welfare. Participants roundly condemned the administration of social aid among the Métis and called for a new rehabilitation program that would address not only Métis economic problems but also their ethereal welfare.[9] The root of the problem, they said, was that provincial social aid was given too freely, even to able-bodied men, and led many to avoid work in order to get government assistance. Of particular concern were those who escaped to the cities to avoid responsibility and get higher welfare payments. This not only undermined cooperative self-help approaches to rehabilitation in the rural municipalities, but also damaged the Métis personality and diminished his or her moral and spiritual standing.[10] The concerns expressed by the meeting may well have been a reaction to the church's loss of control, in that the state had preempted its traditional welfare role and that, by this time, the Métis were moving off the land in favour of city life. But, by inference, it was the CCF that was blamed for the situation and this was underscored in the demand that the provincial government address the group's concerns.

Even more important were the issues pertaining to Native education. Douglas was firmly committed to integrating all Native students, even Indian children, into the provincial school system and he and his ministers made no secret of the fact. In the wake of the Piercy Inquiry into northern education – which itself represented an indictment of the old school system – Douglas was asked to meet with His Grace, Bishop Martin Lajeunesse, of the Diocese of Keewatin, to reach 'a mutual understanding on northern educational matters.'[11] The meeting, in August 1945, was held in Ile-à-la-Crosse and included Joe Phelps, members of the bishop's teaching staff, and the Liberal incumbent for Athabaska who chaired the meeting. From the outset, Douglas seemingly was not prepared to compromise on the principle that it was the state's duty to educate Native children. The bishop pointed out that 1945 marked the 100th anniversary of the arrival of the first Roman Catholic priest at Ile-à-la-Crosse and the 85th year since the founding of the first school there. But Douglas remained unmoved. He insisted that, while the church had exclusive responsibility for the teaching of religion, parents had the first claim upon their children and it was the state's responsibility to enforce school attendance and provide the necessary funding. He also did little to dispel fears about the as-yet secret Piercy Report, although he was emphatic that no schools would be closed as a result of its findings.[12]

While the premier had been circumspect in criticizing parochial schools, people like Morris Shumiatcher left little doubt about their contempt for such education. Three months after the Ile-à-la-Crosse meeting, Shumiatcher, as legal advisor to the Saskatchewan government, delivered a speech to Regina College students in which the past performance of the churches was openly condemned. He insisted that, despite Indian treaty rights, the Department of Indian Affairs had merely 'farmed out' education to volunteer church schools, and these had not only fallen far short of the education received by white children but also had been administered by 'callous treatment verging on cruelty.'[13] The result, he said, was that the vast majority of Indian children in the province remained uneducated.

Shumiatcher's comments invited an immediate disclaimer from the *Indian Missionary Record,* a missionary journal published by the Oblate

Fathers of Saint Boniface in Manitoba. Denying any wrongdoing on the part of the church, the editor insisted that church schools could be compared favourably with those for Euro-Canadians:

> It is historically false to affirm that the Government ... 'farmed out the education' of Indians to the various churches. Before the Government ever took an interest in the education of the Indians the missionaries of the various Churches engaged in Indian work had created schools for the children; ... Moreover the Church ... schools have tried to maintain the educational standards of the province. They are regularly inspected by the provincial inspectors of the Department of Education: the inspectors' reports, which are official, tell a story of progress comparable to that achieved in the rural schools of the province. Many Indian schools show a great improvement in the past years in vocational training which is given the pupils along with purely scholastic training, and thus are superior to many schools for the white children.[14]

He then went on to call for a serious investigation of the matter and challenged the press to give the same publicity to it as it had to Shumiatcher's unfair assessment.

The *Record's* response to Shumiatcher's comments was only one instance of a much larger reaction to an emerging trend toward secularized education, particularly where Indian students were concerned. The USI brief to the federal government, it will be recalled, had roundly condemned church schools, and this proved to be but one part of a much larger criticism across the country as steps to overhaul the Indian Act unfolded in Ottawa. The Catholic community was especially incensed by the recommendation of the 1948 Joint Committee of the Senate and House of Commons, which called for the integration of Indian students into provincial school systems, and even more so by the abortive Bill 267, which provided for such a scheme.[15] As expected, the bill provoked the ire of the Catholic press, both in eastern and western Canada. *The Ensign,* Canada's national Catholic weekly, was among the first to see the connection between what was happening at the provincial level and the new federal bill and castigated both for attempting to 'impede or even eliminate Christian schooling' for Canadian children.[16] In a call to action, the editor urged all Christians to 'abandon the merely defensive attitude into which secularized neo-paganism has driven us and rise in righteous indignation against the comparative handful of determined secularists who ... have ventured to lay hands upon ... the Christian education of our children.'[17] Likewise the *Indian Missionary Record* called upon Christians across the land to protect the rights of parents and children to teach and learn according to the dictates of Christian conscience. It railed against Bill 267 and the public school system it supported because 'It is well known that these ... schools (Quebec excepted) are non-denominational and therefore godless.'[18] And, using an argument that had special meaning for critics of the CCF in Saskatchewan, the *Record* insisted that the fight against Bill 267 was only a small part of the larger struggle against 'the godless forces of communistic revolution in the bloody war of Korea and in the silent cold war in other countries of the world.'[19]

By the early 1950s, the storm in the Catholic community had passed. The Indian Act in its final form did not abolish church schools for Indians as the 1948 JCSHC had recommended, nor did it entirely abandon denominational privilege. Catholics could still enter into contracts with Indian Affairs to teach Indian students and in fact did so, particularly with regard to residential schools in the West. There was also the added benefit that the act firmly established the principle that, where a majority of Indian students were Catholic, they must be taught by a Catholic teacher. Nevertheless, the act also made provision for the integration of Indian children into provincial schools where geography made it feasible. Catholics realized that this provision signaled an inevitable decline in the role of mission schools in the education of Indians. They also recognized that they had no choice other than to accept the situation, although some continued to fight a rearguard action for the remainder of the decade, but did so without reversing the trend. By the early 1960s, the Indian school population in Canada numbered more than 43,000 and, of these, a quarter had been integrated into non-Indian schools.[20]

In Saskatchewan, Catholic educational rights did not figure as a major issue for the remainder of the 1950s. The relationship between the CCF and the church, for the most part, was generally amicable and not unlike that between the government and other religious interests. The lag in Indian school integration in the province, noted above, may also have lessened church reaction to the potential loss of educational prerogative. There were, however, a few small incidents that served as a reminder that a certain sensitivity continued to linger. In 1956, Sister St. Oliva, principal of Lebret School, complained to the deputy minister of the Department of Social Welfare that books, including those on religion, were not being provided to the children from the Métis farm.[21] Religion was normally taught at the school for half an hour a day, and although books for that purpose had been provided in the past, for some reason the Rehabilitation Branch had decided to discontinue the practice for those Métis children directly under the branch's authority. The deputy minister, unaware of departmental policy on the matter, referred the issue to the director of rehabilitation, who simply reported that 'it is not the policy of the Branch to purchase books for religious instruction.'[22] The matter seemingly ended there, but for the principal and her Catholic teachers, the incident undoubtedly was a pointed illustration of the anti-religious bias of state schooling.

A more emotionally charged incident occurred the following year from a similar quarter. In March, John Sturdy, at the time assistant to the premier and a long-time school principal and MLA from the Qu'Appelle area, made a speech in the legislature that was addressed to the issue of Indian education and was broadcast by radio. Among the listeners was Mr. Rodine, who had been appointed by the federal government to the position of superintendent of Indian schools for the province of Saskatchewan. Rodine seemingly liked what Sturdy had to say and so invited him to be the guest speaker at a banquet held as part of a convention of teachers of Indian schools in the province, convened at Lebret. Sturdy accepted the invitation and delivered a speech close to what he had said in the legislature, although it was slightly modified to meet the occasion. Although he paid lip-service to the historic importance of church schools, Sturdy was particularly critical of southern residential schools that continued to be administered by the churches under the auspices of Indian Affairs.[23] He maintained that the type of education they offered was no longer relevant to the new technological age; moreover, he insisted that these schools, like Indian reserves themselves, were basically segregationist and counterproductive to the CCF's goal of Native integration into society. He argued that the only solution to the Native problem was state education; and, as a model, he pointed to the new northern public school system where, as a consequence of cooperation between Indian Affairs and the province, Indian, Métis, and white children mixed together in integrated schools during the formative stages of their lives. In light of this, he said, he was 'much more hopeful of the solution of the Indian ... and the Métis problem in the northern part of the province than [he was] in the southern part, where segregation in education is so much in evidence.'[24]

Sturdy later claimed that both DIA and church officials had complimented him on his banquet speech. But it is evident that it also invited the wrath of at least one Catholic educator. Father Robidoux, the principal of the Qu'Appelle Indian school, was appalled by Sturdy's message and his umbrage was duly expressed in a letter to the premier:

> I, as Official Host of the convention, ... wish to protest most heartily against his entire speech, couched as it was along lines of carping and ironic criticism of the Branch of Indian Affairs, full of disparaging remarks about the set up of Indian schools across Sask., some of which were entirely false and based I presume, on complete misinformation of legal and cultural aspects of the Indian Problem, finally his few remarks about

the personal dedication and devotion of the Teachers present did not atone much for the poor evaluation he made of the results of their work.[25]

Douglas forwarded Robidoux's letter to Sturdy, but instructed him not to reply because technically it had been sent in confidence to the premier only. Sturdy apparently felt he owed Douglas an explanation and so penned a lengthy memorandum in which he basically dismissed the complaint as an expression of entrenched religious interest:

Father Robidoux is, to my mind, very typical of the Oblate Order in his attitude towards educational and religious control of the Indians. In speaking to me after the banquet, he deprecated the day school type of education and any other system other than the residential type of school under the church. I am well aware that any change in the status quo in as far as Indians are concerned will be resented and vigorously opposed, particularly from this quarter.[26]

Douglas, nevertheless, penned a conciliatory reply, not only expressing his sorrow that the address had incurred the principal's displeasure but also inviting the good father to raise the issue with Sturdy himself. As he put it, 'I think he would be glad to receive from you an expression of your viewpoint which emanates from a long and practical experience in the field.'[27] No political consequence of any importance resulted and the matter was smoothed over. But once again, the incident underscored the fact that tension over Catholic educational prerogative was still present.

It would be a mistake to believe that the imposition of state authority was the only explanation of Catholic acquiescence to the education policies of the CCF. While the Douglas government was not willing to compromise on the principle of integrating all Native children into the provincial system, it was entirely conciliatory when it came to the question of Catholic personnel and even Catholic schools operating under provincial guidelines. What the government was opposed to were substandard DIA schools, usually residential schools operated by the church. But at the same time, Douglas realized that he had to accommodate Catholic interests where possible and that it would be dangerous to alienate any one section of society, especially one that represented entrenched religious authority in both the Métis and Indian communities. Before and after coming to power, the CCF did everything in its power to reassure the Catholic community that it could not be equated with communism and its promotion of a godless society. The CCF, it was argued, had been created in the tradition of the British and Australian Labour Parties, and neither represented an assault on private ownership or an attempt to substitute materialist culture for spiritual values.[28] In radio broadcasts and editorials, the premier, in particular, vehemently insisted that the brand of socialism represented by the CCF was in complete harmony with the teachings of the Christian community and, as such, did not represent a threat to Catholic teachings.[29] Ministers in his government also paid attention to the concerns raised in the Catholic community.

One example of this was the government's response to the 1956 Lestock meeting of priests, decrying the delivery of social welfare to the Métis. Government officials, from departments delivering services to the Métis colonies, not only met with the Lestock delegation to iron out differences of opinion, but in the end conceded 'that the question of social aid to Métis should be carefully reviewed, keeping in mind the suggestions made earlier.'[30] Still another example was Douglas's willingness to recommend Catholic appointments to offices associated with Native issues. In 1946, it was rumoured that Douglas was planning to appoint a royal commission to inquire into the whole state of Native affairs in the province, as the government had done in the case of agriculture. In late March, Douglas received a letter from F.V. Rielly, a Catholic lawyer from Rosthern, recommending for strategic reasons the appointment of a Catholic to the royal commission:

Most of the Indians in this neighbourhood are Roman Catholics, and although their French neighbors [Métis] are almost solidly liberal, they have strong progressive leanings. The younger men, more particularly those who have been in service, are now doing their own thinking, and are once more bent on winning back their native independence. I think however that there will be a great deal of opposition on the part of the clergy. This might be offset in part by appointing a Roman Catholic on your commission. In the neighbourhood of the reserves the chief stock-in-trade of the machine is the charge that the C.C.F. is anti-Catholic, and we have found this very hard to combat.[31]

In his reply, Douglas warmly endorsed Rielly's suggestion. He said that his first preference was a federal commission, in which case he promised to recommend to Indian Affairs that a Catholic be appointed. He also added that, were there a provincial inquiry into the state of the Métis, he would likewise act on Rielly's recommendation. As Douglas explained: 'The church has probably done more work among the Indians and the Métis people than any other organization and, therefore, are [sic] better qualified to advise us on future policy on their behalf.'[32]

Douglas's response to Rielly was more than political correctness and spoke to the government's willingness to accommodate Catholic interests. This can be seen not only in the CCF's cooperation with the church in Green Lake, started by their Liberal predecessors, but also in the extension of that cooperation to Métis colonies in the South. Local priests almost invariably sat on the various management committees of the colonies and even served as employees of government departments working with the residents. One of the most important and strategic moves by the government was the appointment of Father E. Blanchard from Willow Bunch. Blanchard had been instrumental in organizing the Lacerte co-op for the Willow Bunch Métis, and his work there had so impressed local officials that the Department of Social Welfare and Rehabilitation hired him to organize co-ops in the other Métis projects as well. According to a memorandum from the deputy minister to the minister of social welfare in 1953, Blanchard's performance was stellar and served to mobilize the support of local interests:

> Father Blanchard has been successful in getting this community [Lestock] away to a good start. He has not neglected other people in the community and has established a good relationship with such persons as the manager of the Co-op store, municipal councillors and Fr. Thetrault, superior and principal of the Indian school, Father Reilly and Father McGrath ... You will be interested to know that Father Campagna from the Duck Lake Mission has visited several communities with Fr. Blanchard and is interested in having something done for Duck Lake Métis. The Bishop at Prince Albert has also talked to Fr. Blanchard regarding several Métis communities in that area and members of our legislature have become very interested in the movement.[33]

As it turned out, Blanchard eventually had a falling out with certain members of the Willow Bunch Co-op and, as a consequence, was summarily fired by the DSWR in 1959.[34] But this did nothing to dissuade the CCF from relying on Catholic personnel. In reality, the Douglas government was quite willing to accommodate Catholic interests out of its own self-interest, and this explains why church participation in the Métis colonies proved to be a fundamental ingredient in the CCF's rehabilitation program.

There can be no doubt that, for a time, Catholic opposition to the CCF was real enough. But much of that opposition was diminished not only by a nationwide transition to secular education but also by a provincial government that saw the advantage of harnessing Catholic sentiment in support of its own reform policies. What the CCF wanted was to include Native people in the larger society. It had no interest in destroying the status quo and certainly no desire to dismantle Christian dominance in the Native community, even if it was Catholic. To that extent, there was a sympathy of interest between the Douglas government and its Catholic constituents.

The Hudson's Bay Company

A similar story can be told about the opposition of the Hudson's Bay Company. The HBC was a natural enemy of the Douglas government, in that its monopolist image was an easy target of socialist rhetoric. As a multinational enterprise with vast holdings in real estate, retail stores, and furs, the company was easily identified as the kind of conglomerate capable of distorting the market economy in its own interests. And, as it turned out, no one was more antagonistic to the Hudson's Bay Company than the fiery Joe Phelps. Phelps had the kind of background and personality that made him extremely sensitive to the 'pretensions' of powerful interests, and as minister of natural resources, he was instantly hostile to the company because of its supposed monopoly, especially over the North. Perhaps even more important, he had a personal axe to grind against the company: as a southern farmer, Phelps had leased land from the HBC only to have the lease peremptorily cancelled by the company on seven-days' notice.[35] The company was entirely within its rights and rationalized the suddenness of the move on the grounds that the land in question had neither buildings nor crops at the time.[36] But for Phelps the cancellation was a personal affront. Never a man to forget a grudge, he was not above using his political office as a means of retaliation. As a minister of the Crown, he wrote a letter to the company in which he threatened to respond in kind: 'However, your company have [sic] a few Agreements with our Government and several of them directly with this Department and I might suggest that some of these same agreements are due to come up for revision very shortly and the same seven days notice in such cases might be quite sufficient to terminate same.'[37] That such a statement represented a conflict of interest on the part of the minister seems not to have troubled Phelps. Nor was the implied threat idle posturing. Personally and ideologically, Phelps hated everything the Hudson's Bay Company stood for, and he was quite prepared to take on the company head to head.

The opening salvo was fired on 19 March 1945 when, as part of the budget debate, Phelps delivered a blistering attack on the company in the Legislative Assembly. A month earlier he had sent out letters to key individuals in the North asking for information about 'the conduct of business of the Hudsons [sic] Bay Company and their exploitations of the native people.'[38] The intent clearly was to dig up anecdotal information that could be used against the company. The speech itself was little more than a diatribe against vested interests, the HBC and the Canadian Pacific Railway being the main targets.

Phelps's main thesis was that the Hudson's Bay Company charter, granted by King Charles II in 1670, was invalid. As a consequence, he argued, title to massive amounts of land the HBC had received in compensation for surrendering Rupertsland (including much of Saskat-chewan) to the dominion in 1869 was also invalid.[39] As he put it, 'I am suspicious that the Hudson's Bay Company people are impostors, masquerading under forged credentials with questionable legal rights and certainly no moral rights to these lands they hold.'[40] He argued that this 'skullduggery' had been aided and abetted by dominion maladmini-stration of Saskatchewan lands prior to their being turned over to the province in 1930 and by provincial Liberal governments, which had given the HBC a free hand in exploiting resources. In the past, he said, the company had defended its charter by employing skilled lawyers; but now, he insisted, 'the tables have been turned and the people are able to engage council [sic].'[41] The unequivocal threat, of course, was that the province might test the charter in the courts. He also hinted at the pos-sibility of calling a special session of the Legislative Assembly to consider revision of old land agreements with various companies. This would include the HBC as well as the CPR, which, he said, operated under 'those shady deals of the past.'[42]

Phelps clearly saw the Hudson's Bay Company as a corrupt vested interest. While its large land holdings in the South made the company immediately suspect, it was its monopolist image in the fur trade that most enraged the minister. What Phelps failed to grasp was that, while the Honourable Company was still the single most important player in the fur trade, it had long-since ceased to operate as a monopoly in the North. Starting with the First World War, the company's old fur-trade preponderance had begun to wither under the pressure of increasing competition, and this trend continued through the Depression years and on into the Second World War.[43] Internally, the company was racked by personnel problems, conflicting business strategies, and divided author-ity; externally, it was confronted by a veritable revolution in communica-tion and transportation technology that made the company's fur domain completely accessible by rival interests, both big and small.[44] The result was a severe decline in the Bay's market share. Indicative was the fact that, in the same year the CCF came to power in Saskatchewan, the company's Fur Trade Department obtained only 23 percent of the total Canadian fur output, representing an overall decline of 13 percent from the 1930s.[45]

It was against this backdrop that the company was now confronted by Joe Phelps. News that the Saskatchewan government might challenge the company's charter in the courts was swiftly communicated to inter-national markets, informed by the press as far away as Buenos Aires.[46] It also led to an immediate drop in the price of the company's shares on the London Exchange.[47] And to make matters worse, Phelps took steps to make good on the threat articulated in his speech in the Assembly.

One of the first measures introduced by the government was a Mineral Taxation Act. The legislation levied an annual fee of three cents an acre on all lands where mineral rights had been retained by private companies or individuals; at the same time, it imposed an annual fee of fifty cents an acre on lands designated by government to be 'producing areas.' The tax affected the Canadian National Railway, the Canadian Saskatchewan Land Company, and other large landowners, but it had special meaning for the CPR and the HBC because both owned vast mineral rights not only to lands they still possessed but also to farm lands they had sold off. In the case of the HBC, the company estimated that it owned some 2,200,000 acres of mineral lands in Saskatchewan and that the tax would amount to a whopping $66,000 a year.[48] At the same time, along with announcing plans for fur conservation blocks in the North and fur marketing services in Regina, Phelps made menacing overtures to the company factors in the North. During visits there, he informed post personnel that he fully intended to take over the licensing, collection, and marketing of all furs in the province.[49] And in March 1945 he sent a threatening letter and telegraph to the Canadian Committee in Winnipeg demanding that the company surrender its Cumberland House Community fur lease. If it did not do so immediately, said Phelps, the legislature would be asked to rescind the lease as well as the company's lease of a private fur preserve in the Cumberland House area.[50]

The Hudson's Bay Company took the CCF threat seriously and dealt with it masterfully. In London, the governor and committee saw the CCF challenge as a serious problem because the CCF's reform program was so ambitious.[51] In Winnipeg, the Canadian Committee estimated that the CCF would probably be in power for at least two terms and therefore recommended that the company, in order to protect its interests, make every effort to appear cooperative.[52] The specific response of the company was devised in Winnipeg and overwhelmingly approved in London. Although the company was quite prepared to defend itself through every legal means available, it also recognized that a political accommodation would have to be found. To that end, the company arranged a private meeting with Phelps in Regina, seemingly in an attempt to beard the lion in his den.

The meeting took place in the premier's office on 24 March 1945. The company sent Philip Chester, the general manager of the Fur Trade Department, Robert Chesshire, Chester's protégé and assistant, and C.E. Joslyn, manager of the company's Land Department. Phelps was there, of course, as was the premier, who attended only intermittently because the Assembly was sitting and he was needed there. The only extant information on the meeting is a lengthy and detailed account penned by the company representatives for the information of the Canadian and London

Committees.[53] Bias notwithstanding, the account not only revealed the contempt the company men had for Phelps personally but also the way in which Phelps was mollified and seemingly out-manoeuvred.

The two parties met at ten in the morning and were joined by the premier fifteen minutes later. The meeting started with 'a brisk exchange of views, with quite a touch of irrelevant comment about the Company from Mr. Phelps when he was worsted.'[54] The company men led off by squarely confronting Phelps, insisting that his actions and threatening correspondence in regard to the Cumberland House leases were little more than 'a venting of spite' against the company.[55] For the benefit of the premier, who seemingly knew nothing about the correspondence, the company delegation read aloud Phelps's March letter and telegraph. Phelps, who was clearly embarrassed both by this and his inability to defend his actions, resorted to 'vague generalities.'[56] Douglas, who had to leave the meeting to address matters in the Assembly, was apparently impressed with the company's views and asked that the discussion be continued when he returned in the afternoon. But before he left, the company men dropped one more bombshell: they pointed out that, if the company's charter had been invalid in 1870, as Phelps had maintained in the legislature, then the title to all the lands subsequently carved out of Rupertsland was also invalid! According to the account, this was an implication that neither Phelps nor Douglas had thought of and both were reportedly taken off guard by the issue.[57]

After Douglas's departure, the meeting continued for close to an hour, only now in a more friendly atmosphere. During that time, Phelps talked openly and frankly about his plans for the North and this afforded the company representatives an opportunity to judge the minister's character. According to their assessment, Phelps was a shallow and ill-informed man prone to thoughtless and biased action: 'Mr. Phelps, a farmer, is not an educated or well informed man, and has practically no experience in the sphere of business or Government affairs. He is full of strong prejudices, a bit of a bully and a ranter, and such a talker that his tongue runs away with him. This combination of characteristics causes him to say many things which he might regret when a realization of their import is impressed upon him.'[58] To make matters worse, it was thought, Phelps was intensely suspicious of 'big interests,' and, knowing almost nothing about the HBC, was 'obsessed' with the idea that the company only squeezed every nickel from its operations. Moreover, he was personally prejudiced against the company 'and was convinced we would do everything in our power to obstruct any action from him that encroached upon our business.'[59] At the same time, he was ruthlessly determined to take action and 'frankly admitted that inexperience would probably cause them to make many blunders, but that they were not going to stop taking action for fear of mistakes.'[60] Indicative was the minister's determination to have the government take over the Cumberland House Community lease. The plan was to combine the lease land with an adjacent area in fulfilment of a muskrat conservation program; and to that end, Phelps had already drawn up a bill that would give the government the power to cancel both HBC leases in Cumberland House.

In light of this assessment, the company delegates decided they would not take an 'immovable stand' because that would only endanger relations with the government and steel Phelps's attacks on the company; instead, they would adopt a conciliatory position and allow Mr. Phelps to save face. To that end, Mr. Chester made a series of proposals that would serve the interests of all concerned: that the company and government make a new start by destroying old correspondence dealing with the dispute; that both parties pledge mutual cooperation because no useful purpose would be served by getting into a series of fights, legal or otherwise; and that, given the HBC's experience and knowledge, the company would actively assist the government, given that both had the same interest in conservation. On the key issue of the Cumberland House leases, Chester offered to relinquish the community lease in return for Phelps's promise to leave the private lease alone.[61] Actually, he was not giving much away because the community lease was due to expire the following year in any event.[62] His gesture, nevertheless, had tremendous symbolic value because it left the impression that Phelps had won the day. In turn, a memorandum of agreement outlining the principle of cooperation and the details concerning the Cumberland House leases was drawn up by the company delegates; and, at a subsequent meeting late in the day, the terms of the memorandum were accepted by both Phelps and the premier. By this time, according to the account, the atmosphere was cordial and friendly and even Phelps was quite pleasant, 'though he probably retains some suspicions of us and wonders if there is a catch somewhere.'[63]

The Regina meeting was important because it had a direct bearing on company-government relations and, hence, on the nature and pace of Native reform in the North. As long as the company was held at arms length by the CCF and seen as a corrupt influence wilfully pursuing its own ends to the detriment of northern Natives, it ran the risk of government intervention and regulation. But were it perceived as a venerable business working in partnership with the government for the benefit of Natives, government would be far less justified in reforming long-standing trade practices in the North. It was clearly in the company's best interest to normalize relations with Phelps and Douglas, and this is exactly what was promised by the results of the Regina meeting.

The memorandum of agreement drawn up in Regina was only an informal mechanism purporting to minimize differences between the two parties, but it had the effect of neutralizing Phelps's personal vendetta against the company. While he continued to distrust the company to the very end, Phelps was forced to be more friendly in his dealings with the Bay managers and far more circumspect in condemning the Honourable Company in the press and legislature. This was all the more so when the company followed up with a series of overtures meant to cement good relations. Two days later, Philip Chester sent a letter to Phelps saying how much he had enjoyed the Regina meeting and inviting the minister to visit him in Winnipeg. Enclosed was a company booklet, *Your Food and Health in the North,* for the benefit of Mrs. Phelps 'in view of her interest in the welfare of people in the north.'[64] In the same letter, Chester promised to forward a copy of a Norway House Nutritional Survey conducted over a four-year period by international experts. The subtext of the letter, of course, was to portray the company's work as a positive, if not altruistic, force in the North. By the same token, when the premier visited London in early May, the governor of the company, Sir Patrick Cooper, sent Douglas a personal invitation to an evening party.[65] A month after that, the company took 22,000 muskrat furs from the Cumberland House private lease and marketed them through the government's fur auction in Regina. It was not required to do so by law because the furs had not been trapped on public crown land. A few weeks later still, the company shipped an additional 20,000 Cumberland House muskrats to the Regina auction. In both cases, the Canadian Committee hoped to protect the interests of the company by winning 'some measure of confidence' from the government.[66] The gesture of goodwill also proved to be good business because, as it turned out, the company furs received higher prices in Regina than they would have had they been sold at auction in Montreal, as originally planned.[67]

The perceived need to cooperate with the government was additionally underscored by the way in which the company handled the troublesome issue of the mineral tax. The Saskatchewan Mineral Taxation Act, along with the Local Government Board Act and the Farm Security Act, had been passed by the government in October 1944 in a special session of the Assembly shortly after the CCF came to power. In draft form, the Mineral Taxation Bill had originally called for a tax of five cents per acre on mineral rights but, as a result of a meeting between the Hudson's Bay Company and the government, the tax had been reduced to three cents.[68] Business interests nevertheless found all three measures distasteful and responded by appealing to the dominion government to have the acts disallowed. The Hudson's Bay Company was one of the appellants and had its lawyers draw up a petition for disallowance. In doing so, however, the company was careful about the wording, declining to include 'any general critical reference in the Petition about the broad policies of the C.C.F. Government.'[69] In October 1945, the HBC's appeal was heard by a special committee of the federal cabinet; a month later, the company learned that the decision of the committee was not to disallow the Saskatchewan Mineral Taxation Act.

In handing down its decision, the federal government did not express any opinion on the constitutionality of the Mineral Taxation Act. This left the door open for legal action against the Saskatchewan government, but both the Canadian Committee and the London Board quickly agreed not to pursue such a course, given that their legal counsel advised against it.[70] Instead, the company took immediate steps to comply with the legislation. C.E. Joslyn met with Phelps personally to discuss the whole issue and together they worked out a deal serving the interests of both parties. The company agreed to an interim tax payment and in return received extra time to complete a survey of its lands to determine which mineral rights would be retained and which would be surrendered in order to avoid taxation of unproductive lands.[71] In the end, the company retained only 297,870 acres of Saskatchewan mineral rights out of the original total of more than two million acres, at an annual cost of $9,600 per year.[72] The cooperation between the Bay and the government was in sharp contrast to the position taken by the Canadian Pacific Railway, which had also petitioned the federal government for disallowance of the mineral tax. The CPR not only refused to pay the tax for more than two years but in 1948 also took the unprecedented step of suing both Phelps and Attorney General J.W. Corman. It did so on the grounds that the tax was prohibitive and meant to injure the company through the confiscation of its lands owing to tax default.[73] But in the end, the CPR's response proved less prudent than that of the HBC, in so far as the railway company lost its suit in the courts, ultimately meeting defeat in the Supreme Court of Canada in 1952.[74]

The rapprochement between the Hudson's Bay Company and the CCF government promised to normalize trade relations. The company, needless to say, was not happy with the compulsory marketing of beaver and muskrat through Regina, nor with policies that removed the Native labour force from the bush in favour of life in settlements. But it had a great deal of experience in dealing with competition in various forms and took measures to protect its market share, not the least of which was the withholding of credit in order to discipline its trappers. It also had experience with government, having worked out an arrangement with the Department of Indian Affairs through which it often delivered government services to Indians in return for federal contracts and favours. The company's new relationship with the CCF was little more than an extension of these past practices and served to minimize disruption to the fur industry. Even the unpredictable Joe Phelps proved to be far less dangerous than his rhetoric and bluster initially had implied, and when he was removed from office following his electoral defeat in 1948, his successor superimposed a more conservative and tempered reform posture on the entire Department of Natural Resources.[75]

Indicative of the new relationship was the issue of government stores in the North. Phelps had wanted government-operated retail outlets in the North in order to make merchandise more accessible and affordable, particularly to support commercial fishing and trapping. But with Phelps's departure, it became clear that the government was not anxious to compete head to head with the Hudson's Bay Company, at least not if it could be avoided. The matter was first raised in April 1949 by George Cadbury, chair of the Industrial Development Board and economic advisor to the Saskatchewan government. Cadbury, operating through the United Kingdom Trade Commissioner, set up a preliminary meeting with company officials in Winnipeg. There, he indicated that the government was interested in expanding retail sales in the North. He suggested that, although he was not interested in setting up 'spheres of operation,' two stores in competition in the same district could be a disadvantage to both.[76] Company officials were not entirely sure what Cadbury had in mind and felt they were not in a position to discuss the matter further. Because the subject was one of 'highest policy and a question of principle,' they insisted that Cadbury take the matter up directly with the managing director, Mr. Chester.[77]

Cadbury's intent was revealed in a letter to the company asking for a meeting with Chester. He indicated that the government planned to expand its retail operations in the North and asked if the company would consider selling some of its trading posts. Not knowing the intentions of the company, he wondered whether such an idea would present an opportunity for 'mutual accommodation.'[78] At a meeting in June, however, Chester made it clear to Cadbury that the company was not interested in downsizing its retail operations, even in areas where the government planned to build stores. In the end, the two men readily acknowledged that both the company and government had 'continuing and substantial interests in the northern portion of Saskatchewan.'[79] They also agreed that the company would be informed when the government planned to establish a competing store, thereby giving it an opportunity to sell out if it was in its own best interests, and that if the company declined to do so, each would be free to establish or maintain its own local operation. In the following year, Cadbury honoured the informal agreement and dutifully notified the company of the government's intent to open stores at Cumberland House, Stanley Mission, and La Ronge.[80] In response, the company politely declined the offer to sell out, thanked Cadbury for the courtesy, and promised to reciprocate in the future.[81] The amicable relationship was a testimony to the 'peaceful coexistence' that now existed; it was also a far cry from the earlier ranting of Joe Phelps who initially had promised to socialize the entire fur industry.

Thus, the Douglas government came to an understanding with the Hudson's Bay Company. Of all the vested interests aligned against the CCF, the company potentially stood to lose the most in any open confrontation with the government. But in adopting a cooperative strategy in their dealings with the Department of Natural Resources, company spokespersons were able to placate, even isolate, radicals like Phelps. At the most fundamental level, the CCF and the company were themselves vested interests in a capitalist society. As such, the Douglas government had no more interest in crippling a powerful economic interest than it had in offending the Roman Catholic Church. The CCF's accommodation to the Honourable Company, in fact, confirmed once again the moderate nature of the government's reform agenda.

Northern Caste Structure
A third example of the opposition to CCF reform policies can be found in the class bias endemic in Saskatchewan society. Although much could be said about social divisions in the municipalities of the South, it was in the North where class stratification was particularly rigid, often mirroring the features of a racially defined caste system. At the top of the social pyramid were the white elite who monopolized most of the power and resources; at the bottom were the Indians and Métis who enjoyed neither. A distinguishing feature of the system was an almost complete lack of social mobility, in that Natives and poor whites in the North seldom, if ever, made their way into the upper ranks.

Unlike in a normal class structure, the northern elite were made up of small business and professional groups who achieved dominance because of the unique nature of the North. After the Second World War there was a tremendous proliferation of commercial, private, government, and church agencies operating in the North, and this led to a concomitant growth in the number of white administrators and business people. The agency sector was predicated on personnel with a certain degree of formal education, experience, and role specialization, and this meant that most of the store managers, conservation officers, and administrators were whites recruited mainly from the South.[82] As a group, these people shared common values, similar status, and comparable income levels.[83] Not surprisingly, they also tended to form close social bonds, knitted together by ethnic and racial self-identification, which sharply set them apart from the Native community. There were, of course, some whites who lived like and socialized with the Indians and Métis, but they were few in number and usually excluded from polite white society.

The sway held by the elite represented a pervasive, if not impene-
trable, obstacle to CCF reforms, particularly those that promised to give
some measure of control to Native people. In theory, community development programs were meant to enhance decision-making by Indians
and the Métis in communities where they constituted a majority, but in
practice this was seldom so. Buffalo Narrows, for example, was predominantly Native and thought to be a progressive community in which its
citizenry exercised a high degree of participant democracy. It had a
number of community associations, including a co-op store, a school
board, a ratepayers association, a credit union, a sawmill co-op, a women's
auxiliary, two different church-associated organizations, a trappers' fur
block council, and a town Advancement Club with three different sports
committees. And yet, despite the fact that three-quarters of the residents
were Native, two-thirds of the office holders in these voluntary associations were white.[84] Among the eighteen people holding more than one
office were five employees of the provincial government and six managers of various business concerns.[85] Indeed, there were only three Métis
and no Indians among the many office holders.[86] It was quite evident
that the devolution of control implied by community development was,
in fact, monopolized by the white elite and fell far short of empowering
Native residents.

The reaction of the white elite to any reform that threatened the established order was poignantly illustrated in attempts to create a co-op store
in Ile-à-la-Crosse in the mid-1950s. In 1953 Vic Valentine, along with his
family, moved to the settlement as an employee of the Department of
Natural Resources. Although he was initially confronted with short-term
suspicion by the Métis fishers, it was the white part of the community
that proved most antagonistic, often dismissing him as a communist, a
Jew, or simply a troublemaker.[87] As he put it: 'The white people some-
how saw me as a threat to their existence in relation to the way in which
they were carrying out their jobs as government, religious, or business
officials.'[88] This antipathy turned to open hostility when Valentine joined
the efforts of the local Métis to organize the Fort Black co-op store, in
competition with the Hudson's Bay Company and a few independent
dealers, thereby interfering with what was basically a local cartel.

At the centre of the monopoly was the Hudson's Bay Company, which
routinely broke the law in order to engross local incomes.[89] The post office
was located in the HBC store and the postmaster was also the company
factor. The factor unilaterally established the price structure for consumer
goods, not only in the HBC store but also in the operations of the two
local free traders, and this monopoly was enforced through the post office.
Income and family allowance cheques addressed to Métis fishers were
simply held by the factor in payment of outstanding debts or as a credit

Vic Valentine, Director of Anthro-
pological Services, Department of
Natural Resources, May 1957.
(Saskatchewan Archives Board
R-A10,764-3)

against the purchase of store goods. Intended recipients were required to
endorse their cheques on the spot to prevent them from shopping elsewhere, and sometimes signatures were forged by company employees
to expedite the process. To maintain the monopoly price structure, the
factor divided the cheques as they arrived into three bundles: the larger
one for the HBC store and the other two for the two small free-trader
stores. The implication was that, if one free trader became too competitive in his pricing of goods, he would not receive his bundle of cheques
for that month; and, because the free trader had already advanced credit
to his customers to the anticipated value of the expected cheques, he
could not afford to lose his share of the cheques. Interestingly enough,
when Valentine discovered this practice, he took the matter up with the
local RCMP officer, who initially proved argumentative and only grudgingly agreed to instruct the Hudson's Bay factor that it was illegal to withhold the cheques. As Valentine explained, the abusive practices he had
unearthed were not confined to Ile-à-la-Crosse because, when word got
out that the company was not legally entitled to withhold cheques, he
received a batch of letters asking him to investigate the operation of the
post office in other areas.

The monopoly also carried over into other activities. When the Métis
fishers attempted to organize cooperative buying by trucking in consumer
goods from Meadow Lake, they ran into opposition from a related
quarter.[90] There was only one trucker in Meadow Lake who had a class
'A' licence, giving him complete control over the trucking industry in the
area, and he bluntly refused to transport Métis goods. He claimed that

the Métis seldom had money to pay and were not always available to receive shipment. But the real reason was something else. The trucker hauled a large portion of the summer and winter freight for the six Hudson's Bay stores in the area and he was afraid that, if he hauled for Indian and Métis individuals who were attempting to circumvent the HBC monopoly, the company would transfer its business to a rival trucking concern operating out of Big River. This was a very real possibility because the rival concern was already hauling a large portion of the HBC's winter freight and it was owned by Waite and Company, for which the HBC acted as a fish-buying agent.

To further reinforce the monopoly, the local white community closed ranks against Valentine and others who supported the creation of a Métis co-op. Al Halvorson, a one-time employee of the Game Branch of the DNR, had tried on a number of occasions to get the local community interested in organizing a co-op, but 'in the process had lost his job and had made enemies of nearly all of the White people in the area.'[91] He subsequently worked as a subcontractor for Bell Telephone Company, which was constructing the radar line in the Ile-à-la-Crosse area, but then discovered that none of the local storekeepers would give his men credit and that he and his family were ostracized by the white community, which refused to speak to even his daughter or wife. According to Valentine, the odium attached to Halvorson was a result of some seemingly unsavoury past practices; nevertheless, he insisted that Halvorson's stigma stemmed from the fact that 'the white people saw him as a threat to the cozy way in which they were doing things.'[92]

Valentine and his family experienced the same treatment. As he explained: 'The only feelings of insecurity which developed were brought about by the pressures placed on me by the local white community. They not only ignored me but my family as well so that life for my wife was very lonely and often depressing.'[93] When his wife was admitted to hospital in Ile-à-la Crosse to deliver their third child, not one person from the white community visited her nor did anyone volunteer to help out Valentine with the other two children. On another occasion, Valentine was angrily confronted on the street by the HBC manager, who claimed that the organization of the local co-op was an invitation to the Métis to refuse paying their bills at the HBC store. Even the conservation officer – a government employee – proved reluctant to assist the co-op and snubbed Valentine socially out of fear of jeopardizing his relationship with the white community.[94]

While the white elite exhibited a fierce resistance to any change in the status quo, the Native component of the class structure likewise proved resistant to CCF reforms, but for different reasons. Relegated to the bottom of the social structure, northern Natives were removed from the avenues of power and decisionmaking through which CCF reforms were conceived and implemented. They were the objects, not the authors of change and, as such, their class interests were neither expressed nor well served in government programs. Through a process of imposed reform they were systematically uprooted from the land and relocated in settlements, only to experience new forms of marginalization, poverty, and ethnic segregation. Many saw the CCF as an alien force threatening their traditional lifestyle and independence, and few were prepared to argue the benefits of government programs. In reality, Native society in the North, as elsewhere, was defined by class and ethnic interests that were anathema to CCF goals. As a result, government programs meant to ameliorate conditions were met with passive indifference or open hostility in the Native community and never achieved the kind of popular support the CCF expected.

It was the caste tendencies of the class system that made a mockery of the good intentions of government. Native people were systematically discriminated against as a result of racist attitudes, entertained in some cases by the very people sent north to reform Native society. Bill Berezowsky, MLA for Cumberland and a sympathetic observer of Native society, clearly recognized this fact in his 1952 submission to the Advisory Committee on Northern Development:

> Particularly noticeable, was a class or racial distinction and prejudice. Individuals of Caucasian origin (white) made it obvious by their general attitude and behaviour that they considered themselves to be superior people. In addition to merchants, trappers, and people of other professions, Government and crown corporation employees were no exception. They all avoid association with the Métis or native Indian people. I observed that the Métis and Indian people appeared willing and anxious to be accepted; nevertheless, they were quite deliberately ignored. However, at times when lackeys or so-called hewers of wood and drawers of water were required, the whites could be interested in the native people.[95]

What Berezowsky was alluding to was a form of segregation that effectively prevented the real benefits of government reform from reaching the Native community. It was a matter of complaint among Natives that government officials routinely gave work preference to whites and almost never trained Natives in the operation of motor vehicles, carpentry, or the other better-paying jobs.[96] As Berezowsky explained, what benefits did accrue to Native society were race and class specific: 'Only when common labor with axe or shovel was required, were they sometimes given work.'[97] The inference was that, government reform notwithstanding, upward social mobility for most Native people was unthinkable.

The solidified nature of the class structure also explains why the CCF was never able to win over the Native leadership. According to Vic Valentine, it was precisely because most Native people realized they could never achieve higher standing in society that they were suspicious and often resentful of those in their midst who attempted to do so by cooperating with government.[98] Those Métis who were selected by government officials as leaders and spokespersons were seldom accepted as such in their own communities and were often dismissed as CCF spies or self-serving big shots.[99] This meant that the real leaders of Métis society, often the elders and trappers, remained largely invisible to government officials and essentially aloof from CCF policies.

At the same time, the caste system operated in still another way to limit popular support for government. The language barrier between the white elite and the Native lower class was fundamental to ethnic segregation in the North and effectively prevented the CCF from articulating their goals to the Native people. As late as 1959, it was still a fact that government officials could not converse in any of the Native languages. As a report to the minister of education by the Council of Lac La Ronge School District complained, 'Our northern administrational apparatus in the field of education, health and natural resources, lack [sic] any effective avenue of communication with the native population, owing to the paucity of bilingual personnel in these administrational spheres. They are thus unable to communicate to the Indians in their own tongue.'[100] In the same report, it was also noted that only a relatively small portion of the Native population of the North spoke English.[101] Even then, most Métis and Indians chose to speak an Indian dialect, often as an expression of ethnic self-identification. According to Bill Berezowsky, because the Métis were not accepted by whites, they preferred to be called Indians or even half-breeds,[102] seemingly as a matter of ethnic pride. At one meeting, for example, a Métis insisted on addressing the audience in his 'beloved Cree tongue' and asked that he and the others not be called Métis 'because we are all Indians and are proud of our origin.'[103] Language, in fact, operated as a buttress to ethnic and class separation and severely limited the ability of government to win approval in the Native community.

The antipathy of Native society was registered in interviews conducted by Vic Valentine. The sentiments expressed tend to be anecdotal in nature, but nevertheless offer valuable insight into the sentiments of local residents. Although not everyone was opposed to the CCF, there was a strong current of disenchantment, especially among the older generation. Those who were dissatisfied bemoaned not only the destruction of their old way of life but also the economic dislocation that accompanied the new order. As an elderly man from Ile-à-la-Crosse explained,

In the old days, we used to work then. As far as livin' was concerned we could get fish meat and berries. It was okay then. We never lived off the store but off the land. The old mans used to tell us what to do how to make a living and all that. They have councillors now. It's not like the old days, when it was free and you could go any place to make a living and now you can't. We were the boss of what we took out of the bush. It belonged to us but now with this compulsory stuff [fur marketing], it doesn't belong to us. The government has just taken everything away from us and never gives us work. There is no wages here. All we got to live on is the rats we catch in the winter for all summer.[104]

According to an interpreted interview with a man in his early sixties from Canoe River,

The trouble with the government is they don't give any work to the people. They come up north here and take away our living. One time, when the liberals were here, there used to be at least work for a man in the summer. But now they send a bulldozer in to do the work. The last work we had was to build a dam up here about three years ago. No, the people don't like the C.C.F. because there is no work and the compulsory rat business. Yes the C.C.F. government has taken away our living. We have to buy a license to catch fish to eat and it has stopped the people killing ducks to eat. Some say they are going to let the people in the north starve because they voted liberal.[105]

By the same token, a married man in his early forties, living at Beaver River, had this to say through an interpreter:

There is nothing here to be got, no work, no roads. We're afraid to set nets to feed our kids – can't hunt nor nothing. We can't even kill nothing to feed our kids with. We're just sitting at home doing nothing. What's feeding our kids right now, to tell the truth is our family allowances, but it isn't enough to buy clothes. If we bought any clothes them kids would have to go hungry. I'd like to see a little work around the country. The C.C.F. never gives us any work that's why we're against them.[106]

It is apparent from these comments that Douglas's developmental model for Canada's last frontier held small promise for Native people displaced from the land. Many did benefit from government policies in ways that were often indirect and not always evident, yet it is equally clear that the traditional poverty and underdevelopment of the Native community had changed little in substance. What was new was the centralization of community life and concomitantly an almost complete dependence on welfare and transfer payments from government.

At its most fundamental level, Native opposition to government was informed by the fact that CCF policies were never meant to alter the established order in the North. In keeping with socialist rhetoric and the pledge to apply 'humanity first' to the new frontier, the CCF's main goal was to develop northern resources for the benefit of all. But in accommodating itself to existing vested interests, the government ensured that, no matter what the nature of development, the overall distribution of wealth and power would remain unchanged. According to Allan Quandt, Douglas was among the first, if not the first, to incorporate into his developmental model the concept of 'trickle-down economics,'[107] implying that wealth generated at the top of the social pyramid would eventually impact in a more limited way at the bottom. It was precisely for that reason that vested interests – including the church, the Hudson's Bay Company, and northern class structure – were never dismantled, or even really threatened, by the CCF. And yet, the wealth and development that did trickle down to the Native community came mainly in the form of government paternalism and welfare payments. More than anything else, Native people resented the loss of their independence and relationship with the land, as well as the extent to which bureaucrats and government officials had preempted control over their lives. For many, the advent of the CCF signaled a significant decline in an already marginal existence.

7
Assessment

In evaluating the policies of the Douglas government, it may be said that the notion of 'walking in Indian moccasins' is an appropriate epitaph. Both in degree and substance, the CCF did express a sympathy and empathy for Native people that was unprecedented in provincial history. The government was genuinely troubled by the plight of an oppressed and disfranchised minority in its midst, and its response was a concerted effort to integrate Métis and Indians into provincial society on a basis of individual equality and fairness. For the most part, but not always, it did so with an appropriate sense of cultural relativism, trying not to be unduly judgmental and appreciating the historic injustices under which Native people had laboured. While the effects of policies were not always positive, and were sometimes disastrous, the intent for the most part was firmly anchored to humanitarian and egalitarian goals. The most characteristic feature of the Douglas era was an entirely new emphasis upon human dignity and rights, not as a function of power or wealth but as a consequence of being a citizen. This was underscored in the revolutionary changes made in the administration of welfare, as well as in the entirely new emphasis on the political and social rights of individuals, both Native and non-Native. Douglas knew how the system worked and his reference to the 'squeaky wheel' being heard spoke not only to the abstract benefits of provincial citizenship but also to the process of socially and politically empowering otherwise disadvantaged people. In keeping with these changes, the CCF also introduced a kinder, more humane, more caring atmosphere in the administration of government policy, and many Natives, like others dependent on welfare and social services, were the beneficiaries.

Conceptually, the overriding policy paradigm for Native reform was integration. But if Natives were to become players in mainstream society, as the concept of integration promised, that would take place in society as it existed, not in some utopia implied by socialist theory. The basic intent was to give Natives the necessary skills, political rights, and services that would allow them to survive in a capitalist world dominated by white people and powerful interests. It was never understood that society would be fundamentally altered in order to accommodate Natives; on the contrary, it was always assumed that the Native would have to be retooled to fit into the existing social framework. It was for this very reason that, as much as the CCF may have deplored the monopolist tendencies of the Hudson's Bay Company, the church, or the northern white elite, there was little attempt to destroy the vested interests that historically had benefited from Native marginalization. This explains why the CCF did not find it difficult to align its own reform agenda with those interests. And it also explains why, in the end, most Natives, whether in Métis colonies and cities of the South or settlements of the North, found themselves living in dramatically altered circumstances but nevertheless still trapped in a marginalized existence. However well meaning CCF reforms may have been, classism, racism, and the other structural barriers that historically had conspired against Native society remained largely untouched. Indeed, the CCF was itself a colonizing force in its treatment of Native people!

At the same time, the empathy promised by 'walking in Indian moccasins' was riddled with paternalism. In one sense, this should not be surprising. The CCF was a would-be socialist party that, in theory at least, promised unprecedented state intervention and regulation as a panacea for social and economic ills. As a government, it was steeped in the doctrine of human progress writ large in the principles of social gospel; to that end, it sought to manipulate the physical and human environment to produce the desired results. Métis colonies in their most pristine form were little more than experiments in social engineering. The operative instrument of change was the government, strategically employing professional administrators, bureaucrats, and experts of various descriptions. Although government rhetoric acknowledged the importance of community development and a bottom-up approach to development, in reality the CCF was much more comfortable with a heavy management hand in manipulating events. Community development itself, especially in the Métis colonies of the South but also in the North, was overseen by a battery of bureaucrats and social animators who prodded and mobilized the local community in the desired direction. Equally indicative of the government's management style was the reluctance of the CCF to substitute cooperative organization for the corporate structure that continued to dominate the northern fishing industry throughout the Douglas years. And of course the total rejection of the single agency concept for the North was a blatant confirmation of Douglas's determination to centralize power in Regina. In truth, the statism inherent in CCF ideology dictated a thoroughgoing paternalism that often overrode

democratic impulses at the community level and contributed to the imposition of a colonial structure in the North.

Although the paternalism of the CCF was not confined to the Native
community, it had special meaning there. In the Métis colonies and in
the North generally, the CCF made little attempt to actually consult
Native people about their wishes and apparently distrusted their views.
The logic of this was that Natives generally lacked formal education and
historically had been unable to find a solution to their own problems;
hence the need for government to impose a solution on their behalf. In
an interview in 1976, Douglas candidly admitted that his government
did not know what the Métis and Indians actually wanted and that his
policies were based on what white people thought would be good for
them.[1] The justification for not consulting Native people, according to
the premier, had to do with both process and timing. Commenting on
the 1946 Indian conference in Regina, Douglas said that Indian delegates
could not come to any consensus as to what they wanted for themselves.
He insisted that had the government waited for Indians to formulate the
course of action, the government would have been into its second or
third term in office before something was done.[2] He maintained that,
although there was an awareness that solutions were being imposed, it
was 'a necessary evil' dictated by the need to act quickly.[3] It seems more
likely, however, that the whole process was driven by administrative convenience and a racial arrogance that fit well with the CCF's inherent paternalism and seeming adherence to the notion of the white man's burden.

In the course of framing its integration policy, the CCF often misread
the nature of Native society and, of course, made mistakes. But this must
be placed in context. As the first government ever to address seriously
the problems confronting Native people, the CCF committed itself to an
administrative voyage through uncharted, and at times turbulent, waters.
Apart from the wholesale destruction of government files by the outgoing
Liberal government in 1944, the plain fact is that the CCF had very
little information to use in fashioning its Native policies. Because past
governments had ignored the very existence of the Métis and dismissed
Indians as a federal responsibility, there was no statistical or demographic
information on Natives, no qualitative comment on the nature of Native
society, no management studies, and no evaluations of the success or
failure of past policies. Moreover, because the CCF was committed to
an expanded role and purview for government, it found itself exercising
jurisdiction in new and untried areas. It is noteworthy, for example, that
in expanding into the North, the DNR was entirely new and Phelps and
Brockelbank were only its first and second ministers.

It is true that there were some precedents. The Patterson government
had introduced the idea of colonies, at least in embryonic form, and this

served to inform CCF Métis policy. It also seems likely that Douglas and Shumiatcher took heart from the New Deal experiment that had taken place in the United States during the 1930s. There, the reforms of Ickes and Collier had sought to regenerate and reconstitute Indian society; they aimed at Indian cultural integrity, an expanded reserve land base, and a degree of tribal self-government, largely functioning under liberal democratic constitutions. Although the link between cultural pluralism and liberal democracy may have had meaning for Douglas, there is no evidence that the premier saw direct parallels between the Indian situation in the United States and that in Canada, or that he ever sought to emulate American policy. At best, the Indian Reorganization Act established a benchmark for experimentation, but it was never seen as instructive nor as prototype legislation for Saskatchewan. Hence, the precedents that did exist were limited in both application and import. This meant that CCF policy was mostly experimental, responding in a commonsense way to perceived problems, using whatever information was available at the time. To garner more information about Natives, the CCF was instrumental in establishing the Centre for Community Studies (CCS) at the University of Saskatchewan and attempted to persuade the federal government to fund a comprehensive study of all Native people in the province. Although the CCS eventually produced a number of relevant and useful studies, its research reports mostly came on-stream only after Douglas had left the province, and the federal government, it will be recalled, ultimately refused to cooperate on a provincewide study of any sort.

Given the absence of Native input, as well as the lack of empirical information on Native society, it should come as no surprise that the Native policies of the CCF were often based on stereotypical, and sometimes racist, understanding. The development of rural-based farm colonies, in which the Métis were programmed to become farm labourers rather than business people as the Métis themselves often wanted, was essentially the result of a stereotypical, racialized image of the Métis. They were seen mainly as a collectivist rural peasantry whose only hope of integration was as an underclassed minority working the land. The more overt and blatant expressions of racism were particularly evident at the local level, a fact noted by Bill Berezowsky in reference to northern field workers and managers. But it also functioned at the ministerial level and, in point of fact, was especially instrumental in the formulation of Métis reform.

The racism inherent in Métis policy was reflected in the fact that, although integration was the stated purpose, the actual goal was complete assimilation. The CCF was prepared to acknowledge the Aboriginal status of the Métis only so long as it served the government's own political ends. For the purposes of raiding the federal treasury or passing the Métis off as federal responsibility, Douglas seldom missed an opportunity to acknowledge the Aboriginal status of the Métis as part of a general problem associated with Indians. It was well known that the Métis were Aboriginal people descended from Indians, a fact conceded in federal legislation and Scrip Commissions and one subsumed in Ray Woollam's view that the Métis might someday be represented by the FSI. But when it came to provincial policy, the CCF, in effect, blatantly denied the Aboriginal status of Métis people. This was explicit in a statement made by O.W. Valleau, minister of social welfare, to delegates who attended the 1946 Métis conference in Regina. In outlining the reforms he was contemplating for the Métis, the minister not only displayed a contemptuous and paternalistic attitude toward the Métis as people but also dismissed their existence as a special and distinctive ethnic group:

> You must get a certain pride in yourself and a pride in the group. That is absolutely necessary. You must get from under what you have been suffering from, the idea that you are not as good as the other fellow ... We can possibly help the younger generation in education. We hope to be able to do that. We haven't made any definite start towards it yet, but we hope to educate them in some of the schools, possibly with some technical schools. I don't know yet, I have not yet had the opportunity of seeing any of your people trying to learn things as being in an office, accounting or anything like that. I don't know whether you have any ability along that line or not, but I think likely you would have ... I can ... start in to educate, and through practical farm education – and when I speak of education I am thinking not only of the school, but of the farm, and the work shop and garage, and so on, give to your people a knowledge of how to go out and earn a living ... I am not at all sure myself that the idea of group settlement is the wisest thing. You see, you people are not a definite race apart. The ultimate solution will be absorption into the general population. I don't think there is any doubt about that. There will come a time when there will be no distinction between the Métis and the white man. You will be absorbed through inter-marriage.[4]

The subtext of the statement contained an unmistakable strain of racism, denoted in references to 'you people,' the doubts raised about the ability of the Métis to learn, the suggestion that earning a living would be a novel experience, and the denial of Métis ethnicity. Valleau, in effect, simply dismissed the right of the Métis to exist as a historically and culturally defined group with unique Aboriginal status.

Valleau was one of the first to enunciate publicly the idea that the ultimate fate of the Métis would be complete assimilation. But it was an idea that found its most concrete expression as the cornerstone of Métis colonies. There, services were delivered not to a distinctive group with Aboriginal rights but to a disadvantaged minority destined for absorption into rural society. Few people in Douglas's day believed that the Métis constituted a viable ethnic community and fewer still believed that they had any special rights that needed protection. Unlike Indians, the Métis had no written treaties with government; they were politically fragmented and lacked an effective organization through which they could articulate demands and rights; they had no land base analogous to that of reserves; they could not boast of any special constitutional status; they had no recognized language that clearly defined their separate ethnicity; and like most others in the province, they already enjoyed full citizenship rights, including the right to vote and consume alcohol. From the perspective of the province, the only trait that defined the Métis collectively was their common poverty, the amelioration of which was the main purpose of government policy. Hence, it seems to have been a foregone conclusion by government that the success of that policy would mean the total assimilation of the Métis. This is why Métis colonies were never given legislative sanction, as Shumiatcher had recommended. They were merely a temporary expedient until the Métis disappeared as a people.

The issue of Métis assimilation also raises a related question: Did the CCF's integration policy mean the assimilation of Indians as well? James Pitsula, in an article dealing with the relationship between the CCF and treaty Indians, argues that this in fact was the case.[5] He maintains that most politicians in the postwar period used the term 'assimilation' in reference to government's goals for Indians but that, in the interest of political correctness, in the late 1950s substituted the word 'integration,' all the while retaining the original meaning.[6] He suggests that the liberal ideas of the CCF were philosophically akin to the Trudeau liberalism expressed in the so-called White Paper of 1969.[7] The latter was a proposed policy statement by the federal Liberal government that was seen in the Indian community across Canada as a racist assault on the very survival of Indian people. The paper called for the dismantling of the Department of Indian Affairs, the formal abolition of Indian status, the repeal of the Indian Act, the breakup of reserves and the transfer of land to Indians as individuals, the abrogation of Indian treaties, and the complete transfer of service delivery to the provinces. As the hallmark of assimilationist policy, the White Paper was rooted in a liberal democratic philosophy that emphasized the sanctity of individual rights and the equality of all people, independent of ethnic or national origins. Theoretically, it stood in complete repudiation of special status and group rights, particularly when legal protection to ethnic minorities overrode the rights of individuals. Thus the White Paper anticipated the day when Indians would be like everyone else, with no special ethnic or national rights but nevertheless would enjoy with other citizens equality under the law. According to Pitsula, the integrationist policies of the CCF government were based on the same political principles and long-term goals as outlined in this 1969 policy statement.[8] He further suggests that in the 1970s, as a result of the massive Indian reaction to the White Paper, liberal integrationist policy aimed at assimilation had become obsolescent and was jettisoned in favour of a new progressive orthodoxy, a policy paradigm emphasizing Indians' inherent right to self-government.[9]

Pitsula is undoubtedly correct in his assessment that CCF policy was based on liberal principles. Among other things, this was underscored in the CCF's precedent-setting provincial Bill of Rights, a document that constitutionally enshrined human or individual rights, as opposed to the ethnic or national rights of Indians. Indeed, the whole debate about the vote, the use of alcohol, and the delivery of social services to Indians was a reflection of the CCF's commitment to extending individual rights and equality to the Indian community. He is also correct that politicians and technocrats – including Morris Shumiatcher – sometimes used the term 'assimilation,' although usually somewhat indifferently and seldom with precise meaning. Nevertheless, Pitsula's interpretation is not entirely convincing and is problematic on a number of accounts.

First, as part of his argument, Pitsula insists that: 'The notion that Indians should constitute a distinct, self-governing entity separate from the rest of the population was completely alien to the Saskatchewan CCF.'[10] The problem with this assertion is that it tends to be ahistorical, in that no one in Canada – not even Indians themselves – saw self-government as giving complete control to reserve residents. During the postwar period, Indians did demand self-government, a fact registered in contemporary newspaper accounts and Indian briefs to Ottawa, but the demand was not based on the comprehensive empowerment associated with the cry for self-determination that existed during the 1970s and today. In substance, what Indians were demanding was a devolution of authority from Indian Affairs whereby Indians would exercise municipal-like powers on reserve. There was little in such a demand that would have troubled the CCF, especially given Douglas's consistent condemnation of the way in which reserves had been administered by Indian Affairs in the past and the fact that such a transfer of powers would have been consistent with the authority exercised by municipalities elsewhere in the province. Indeed, Morris Shumiatcher, it will be recalled, was on record in favouring just such authority for Indians living on reserves as a precondition to their playing a role in provincial society: 'The Indian must first be free to develop his own culture and not merely to imbibe ours; to learn his own history, and not to rely on our interpretation of it; to practice his own religion, and not to be coerced into another; to devise his own means to self-government, and not be cowed by ours.'[11] What Shumiatcher was saying was completely consistent with the American New Deal emphasis on Indian cultural renewal and local self-government. It is also a far cry from the assimilationist policies of the White Paper. If assimilation were the goal of CCF policy, why would the main policy advisor to Douglas and the cabinet support Indian cultural integrity and political self-determination?

Second, Pitsula points to a 1959 speech by Douglas, delivered to the Regina Welfare Council, in which the premier questioned the value of reserves: 'Reservations are becoming insufficient to hold the increasing Indian population. The solution is for the Indian to integrate into white society.'[12] It is certainly true that Douglas and others questioned the value of reserves, but the premier was not recommending to the Regina Council the wholesale dismantling of reserves, as would the White Paper. He believed that integration ultimately would mean that Indians would pay taxes and receive service like anyone else – as is often the case of off-reserve Indians today – but he insisted that, were Indians to leave the reserve, the process would be entirely voluntary. As he put it, 'this is not the kind of thing you can force on people.'[13] Douglas knew full well that Indian reserves were a precious treaty right, jealously guarded by Indians and sanctioned by federal legislation, and he also knew that any recommendation on his part to end reserves would have jeopardized his relationship with the Indian community. His main concern, based on empirical evidence, was that reserves were not economically viable. This was the message communicated in the Saskatchewan submission to the 1959 federal JCSHC and one borne out by the acceleration of Indian migration to the cities throughout the 1950s and afterwards. What Douglas was concerned about, and seemingly expressed to the Regina Council, was that once Indians had left the reserve, they would need the employment skills, citizenship rights, and services that would place them on an equal footing with others and make them competitive in the job market.

Whether this necessarily meant that Indians ultimately would be assimilated was never made explicit by Douglas or anyone else in the CCF and seems unlikely. Today, Indians not only support the notion of integration but also demand it as a function of Aboriginal rights and the fact that some 50 percent of Indians in Saskatchewan now live off the reserve. They insist on being players in mainstream society and making a contribution to provincial development, a fact recently mirrored in the creation of Indian reserves in cities by rural-based bands. They want to participate, however, not as brown white-men but as Indians with a unique culture and national rights. There is no indication that such a goal was ever repudiated by Douglas or out of step with what Douglas was proposing for both on- and off-reserve Indians. Indeed, it is entirely in keeping with what Shumiatcher was alluding to when he argued the importance of Indian cultural integrity and self-government as a pre-condition of integration.

Third, and perhaps the strongest evidence that CCF integration policy did not necessarily mean assimilation for Indians, was the fact that the CCF made no attempt to undermine the foundations on which the special status and collective rights of Indians existed. Were Indian assimilation the goal of CCF policy, it is hard to believe that Douglas would have supported the creation of a provincial Indian association, knowing full well that its only raison d'être was the enhancement of Indian ethnicity and the protection of Aboriginal and treaty rights. This objective was enshrined in the USI constitution and in briefs to Ottawa, and John Tootoosis and other Indian leaders seldom let anyone forget it; and yet Douglas until the very end of his tenure in office continued to embrace the union and later the FSI with moral, political, and financial support.

It is true that John Sturdy saw Treaty 4 as an 'insurmountable road-block' to Indian progress and called for its removal,[14] but his was a voice in the wilderness. For the most part, the CCF was steadfast in support-ing Indian demands that nothing be done to undermine Indian treaties. Indicative is the fact that, in his message to Indian delegates at the Saska-toon conference where the USI was created, Douglas was unequivocal in his support of special Indian rights. As he put it: 'This conference is called by the representatives of the people of Saskatchewan, who wish to sup-port you in your claims for the fulfillment of your Treaty Rights, and the establishment of a better life for you in this Province and throughout Canada.'[15] Seemingly in Douglas's mind, the honouring of Indian treaties and a better life for Indians were not only compatible but also inexorably linked. The importance of treaties was also enshrined in the government's 1946 publication of the Saskatoon conference proceedings. Particularly revealing was the fact that the printed minutes of those meetings were preceded by a copy of Alexander Morris's account of the negotiation and texts of Treaties 3 and 4; and that the compiler of the information was none other than Douglas himself![16] Likewise, in the mid-1950s, it will be recalled, Bill Berezowsky introduced into the Saskatchewan Assembly two resolutions calling for upgraded services for Indians on a par with those enjoyed by other citizens; both were based on the proviso that this would be done 'without abrogation or loss of their [Indian] hereditary or treaty rights,' and both passed the house unanimously.[17] And throughout the entire citizenship debate, Douglas and others went out of their way to reassure Indians that the vote and liquor privileges would in no way undermine or endanger treaties. In a keynote address at the 1958 Fort Qu'Appelle conference of Indians, for example, Douglas insisted that the franchise in no way imperilled the inviolate nature of Indian treaties:

'I want to begin by saying that I believe the central strong point of the Indian life in Saskatchewan and in Canada lies in the treaties which you have with the Great White Queen. Nothing which we are suggesting to you is intended to weaken those treaties ... They were signed in good faith. They are to last as long as the sun shines and the rivers flow.'[18] Evidently, the CCF saw no contradiction whatsoever in granting Indians liberal democratic rights on the one hand and honouring treaties as the bedrock of Indian collective and ethnic rights on the other.

In essence, at least where Indians were concerned, the stated policy objective of the CCF was integration, not assimilation, and at the time that was what was meant. A careful reading of the manuscript material covering the CCF era leaves the unmistakable impression that the CCF leadership was extremely sensitive about the whole issue of people's rights, whether of an individual or collective nature; it also clearly contradicts any suggestion that Douglas was either personally or ideologically moti-vated to attack Indian ethnicity and special status. Unlike that of the Métis, the special status of treaty Indians was acknowledged by almost everyone and the CCF was no exception. There was little in the govern-ment's Indian policies that would tie it intellectually to the mean-spirited and destructive nature of the later White Paper, nor is there evidence that the Douglas government ever lobbied the federal government for the abolition of the Indian Act, treaties, or special Indian status. Pitsula in fact admits as much, but suggests that the CCF was prepared to wait for Indians to assimilate voluntarily in order for them to receive the benefits of full citizenship.[19] Why Indians would do so, particularly when the government urged them to accept citizenship without requiring that they surrender their special status, is not made explicit by Pitsula. The fact nevertheless remains that there was nothing in the actions of the CCF that would marry CCF policy to the intentions of the White Paper.

To argue otherwise is to ignore a related fact, namely that the CCF never endorsed the assimilationist Indian policies put in place in the United States in the postwar period. At the precise moment that the CCF was fashioning its own reform program, Americans were systematically dismantling the New Deal reforms in favour of a new policy known as Indian 'termination.' The policy sought to cancel Indian status and federal responsibility for Indians, to end all treaty obligations to Indians and settle outstanding land claims, to wipe out reserves as anomalous political enclaves in the States, to eradicate tribal governments, and, in effect, to absorb Indians into the American melting pot.[20] If, in fact, the goal of CCF policy had been to assimilate Indians, one would have thought the American example would have provided a convenient and timely justification for assaulting Indian status and group rights in Saskatchewan. But termination, as the intellectual precursor of the White

Paper, was never viewed by the CCF as something worth imitating. To the extent that the American experience had any relevance whatsoever, Shumiatcher and Douglas familiarized themselves with the New Deal reforms of the 1930s, not with the termination policies of the 1950s. Within that context, the continuity in policy was not between that of the CCF and the White Paper of 1969, as Pitsula has argued; rather, it was between the CCF policies and what Pitsula has described as the new progressive orthodoxy of the 1970s. The common thread tying the CCF era to the post-White Paper period was that integration for Indians (although not for the Métis) meant integration, not assimilation.

It was under the umbrella of CCF integrationist reform that the precursor to the modern-day Federation of Saskatchewan Indian Nations was born. Certainly the Douglas government did not create the Union of Saskatchewan Indians, nor did it dominate its agenda, although it made efforts to do so. The USI was organically linked to an Indian rights movement that ran deep in the Indian psyche and can be traced back to the early reserve period in western Canada. Nevertheless, the Douglas government deserves some credit for fostering an organization meant to be an effective voice for the province's Indian people. Unlike in other jurisdictions, such as Alberta, the CCF created a political climate that actually nurtured the right of Indians to organize politically, and it did so in a way and to an extent that was unprecedented. The result was the creation of an Indian federation that would play a leadership role in the Indian self-government movement that would last right up to the present.

The CCF was not a saviour of Native people and in some cases its policies proved to be destructive of Native interests. But the Douglas regime is nevertheless historically important. It was the first government in Saskatchewan to attempt to integrate Native people into provincial society and it did so with an intensity and sincerity that makes the CCF's efforts remarkable by any standard. Driven by postwar ideology and a burning sense of social justice seldom seen in government, the Douglas regime was determined to confront the problems tormenting Native society, at least as it saw them. In doing so, the CCF elevated Native issues to an entirely new level of public consciousness in Saskatchewan. That the government's policies would be judged wanting by the standards of today's discourse on Aboriginal self-government is testimony to the fact that leaders like Douglas, Shumiatcher, and Sturdy, although progressive thinkers in their own day, were nevertheless men of their times and bound by limitations imposed by existing social understanding. This should not obscure the reality, however, that in their own day these men attempted to do what others had ignored.

Notes

Introduction

1 Douglas was first elected to the House of Commons where, despite his status as a mere freshman in politics, he did battle with such giants as Mackenzie King and R.B. Bennett, both of whom came to respect and like Douglas. A few years later, an Ottawa correspondent wrote of Douglas that 'all in all, he's the best debater we have in the House.' Cited in Chris Higginbotham, 'The Tommy Douglas Story,' Public Archives of Canada, T.C. Douglas Papers, vol. 135, file 5.

2 For a fairly extensive bibliography on the CCF in Saskatchewan, see Anne Scotton, ed., *Bibliography of All Sources Relating to the Co-operative Commonwealth Federation and the New Democratic Party in Canada* (n.p.: Woodsworth Archives Project 1977), 149-96; and Lawrence Glen Thompson, 'The CCF/NDP in Saskatchewan: A Case Study of Social Democracy' (MA thesis, University of Regina 1986), 192-209.

3 S.M. Lipset, *Agrarian Socialism: The Cooperative Commonwealth Federation in Saskatchewan: A Study in Political Sociology* (Berkeley: University of California Press 1950; reprint 1968 and 1971).

4 Ibid., 355.

5 The discussion of Silverstein is taken from ibid., 452-4, 456.

6 Robert Tyre, *Douglas in Saskatchewan: The Story of a Socialist Experiment* (Regina: Mitchell Press 1962).

7 Ibid., 4, 41.

8 Doris French Shackleton, *Tommy Douglas* (Toronto: McClelland and Stewart 1975).

9 Ibid., 199.

10 Thomas H. McLeod and Ian McLeod, *Tommy Douglas: The Road to Jerusalem* (Edmonton: Hurtig Publishers 1987).

11 Shackleton, 200-7.

12 One example is the fact that Shackleton, on page 205, implies that Douglas first met Dan Kennedy after a pipe ceremony on the Assiniboine Reserve near Montmartre. The Douglas Papers, however, indicate that the two men first met weeks before that event and that it was at that initial meeting that Kennedy invited Douglas to attend the pipe ceremony. See Saskatchewan Archives Board, T.C. Douglas Papers, Files of the Premier, 'Indians,' file XLV.864 a(49), C.C. Williams to T.C. Douglas, 12 July 1945.

13 An example is the work of Murray Dobbin. In 1978, Dobbin published an account of the Métis Society and, three years later, a book entitled *One-and-a-Half Men*, focusing on the lives and careers of two Métis patriots, Jim Brady and Malcolm Norris. Both men were instrumental in organizing and mobilizing Native communities in Alberta and Saskatchewan and both, for a time, worked among Native groups of the North as employees of the CCF government. Dobbin also published a short article on the CCF's policies in the North, as well as a couple of two-page commentaries recapping much of the content of the article. In his work, Dobbin makes no secret of either his own leftist

political sympathies or the fact that he was personally disappointed with what he described as the CCF's continuation of the neo-colonial policies of previous governments. Generally, the material is well researched and worthwhile, but limited in scope and application. The book, for example, treats the CCF as merely incidental to the lives of Brady and Norris. The article on the North is only thirty-odd pages in length and tends to over-simplify northern developments, while naturally saying nothing about Indian policy or about Native society in the southern portion of the province. More recently, James Pitsula wrote two articles addressed to the relationship between the CCF and Saskatchewan Indians. Both are well researched and thoughtful, but are also problematic. The author tends to give too much credit to the CCF in the organization of the provincial Indian organization; he focuses exclusively on Indian issues and fails to appreciate the extent to which and the ways in which Métis issues impacted on the government's Indian policy; and his conclusion that the CCF's Indian reform was basically assimilationist is questionable. See Murray Dobbin, 'The Saskatchewan Métis Society – 1935-1950 [in four parts],' *New Breed* (August 1978; September 1978; October 1978; November-December 1978); *One-and-a-Half Men: The Story of Jim Brady and Malcolm Norris, Métis Patriots of the Twentieth Century* (Vancouver: New Star Books 1981); 'Prairie Colonialism: The CCF in Northern Saskatchewan, 1944-1964,' *Studies in Political Economy* 16 (1985): 7-40; 'CCF-NDP Northern Policies Continuation of Neo-Colonialism,' *Briarpatch* 12, no. 10 (1983): 17-19; and James M. Pitsula, 'The Saskatchewan CCF Government and Treaty Indians, 1944-64,' *Canadian Historical Review* 75, no. 1 (1994): 21-51; 'The CCF Government and the Formation of the Union of Saskatchewan Indians,' *Prairie Forum* 9, no. 2 (1994): 131-51.

14 See the comments by Silverstein above.

15 Arthur K. Davis, 'The Saskatchewan CCF: The Unfinished Battle for the Shire,' unpublished manuscript in Public Archives of Canada, T.C. Douglas Papers, vol. 152, file 16.2, 18.

16 Ibid., 18, 25.

17 This conclusion is based on the popular vote. In the election of 1960, when the CCF was still led by Douglas, the party received 40.8 percent of the vote; in 1964, after Douglas's departure, it still captured 40.3 percent, while the Liberals, who won the election, got a 40.4 percent endorsement. As one columnist observed, 'The Saskatchewan people defeated the CCF, not decisively but almost reluctantly, with a trace of regret that will be felt in many a non-Socialist heart across Canada.' See the voting patterns outlined in Davis, 'Saskatchewan CCF,' 5. The quotation is by Don McGillivray, 'Era Ends on the Plains,' *Ottawa Citizen*, 23 April 1964.

18 Pitsula, 132.

19 Saskatchewan Archives Board, T.C. Douglas Papers, Files of the Premier, 'Indians,' file XLV.864 E(49), to Dear Candidates from John H. Sturdy, 15 April 1960.

Chapter 1: Historical Setting

1 F. Laurie Barron, 'A Summary of Federal Indian Policy in the Canadian West, 1867-1984,' *Native Studies Review* 1, no. 1 (1984): 28.

2 Ibid.

3 John L. Taylor, 'Canada's Northwest Indian Policy in the 1870s: Traditional Premises and Necessary Innovations,' in *Spirit of the Alberta Treaties,* ed. Richard Price (Montreal: Institute for Research on Public Policy 1980), 3, 7.

4 See Andre N. Lalonde, 'Colonization Companies and the North-West Rebellion,' in *1885 and After: Native Society in Transition,* ed. F. Laurie Barron and James B. Waldram (Regina: Canadian Plains Research Center 1986), 53-65; also Donald McLean, '1885: Métis Rebellion or Government Conspiracy?' in Barron and Waldram, eds., *1885 and After,* 79-104.

5 The *Manitoba Act* of 1870, by which Manitoba was admitted to Confederation, clearly stated in Section 31 that lands were granted to the Métis of that province in acknowledgment of their Aboriginal status. Later, Macdonald denied that Aboriginal rights had been recognized in the Act and insisted that the land grants were simply a policy to 'put down turbulent feelings' in Manitoba. See Joe Sawchuk, *The Métis of Manitoba: Reformulation of an Ethnic Identify* (Toronto: Peter Martin Associates 1978), 32-3.

6 Lalonde, 54-5.

7 Peter Cumming and Neil Mickenberg, eds., *Native Rights in Canada* (Toronto: Indian-Eskimo Association of Canada 1977), 149, 167-8.

8 Barron, 29.

9 John L. Tobias, 'Indian Reserves in Western Canada: Indian Homelands or Devices for Assimilation,' *Approaches to Native History in Canada: Papers of a Conference Held at the National Museum of Man, October 1975*, ed. D.A. Muise (Ottawa: National Museum of Man 1977).

10 The rations program and implications are discussed in F. Laurie Barron, 'Indian Agents and the North-West Rebellion,' in Barron and Waldram, eds., *1885 and After*, 148.

11 F. Laurie Barron, 'The Indian Pass System in the Canadian West, 1882-1935,' *Prairie Forum* 13, no. 1 (1988): 25-42.

12 John L. Tobias, 'Canada's Subjugation of the Plains Cree, 1879-1885,' *Canadian Historical Review* 64, no. 4 (1983): 536-42.

13 Ibid., 538-46.

14 McLean, 79-104.

15 Ibid.

16 Tobias, 546-8.

17 Diane Payment, 'Batoche after 1885, a Society in Transition,' in Barron and Waldram, eds., *1885 and After*, 173-87.

18 Ibid., 179-84.

19 Ibid., 179.

20 This phrase not infrequently appears in the title or subtitle of books on the Métis, especially in reference to Manitoba. See D. Bruce Sealey and Antoine S. Lussier, *The Métis: Canada's Forgotten People* (Winnipeg: Manitoba Métis Federation Press 1975).

21 In theory, the federal government issued to the Métis what was known as 'scrip,' a certificate that could be exchanged for land or money, in compensation for the surrender of whatever rights to western lands the Métis may have had; thereafter, the federal government insisted that Métis people, although of Aboriginal ancestry, no longer had any special claims against the government and that, like everyone else, they were merely citizens of the province with all the rights that provincial citizenship implied. By contrast, Section 91(24) of the BNA Act stipulated that the federal government, not the provinces, was responsible for Indians and the lands of Indians. In effect, Indians were deemed to have special Aboriginal status as wards of the federal government.

22 The policies outlined in this paragraph are taken from Barron, 'The Indian Pass System,' 26.

23 See Sarah Carter, 'Two Acres and a Cow: Peasant Farming for the Indians of the Northwest, 1889-1897,' *Canadian Historical Review* 70, no. 1 (1989): 27-52.

24 Indian resistance and the cultural integrity of Indian reserves are described in Barron, 'A Summary of Federal Indian Policy,' 31-3.

25 Barron, 'The Indian Pass System,' 34-7.

26 The opposition to enfranchisement is discussed in Barron, 'A Summary of Federal Indian Policy,' 32-3.

27 Ibid.

28 Noel Dyck, 'An Opportunity Lost: The Initiative of the Reserve Agricultural Programme in the Prairie West,' in Barron and Waldram, eds., *1885 and After*, 133-4.

29 Jean Barman et al., 'The Legacy of the Past: An Overview,' *Indian Education in Canada, volume 1: The Legacy*, ed. Jean Barman et al. (Vancouver: UBC Press 1986), 8-9. Most of the industrial schools were closed between 1914 and 1922, their formal abolition as an administrative category being effected in 1923.

30 Ibid.

31 Arthur K. Davis, 'The Saskatchewan CCF: The Unfinished Battle for the Shire,' unpublished manuscript in Public Archives of Canada, T.C. Douglas Papers, vol. 152, file 16.2, 25.

32 Ibid., 22.

33 Ibid., 24.

34 Ibid.

35 See the discussion of municipalities in the 'Métis Poverty and Government Responses' section of this chapter.

36 The exclusion of Métis children from school for health and other reasons is discussed below in the 'Métis Poverty and Government Responses' section of this chapter.

37 Population data showing the decline in the Native community are discussed below.

38 K.A. MacKirdy et al., eds., *Changing Perspectives in Canadian History* (Toronto: J.M. Dent and Sons 1967), 318.

39 For a discussion of Indian life in the West during the interwar years, see Stan Cuthand, 'The Native Peoples of the Prairie Provinces in the 1920's and 1930's,' in *One Century Later,* ed. Ian A.L. Getty and Donald Smith (Vancouver: UBC Press 1978), 31-42.

40 The actual number of Indian volunteers was much higher than is generally appreciated owing to the fact that many were turned down because of ill health. According to an Indian elder at James Smith reserve, recruitment teams made a point of regularly attending summertime picnics and fairs. He recalled that on one Sunday afternoon alone, some seventeen Indian youths signed up for service, but that subsequently virtually all of them were refused admission for health reasons, usually tuberculosis. This undoubtedly explains why, according to official records, only five war veterans came from that reserve. Respondent A, interviewed on James Smith Reserve as part of a Native Studies 404.6 course project, University of Saskatchewan, March 1987.

41 Cuthand, 31-5.

42 The denial of Native status is nicely illustrated in the case of Métis people living in Manitoba. Jean Lagasse's study cites dominion census figures to the effect that there were fewer 'reported' Métis people in that province in the census years 1886 and 1941 than in 1870. See Jean H. Lagasse et al., *The People of Indian Ancestry in Manitoba,* vol. 3 (Winnipeg: Manitoba Department of Agriculture and Immigration 1958), 54.

43 *General Review and Summary Tables,* vol. 1 of *Eighth Census of Canada, 1941* (Ottawa: Dominion Bureau of Statistics), 222, notes 9, 10.

44 Ibid., 222.

45 Canada's population in 1941 was 11,506,655. Ibid., 239; also see the discussion of the Native population in Doris French Shackleton, *Tommy Douglas* (Toronto: McClelland and Stewart 1975), 200.

46 Saskatchewan Archives Board, T.C. Douglas Papers, Files of the Premier, 'Indians,' file XLV.864 D(49), 'Brief of the Government of Saskatchewan Presented to the Joint Committee of Senate and House of Commons on Indian Affairs (1959),' chap. 2, p. 2.

47 These totals are based on a 1941 population of 13,384, cited in Shackleton, 200; and on the percentages cited in the text of this discussion.

48 'Brief of the Government of Saskatchewan,' chap. 2, p. 3.

49 Ibid.

50 Ibid., 4.

51 Underscoring the urban Native presence was the organization of service councils designed to implement and oversee various training programs for Natives in cities such as Prince Albert and Regina. See the discussion of the conference on Indians and Métis organized by the Regina Welfare Council, in a letter from I. Russell to H.F. Foster, 9 Aug. 1958; Saskatchewan Archives Board, Saskatchewan Social Welfare and Rehabilitation Branch, Métis – General Correspondence, 933 file III 23.

52 See the reference to Reeve Pachel of Orkney to the effect that he 'object[ed] to paying anything in way of relief or medical care for these Métis, claiming they pay no taxes, are squatters and practically transients as they move about so much.' Saskatchewan Archives Board, Douglas Papers, Files of the Premier, 'Métis,' file XL 859 a(44), Report of Dr. F.C. Middleton on the health situation at Crescent Lake (1942), 4.

53 'Indian Half-Breeds Cause Concern,' *Yorkton Enterprise,* 21 January 1943.

54 Ibid.

55 The details of the account are taken from an editorial entitled 'Condition of the Indian Half-Breeds Appalling· Says Magistrate Potter,' *Yorkton Enterprise,* 13 August 1942.

56 Ibid.

57 Ibid.

58 Saskatchewan Archives Board, Douglas Papers, Files of the Premier, 'Métis,' file XL 859 a(44), Special Sanitation Report by J.E. Hockley, 1 February 1943, p. 2.
59 See the memorandum from the Deputy Minister of Health to T.C. Douglas, 25 July 1944; Saskatchewan Archives Board, Douglas Papers, Files of the Premier, 'Métis,' file XL 859 a(44).
60 Cited in the memorandum from F.C. Middleton to the Deputy Minister of Public Health, 9 December 1942; Public Archives of Canada, T.C. Douglas Papers, Files of the Premier, 'Métis,' file XL 859 a(44).
61 The details about the appointment are taken from 'Government Picks Métis Investigator,' *Regina Leader-Post*, 24 April 1938.
62 Cited in Catherine I. Littlejohn, 'The Historical Background of the Indian and Northern Education Program' (Ph.D. diss., University of Calgary 1983), 54.
63 The 1938 estimate is taken from a memorandum addressed to the deputy minister of education, J. H. McKechnie, 26 October 1938; Saskatchewan Archives Board, Department of Education, Ed. Addendum, File 49, Métis Schools. The actual population, however, is difficult to determine. The 1941 census identified only 9,169 Métis in the province, but this statistic is generally recognized as being unreliable. Only three years later, the Métis themselves estimated their population at over 50,000. See Shackleton, *Tommy Douglas*, 200, 202.
64 Saskatchewan Archives Board, Department of Education, Ed. Addendum, File 49, Métis Schools, J.T. Tomlinson to Dr. McKechnie, 17 April 1942.
65 Ibid., Dr. McKechnie to J.T. Tomlinson, 22 August 1942.
66 See the reference to John Ross's intervention below.
67 Saskatchewan Archives Board, Department of Education, Ed. Addendum, File 49, Métis Schools, Director of School District Organization to the Inspector of Schools, 8 October 1939.
68 Ibid.
69 Ibid., Director of School District Organization to the Inspector of Schools, 22 November 1939.
70 The Klan, which was imported from Indiana in 1926, established locals in Regina, Moose Jaw, and a number of smaller communities. The main purpose was to preserve Saskatchewan as an Anglo-Saxon and Protestant domain. The target of the Klan's hatred was the heavy influx of European immigrants, many of whom were Catholic. See W. Calderwood, 'The Rise and Fall of the Ku Klux Klan in Saskatchewan' (Ph.D. diss., University of Saskatchewan 1968).
71 Saskatchewan Archives Board, Department of Education, Ed. Addendum, File 49, Métis Schools, 'Re Métis and the St. Vital RCSSD No. 3.'
72 Ibid., Special Report, 30 July 1943.
73 Saskatchewan Archives Board, T.C. Douglas Papers, Files of the Premier, 'Métis,' R-33.1, File XL 859 a(44), 'Re. Half-Breeds – Crescent Lake.'
74 Saskatchewan Archives Board, Department of Education, Ed. Addendum, File 49, Métis Schools, Special Report, 30 July 1943.
75 Ibid., Superintendent of Schools to Deputy Minister of Education, Re. Pebble Lake SD 316, 28 October 1941.
76 Ibid.
77 Ibid., 'Re. Métis and St. Vital RCSSD No. 3.'
78 Ibid.
79 Ibid.
80 Ibid.
81 Ibid., Deputy Superintendent McKechnie to Hon. Hubert Staines, 15 July 1942.
82 Located thirty-five miles northeast of Meadow Lake, Green Lake was located on the northern fringe of Saskatchewan agricultural settlement. The soil was light and sandy and, at the time, the main crops were oats, barley, and wheat. 'Experiment with Metis,' *Saskatoon Star-Phoenix*, 21 September 1949.
83 Saskatchewan Archives Board, Department of Education, Ed. Addendum, File 49, Métis Schools, Hon. J. Estey to Hon. I. Schultz, 17 June 1941.
84 Ibid., Commissioner G.J. Matte to the Hon. I. Schultz, 19 June 1941.

85 Ibid.
86 Ibid.
87 Ibid.
88 Ibid.
89 Ibid.
90 Archives Deschâtelets, *Indian Missionary Record* [Lebref], November 1945.
91 Historically, the idea of a Métis colony or reserve was closely associated with Catholic missions in the West. During negotiations ending the Riel Resistance in Manitoba, Father Ritchot had broached the idea to Prime Minister Macdonald. Likewise in 1879, Bishop Tache of St. Boniface once more raised the issue, this time with the minister of the interior, as a solution to the destitution of the Métis throughout the West. But the most determined advocate of Métis reserves was the Reverend Albert Lacombe, one of the first Oblates to be sent to the Territories and a man devoted to the welfare of Indians and Métis alike. In support of Métis colonization, Lacombe was able to win over his ecclesiastical superiors, Bishops Langevin and Grandin, and in 1895 he drew up a comprehensive plan, which was forwarded to the federal government. The scheme called for a reserve on which the landless destitute Métis of the West would be relocated, and it included provision for voluntary residence (unlike Indian reserves), usufruct land tenure, government assistance, and an agrarian sedentary existence. Almost immediately, the Ministry of the Interior agreed to the plan and set aside two townships in the vicinity of Egg and Saddle Lakes (modern-day Alberta). The new colony, which Lacombe named Saint Paul-des-Métis, was placed directly under the authority of the Catholic Church. Father Adeodat Therien was appointed resident manager of the project; the Board of Management included Lacombe, the three western bishops, and two lay members appointed by them; and the Episcopal Corporations of the three Catholic dioceses were granted four sections of lease land to support the creation of a residential school. For more than a decade, Saint-Paul struggled for its existence, only to collapse in 1909. But the idea of Métis colonies persisted, especially in ecclesiastical political circles, and it was within that context that the Patterson government inaugurated the Green Lake colony. See G.F.G. Stanley, 'Alberta's Half-Breed Reserve Saint-Paul-des Métis 1896-1909,' *The Other Natives: The Métis*, vol. 2 (Winnipeg: Manitoba Métis Federation Press 1978) 75-107.
92 Archives Deschâtelets, *Indian Missionary Record* [Lebret], November 1945. Saskatchewan Archives Board, Department of Education, Ed. Addendum, File 49, Métis Schools, Commissioner Matte to Hon. I. Schultz, 19 June 1941.
93 Saskatchewan Archives Board, Department of Education, Ed. Addendum, File 49, Métis Schools, Commissioner G.J. Matte to the Hon. I Schultz, 19 June 1941.
94 Ibid.
95 Ibid.
96 Ibid.
97 That Green Lake was meant to achieve municipal status was underscored by the fact that it was later held up as a model to be emulated by Indian bands in making their transition to municipal status. See the report on the Indian-Métis Conference, *Saskatoon Star-Phoenix*, 25 September 1964.
98 The reasoning behind this conclusion, according to the deputy minister of education, was that 'the Métis want to be where there are white people and more or less commotion and stir.' Saskatchewan Archives Board, Department of Education, Ed. Addendum, File 49, Métis Schools, J.H. McKechnie to Hon. J.W. Estay, 13 March 1941.
99 Ibid., 'Re. Métis and St. Vital RCSSD No. 3.'

Chapter 2: The CCF and the Evolution of Métis Policy
1 Thomas H. McLeod and Ian McLeod, *Tommy Douglas: The Road to Jerusalem* (Edmonton: Hurtig Publishers 1987), 107.
2 Murray Dobbin, 'The Saskatchewan Métis Society – 1935-1950,' part 4, *New Breed* (November-December 1978): 11.
3 McLeod and McLeod, 115.
4 Ibid., 112.
5 Ibid., 115.

6 'Resolutions of Convention: Constituencies Offer Many Suggestions to Govt,' *Saskatchewan Commonwealth*, 19 July 1944.
7 Ibid.
8 See the discussion of CCF philosophy and Métis colonies below.
9 Saskatchewan Archives Board, Department of Education, Ed. Addendum, File 49, Métis Schools, Report by M.F.A. Linday, S/Insp., Indian Head Detachment, Regina Sub-Division, 18 May 1944.
10 Ibid.
11 Ibid., F.E. Spriggs, Supt., Asst. CIB Officer, Regina, to Deputy Attorney-General, 31 May 1944.
12 Ibid., L.B. Ring, Director of Child Welfare, to School Attendance Branch, 2 June 1944.
13 Ibid., Sec. Treas. of Rural Municipality of Abernethy, to Chief Attendance Officer, Department of Education, 20 July 1944.
14 Ibid., W.S. Lloyd to Dr. F.C. Middleton, Director of the Division of Communicable Disease, 31 July 1944.
15 Doris French Shackleton, *Tommy Douglas* (Toronto: McClelland and Stewart 1975), 200.
16 Saskatchewan Archives Board, T.C. Douglas Papers, Files of the Premier, 'Métis,' R-33.1, File XL 859 a(44), R.O. Davison, MD, Deputy Minister, to T.C. Douglas, 25 July 1944.
17 Saskatchewan Archives Board, Department of Education, Ed. Addendum, File 49, Métis Schools, Ivan Schultz to Hon. J.W. Estey, 2 June 1941.
18 Saskatchewan Archives Board, T.C. Douglas Papers, Files of the Premier, 'Métis,' R-33.1, File XL 859 b(44), Métis, 13 July 1949, 3.
19 Ibid.
20 Ibid.
21 Cited in T.C. Pocklington, *Alberta Métis Settlements* (Regina: Canadian Plains Research Center 1991), 19.
22 Saskatchewan Archives Board, T.C. Douglas Papers, Files of the Premier, 'Métis,' R-33.1, file XL 859 a(44), J.H. Brockelbank, Minister of Municipal Affairs, to T.C. Douglas, 17 July 1944, re. representations of Mrs. Allary on behalf of the Métis association.
23 See the discussion of the Union of Saskatchewan Indians in Chapter 3.
24 Dobbin, 'The Saskatchewan Métis Society – 1935-1950,' part 1 (August 1978), 16-18.
25 Ibid.
26 Ibid., 16.
27 James M. Pitsula, 'The CCF Government and the Formation of the Union of Saskatchewan Indians,' *Prairie Forum* 19, no. 2 (1994): 134.
28 Ibid.
29 Dobbin, 'The Saskatchewan Métis Society – 1935-1950,' part 2 (September 1978), 11.
30 Ibid., part 2, 11; and part 3 (October 1978), 10.
31 Ibid., part 2, 13.
32 Ibid., part 2, 12.
33 Cited in ibid., part 3, 14.
34 Cited in ibid.
35 Ibid.
36 Cited in ibid., part 1, 18.
37 Ibid., part 3, 12.
38 Cited in ibid., part 1, 18.
39 There is a language spoken by some Métis in both the North and South: Michif today is recognized as a separate and distinctive language melding both Cree and French forms and vocabulary. See Guy Lavallee, 'The Michif French Language: Historical Development and Métis Group Identity and Solidarity,' *Native Studies Review* 7, no. 1: 81-93.
40 Dobbin, 'The Saskatchewan Métis Society – 1935-1950,' part 1, 18.
41 Shackleton, 200.
42 Cited in Dobbin, 'The Saskatchewan Métis Society – 1935-1950,' part 3, 12.
43 Ibid.
44 Ibid., part 3, 13.
45 Ibid.
46 Ibid., part 2, 11; and part 3, 11.

47 Ibid., part 2, 11.
48 Ibid., part 4, 11.
49 Ibid.
50 Ibid.
51 Dobbin has claimed that the underlying reason for the CCF's half-hearted effort to attract the Métis vote was racism. He offers no evidence, however, to support this assertion. See ibid., part 4, 11.
52 Saskatchewan Archives Board, T.C. Douglas Papers, Files of the Premier, 'Métis,' R-33.1, file XL 859 a(44), O.W. Valleau to T.C. Douglas, 21 March 1946.
53 This conclusion was underscored in the creation of the Committee on Minority Groups (CMG). The committee, set up by government in the late 1950s, was designed to plan and coordinate social assistance delivered to disadvantaged minorities, including Native groups. See the discussion of the CMG below in this chapter.
54 See the discussion of schools within the context of Métis colonies below in this chapter.
55 Saskatchewan Archives Board, T.C. Douglas Papers, Files of the Premier, 'Métis,' R-33.1, file XL 859 b(44), James Gray to Harold Chapman, 19 March 1952.
56 Ibid., DeLorande to T.C. Douglas, 12 March 1945.
57 Ibid.
58 Ibid., Delorande to T.C. Douglas, 16 April 1945.
59 Ibid., Valleau to DeLorande, 20 July 1945.
60 Ibid., DeLorande to Bowerman, 20 August 1945; Bowerman to Douglas, 21 August 1945; and Van Eaton to Douglas, 2 September 1945.
61 Ibid., Unaddressed letter from DeLorande, 25 February 1946.
62 Ibid., Douglas's Secretary to Bowerman, 23 August 1945.
63 Ibid., Bowerman to Douglas, 10 September 1945.
64 Ibid., Douglas to Van Eaton and Bowerman, 25 September 1945.
65 Ibid., Douglas to Valleau, 22 November 1945.
66 Ibid., Douglas to Bowerman, 22 November 1945.
67 Ibid., Valleau to Douglas, 21 March 1946.
68 Ibid., Douglas to Bowerman, 22 November 1945.
69 Ibid., Douglas to DeLorande, 15 May 1946.
70 Saskatchewan Archives Board, J.H. Sturdy Papers, M14 file 198, Conference of the Metis of Saskatchewan Proceedings, 30 July 1946, Douglas's Invitation, 18 July 1946. (Hereafter referred to as the Métis Conference, 1946.)
71 A caption, accompanying a photograph published by the *Saskatchewan Commonwealth*, 7 August 1946, estimated the attendance at 40 to 50. However, this is refuted by the list of delegates cited in the proceedings of the conference. See the Métis Conference, 1946, n.p.
72 McLeod and McLeod, 120.
73 Pitsula, 138.
74 'Shumy' enjoyed the distinction of having earned the first doctorate in jurisprudence ever granted by the University of Toronto. In his service to Douglas, he was a jack-of-all-trades and sometimes even acted as chauffeur for the premier.
75 The Métis Conference, 1946, 2.
76 Ibid., 7-16.
77 Ibid., 64-8.
78 Ibid., 67-8.
79 Ibid., 21-3.
80 Ibid., 24.
81 Ibid.
82 Ibid., 37.
83 Ibid., 51.
84 'Publicized Métis Pair Not Official Delegates,' *Saskatchewan Commonwealth*, 4 December 1946.
85 Saskatchewan Archives Board, T.C. Douglas Papers, Files of the Premier, 'Métis,' R-33.1, file XL 859 a(44), Report and Recommendations Submitted to Saskatchewan Provincial Government, by M.W. Knudson and R.O. St. Dennis, 16 November 1946.

86 Ibid., Valleau to C.M. Fines, Provincial Treasurer, 30 December 1946; also 'Publicized Métis Pair Not Official Delegates,' *Saskatchewan Commonwealth*, 4 December 1946.

87 Dobbin, 'The Saskatchewan Métis Society – 1935-1950,' part 4, 14-15.

88 Ibid., 16; see also 'Métis Plan Convention,' *Saskatchewan Commonwealth*, 23 February 1949.

89 There was an instance in 1947 when John Tootoosis, President of the Union of Saskatchewan Indians, sent a letter to Morris Shumiatcher asking for welfare aid for John Kennedy and his wife. Kennedy's father had enfranchised, thereby giving up Indian status, and this meant that Kennedy too was a non-status Indian. His wife was a Métis from Lebret. Given their legal status, the couple normally would have worked through a Métis association, but in light of the demise of the SMS they appealed for assistance through the USI. Ultimately, they received welfare assistance funded entirely by the province. Saskatchewan Archives Board, T.C. Douglas Papers, Files of the Executive Assist, R-33.2 XXII 403 (24-1-11), Tootoosis to Shumiatcher, 1 February 1947; and Shumiatcher to Tootoosis, 1 April 1947.

90 According to the minister of welfare, the federal government's decision that the Métis were a provincial responsibility was generally accepted by all the provinces. Saskatchewan Archives Board, T.C. Douglas Papers, Files of the Premier, 'Métis,' R-33.1, file XL 859 a(44), Valleau to Douglas, 21 March 1946.

91 'Status of Métis Studied at Meeting,' *Regina Leader-Post*, 25 June 1949.

92 Dobbin, 'The Saskatchewan Métis Society – 1935-1950,' part 4, 14. See also Dobbin, 'The Blurry Vision of the CCF-NDP,' *Briarpatch* 12, no. 10 (1983): 18.

93 It was common to dole out relief just before an election and cut it back afterwards, especially in constituencies that had returned an opposition candidate. See the reference to the plight of the Métis in the Lebret area following the election of 1944. Saskatchewan Archives Board, DSWR, T.C. Douglas Papers, Files of the Premier, 'Métis,' R-33.1, file XL 859 a(44), Premier's Office to J. Brockelbank, 18 September 1944.

94 James Pitsula, 'The CCF Government in Saskatchewan and Social Aid, 1944-1964,' *Building the Co-operative Commonwealth: Essays on the Democratic Socialist Tradition in Canada*, ed. J. William Brennan (Regina: Canadian Plains Research Center 1984), 205.

95 Ibid., 205-6.

96 Ibid., 206.

97 Ibid.

98 Ibid., 207.

99 Ibid., 208.

100 Ibid.

101 Ibid., 211.

102 Saskatchewan Archives Board, T.C. Douglas Papers, Files of the Premier, 'Métis,' R-33.1, file XL 859 a(44), Lloyd to Douglas, 21 August 1944.

103 Ibid., Jos. Aubichon to Hon. T.C. Douglas, 25 July 1944.

104 See, for example, Saskatchewan Archives Board, Department of Education, Ed. Addendum, file 49, Métis Schools, G. Matte to Hon. I. Schultz, 19 June 1941.

105 S.M. Lipset, *Agrarian Socialism: The Cooperative Commonwealth Federation in Saskatchewan: A Study in Political Sociology* (Berkeley: University of California Press 1950; reprint 1968 and 1971), 187-8.

106 Arthur K. Davis, 'The Saskatchewan CCF: The Unfinished Battle for the Shire,' unpublished manuscript, in Public Archives of Canada, MG 32 C28, vol. 152, File Davis, 24.

107 Ibid., 25.

108 Dobbin, 'The Saskatchewan Métis Society – 1935-1950,' part 4, 12.

109 Saskatchewan Archives Board, T.C. Douglas Papers, Files of the Premier, 'Métis,' R-33.1, file XL 859 a(44), Shumiatcher to the Minister of Social Welfare, 11 September 1945.

110 Archives Deschâtelets, Province of Manitoba, L 282.M27T 41, Edmund Bridges to Carl P. Frank, 20 January 1945.

111 *Annual Report of the Department of Social Welfare of the Province of Saskatchewan for the Fiscal Year 1955-56* (Regina: King's Printer), 32.

112 *Annual Report of the Department of Social Welfare of the Province of Saskatchewan for the Fiscal Year 1953-4* (Regina: King's Printer), 39.

113 This is only a rough estimate. There were about 1,500 Métis receiving 'direct assistance' in organized areas in 1948, while Green Lake had an estimated population of 850 in 1953. This would place the total figure at slightly less than 2,500, representing approximately 20 to 25 percent of the provincial Métis population by the late 1940s. Saskatchewan Archives Board, T.C. Douglas Papers, Files of the Premier, 'Métis,' R-33.1, file XL 859 b(44), Minutes of Prairie Inter-Provincial Conference, held on 13 July 1949.

114 This is a reference to Lebret.

115 The contrast in perspective is indicated in the 1941 comments of the commissioner of the Northern Areas Branch in reference to the establishment of Green Lake. The commissioner argued that adults could only be educated in gardening and small-scale farming as a supplement to their meager returns in trapping and fishing, and that the only real hope in absorbing the Métis was the education of their children. Saskatchewan Archives Board, Department of Education, Ed. Addendum, file 49, Métis Schools, Commissioner Matte to Hon. Ivan Schultz, 19 June 1941.

116 The importance of an altered curriculum for the Métis had been recognized earlier by the Patterson government in establishing Green Lake. In 1941, the commissioner of the Northern Areas Branch noted how inadequate the regular public school course was where Métis people were concerned. He went on to say that 'it is my hope that a more practical curriculum for the school will be put into effect. I believe it is obvious that what is needed more for these people in the matter of education is moral and manual instruction.' Ibid.

117 At Lebret, for example, small children were bused to the local school in the village where they received a basic education in the three 'Rs,' but teenagers seem to have received very little academic training. According to a DSWR report, the Lebret colony 'provides some instruction in homemaking and health care. It provides training in modern farm methods and helps to develop knowledge, skills and work habits among teen-age boys living on the farm. In view of the increasing mechanization of farm operations the training of teen-agers is aimed at helping the Métis find a place in the economy of the province.' *Annual Report of the Department of Social Welfare of the Province of Saskatchewan for the Fiscal Year 1955-6*, 32.

118 Ibid., 31-2.

119 Saskatchewan Archives Board, T.C. Douglas Papers, Files of the Premier, 'Métis,' R-33.1 XL.859 c(44), Correspondence between John Sturdy and J.S. White, 10/14 June 1954.

120 Ian MacPherson, 'The CCF and the Co-operative Movement in the Douglas Years: An Uneasy Alliance,' in Brennan, 190-1.

121 Ibid.; and John Bennett and Cynthia Krueger, 'Agrarian Pragmatism and Radical Politics,' in Lipset, 355-6.

122 Saskatchewan Archives Board, Sask. Social Welfare – Rehabilitation Branch, Canwood Métis Study, R-85-308 933 file III 1b, 1956 Report by K. Forster, Director of Rehabilitation.

123 Saskatchewan Archives Board, T.C. Douglas Papers, Files of the Premier, 'Métis,' R-33.1 XL.859 c(44), Douglas to Alex Bishop, 4 May 1954.

124 All details of the 1948 revisions in land allotment are taken from Saskatchewan Archives Board, DSWR, Green Lake Project, R85-308 933, file III 30.

125 Saskatchewan Archives Board, Sask. Social Welfare – Rehabilitation Branch, Lebret Co-operative, R85-308 933, file III 40, W. Guthrie to K. Forster, 26 January 1956.

126 Saskatchewan Archives Board, Sask. Social Welfare – Rehabilitation Branch, Lestock Project, R85-308 933, file III 31b, K. Forster to J.S. White, 12 March 1956; and W. Guthrie to K. Forster, 20 December 1956.

127 Ibid., W. Guthrie to K. Forster, 27 September 1957.

128 Ibid., W. Guthrie to K. Forster, 27 January 1956.

129 Ibid., W. Guthrie to K. Forster, 20 December 1956.

130 Ibid., Father Blanchard's Report on the Lestock Project in regard to local meetings held in December 1954.

131 Ibid., W. Guthrie to K. Forster, 27 January 1956.

132 Ibid., W. Guthrie to K. Forster, 27 September 1957.

133 Saskatchewan Archives Board, T.C. Douglas Papers, Files of the Premier, 'Métis,' R-33.1, file XL 859 b(44), James Gray to Harold Chapman, 19 March 1952.

134 In the mid-1940s, the government made provision for an advisory council at Green Lake. The council was to be elected annually by secret ballot and represent the settlement in discussions with the inspector appointed by Municipal Affairs to supervise the community. But the council never functioned according to plan and quickly fell into disuse. A decade later, the lack of a local council figured in DSWR's criticism of the LID Branch's administration of Green Lake: 'there does not appear to be any plan whereby the Métis can participate in planning community life. It was felt that the Métis should have a part in decision-making and planning their future as much of the planning was superimposed on them.' In response, the branch did agree to establish a committee of eight Métis with limited authority over local matters. See *Saskatchewan Commonwealth*, 23 January 1946; and Saskatchewan Archives Board, Sask. Social Welfare – Rehabilitation Branch, Green Lake Project, R85-308 933, file III 30, Report of Pre-Conference Meeting of 26 August 1955; and Report on 1955 Green Lake conference.
135 Saskatchewan Archives Board, Sask. Social Welfare – Rehabilitation Branch, Canwood Métis Study, R85-308 933, file III 1b, 1956.
136 A resolution calling for government loans for business and other purposes was passed unanimously at a Métis convention in Regina in 1949. 'Sturdy Addresses Métis Convention,' *Regina Leader-Post*, 16 July 1949.
137 Saskatchewan Archives Board, Sask. Social Welfare – Rehabilitation Branch, Green Lake Project, R85-308 933, file III 30, R. Talbot to J. White, 16 December 1959.
138 Ibid.
139 There was one case in the Baljennie area where the Métis were used as cheap labour by another Métis who was a large landowner. Saskatchewan Archives Board, Sask. Social Welfare – Rehabilitation Branch, Baljennie Settlers, R85-308 933, file III 2, J. Elliott to Administrator of the LID Branch, 10 February 1955.
140 Ibid.
141 Saskatchewan Archives Board, Sask. Social Welfare – Rehabilitation Branch, Green Lake Project, R85-308 933, file III 30, W. Haggett to K. Forster, 28 October 1953.
142 Ibid., Green Lake (Conference), 3.
143 Ibid.
144 Ibid.
145 Saskatchewan Archives Board, Sask. Social Welfare – Rehabilitation Branch, Métis – General Correspondence, R85-308, file III 23, K. Forster to R. Talbot, 19 April 1960.
146 Ibid.
147 Ibid.
148 Saskatchewan Archives Board, Sask. Social Welfare – Rehabilitation Branch, Green Lake Project, R85-308 933, file III 30, Report by L.E. Brierley RE. Green Lake Community (1955).
149 Ibid.
150 It is ironic that, in 1961, almost at the very moment that colonies were being rejected as a solution to Métis problems, Indian Affairs personnel were investigating the Lebret and Willow Bunch colonies as prototypes for the economic development of Indian reserves. Three years later, the minister of municipal affairs, D.T. McFarlane, suggested to an Indian-Métis conference that the colony of Green Lake should be seen as a model for Indian reserves looking to make the transition to municipalities. See ibid., H. Talbot (Director of Welfare) to J.S. White (Deputy Minister of DSWR), 16 October 1961; and 'Indians Asked to Consider Joining Municipal System,' *Saskatoon Star-Phoenix*, 25 September 1964.
151 Saskatchewan Archives Board, Sask. Social Welfare – Rehabilitation Branch, Métis – General Correspondence, R85-308 933, file III 23, K. Forster to R. Talbot, 19 April 1960.
152 Saskatchewan Archives Board, Sask. Social Welfare – Rehabilitation Branch, Green Lake Project, R85-308 933, file III 30, R. Talbot to J. White, 16 December 1959.
153 Saskatchewan Archives Board, T.C. Douglas Papers, Files of the Premier, 'Métis,' R-33.1 XL.859 c(44), J. White to A. Nicholson, 5 August 1960.

Chapter 3: Provincial Indian Policy
 1 In the census year 1946, the on-reserve population of the province was 13,978, representing a 9 percent increase since the last census year of 1941. For a tabular summary of population growth up to 1956, see the 1959 Indian Affairs Submission of the

Saskatchewan Government to the Joint Committee of the Senate and House of Commons on Indian Affairs, *Minutes of Proceedings and Evidence No. 12* (Ottawa: Queen's Printer and Controller of Stationery 1960), Table 1, 1073. (Hereafter referred to as the 1959 Indian Affairs Submission of the Saskatchewan Government.)

2 Saskatchewan Archives Board, T.C. Douglas Papers, Files of the Premier, 'Indians,' R-33.1, file XL.859 b(44), Minutes of Social Welfare Conference, Regina, 13 July 1949.

3 Ibid.

4 Ibid.

5 Doris French Shackleton, *Tommy Douglas* (Toronto: McClelland and Stewart 1975), 205.

6 Morris Shumiatcher, 'Indian Smoke on the Western Sky,' *Canadian Forum* (March 1946): 283.

7 Ibid. It was also reported that Indian observers at the Sintaluta ceremonies were 'deeply impressed' with the sincerity of the premier. See Saskatchewan Archives Board, T.C. Douglas Papers, Files of the Premier, 'Indians,' file XLV.864, a(49), Zacharias Hamilton to Douglas, 31 July 1945.

8 This policy analysis is based on the general thrust of comments found in the papers of the premier and of other officials. Specifics are discussed in detail in the remainder of the chapter. For an example of the indictment of the federal government, see ibid.

9 Ibid.

10 Arrell Morgan Gibson, *The American Indian* (Toronto: D.C. Heath 1969), 531.

11 Ibid., 539.

12 Ibid., 541.

13 Ibid., 539.

14 Ibid., 550-5.

15 See Saskatchewan Archives Board, T.C. Douglas Papers, Files of the Premier, 'Indians,' R-33.1, file XLV.864 a(49), Douglas to Malcolm Norris, 5 April 1946.

16 Ibid., Department Memo from Shumiatcher to Douglas, 3 January 1946.

17 This conclusion is based on the fact that the Douglas papers focus almost exclusively on what was happening in Canada and contain few references to the American experience. There is no indication whatsoever that the premier actively considered the New Deal reforms as a prototype for action in Canada.

18 Saskatchewan Archives Board, T.C. Douglas Papers, Files of the Premier, 'Indians,' R-33.1, file XLV.864 a(49), Hamilton to Douglas, 31 July 1945.

19 Ibid.

20 Ibid. Both Hamilton and Kennedy were members of the Saskatchewan Historical Society and often co-researched topics pertaining to Indian history.

21 James M. Pitsula, 'The CCF Government and the Formation of the Union of Saskatchewan Indians,' *Prairie Forum* 19, no. 2 (1994): 136.

22 Ibid.

23 Ibid., 137.

24 Ibid.

25 Norma Sluman and Jean Goodwill, *John Tootoosis: A Biography of a Cree Leader* (Ottawa: Golden Dog Press 1982), 148.

26 Ibid.

27 Saskatchewan Archives Board, T.C. Douglas Papers, Files of the Premier, 'Indians,' R-33.1, file XLV.864 a(49), Brief of the Protective Association for the Indians and Their Treaties to the Honorable the Minister of Indian Affairs for Canada, September 1945, 1.

28 Ibid.

29 Sluman and Goodwill, 148.

30 Ibid.

31 Pitsula, 134.

32 Saskatchewan Archives Board, T.C. Douglas Papers, Files of the Premier, 'Indians,' R-33.1, file XLV.864 a(49), Bulletin No. 47, 20 February 1946, League of Nations of North American Indians.

33 Ibid.

34 See ibid., letter of thanks to the premier from Lawrence Twoaxe, Chairman of the League's National Organization Council, for the government's support of the league's meeting in Regina 1946.

35 Ibid., NAIB Grand National Convention Call, 16 July 1945.
36 Ibid.
37 Ibid.
38 See Peter Kulchyski, '"A Considerable Unrest": F.O. Loft and the League of Indians,' *Native Studies Review* 4, nos. 1 and 2 (1988): 95-117.
39 Kulchyski, 100. Most writers argue that the Alberta branch of the league became the Indian Association of Alberta in 1939 (see Kulchyski, 100; and Sluman and Goodwill, 175). However, in a taped interview in 1977, Tootoosis disputes this, arguing that the IAA had that name from the beginning and was distinct from the League of Indians of Alberta. See Saskatchewan Archives Board, Oral History Project 21, Interview of John Tootoosis by Murray Dobbin, 9 November 1977.
40 Sluman and Goodwill, 183.
41 Saskatchewan Archives Board, T.C. Douglas Papers, Files of the Premier, 'Indians,' R-33.1, file XLV.864 a(49), Douglas to Paull, 11 September 1945; Douglas to Lawrence Twoaxe, 29 April 1946.
42 Cited in Special Joint Committee of the Senate and House of Commons on the Indian Act, *Minutes of the Proceedings and Evidence*, no. 20, 9 May 1947, 1054-5. Also cited in Pitsula, 137.
43 'Premier Urges Indians Unite,' *Regina Leader-Post*, 28 December 1945.
44 Ibid.
45 'Saskatchewan Indians Join in One Federation,' *Regina Leader-Post*, 5 January 1946.
46 Ibid.
47 'Indians Form Federation,' *Saskatchewan Commonwealth*, 9 January 1946.
48 The *Saskatchewan Commonwealth* (9 January 1946) reported that Shumiatcher chaired the meeting; however, according to the *Regina Leader-Post* (2 February 1946), the president of the AIS, Joe Dreaver, presided. The accuracy of the former account is confirmed by the Proceedings of the Regina Conference, subsequently published by the Douglas government. See Saskatchewan Archives Board, Indians of North America – Societies, R834 file 37, Union of Saskatchewan Indians, Report of the Establishment of Indian Unity in Saskatchewan, Prepared by T.C. Douglas, March 1946, 48. (Hereafter referred to as Report of ... Indian Unity.)
49 Phelps's comments are cited in 'Indians Form Federation,' *Saskatchewan Commonwealth*, 9 January 1946.
50 This promise was reported in ibid., but does not appear in the abridged proceedings of the meeting.
51 Ibid.
52 Ibid.; and Report of ... Indian Unity, 46.
53 Ibid. See Shumiatcher's briefing notes, entitled 'Indians,' in Saskatchewan Archives Board, T.C. Douglas Papers, Files of the Premier, 'Indians,' R-33.1, file XLV.864 a(49). Also, see Report of ... Indian Unity, 47.
54 'Indians Form Federation,' *Saskatchewan Commonwealth*, 9 January 1946. This comment does not appear in the abridged proceedings.
55 Report of ... Indian Unity, 48.
56 Ibid., 49.
57 Ibid.
58 Ibid.
59 Ibid., 51. The IAA constitution was probably forwarded to Shumiatcher by John Laurie, Secretary of the IAA. The latter was an old friend of Shumiatcher and attended the Regina conference at Shumiatcher's invitation.
60 Report of ... Indian Unity, 52.
61 These resolutions received little attention in the press coverage of the Regina meeting, but were subsequently discussed in reference to the Duck Lake conference. See 'Report on the Indian Meeting at Duck Lake, Sask.,' *Indian Missionary Record Supplement* [Lebret], February 1946. The resolutions were also delineated in the Report of ... Indian Unity, 50-1.
62 This, in fact, was the first resolution debated and passed.
63 'Indians Seeking Plan of Self-Sufficiency,' *Regina Leader-Post*, 2 February 1946.

64 Cited in 'Indians form Federation,' *Saskatchewan Commonwealth*, 9 January 1946. Dreaver's statement is not contained in the abridged publication of the proceedings of the conference.

65 Ibid.

66 'Report on the Indian Meeting at Duck Lake, Sask.,' *Indian Missionary Record Supplement* [Lebret], February 1946.

67 The delegate count was cited in ibid., but seems high. The number cannot be confirmed by the conference proceedings, which list only a selected group included among the total. See Report of ... Indian Unity, 53.

68 Ibid.

69 'Another Indian Pow-Wow Called,' *Regina Leader-Post*, 28 January 1946.

70 'Report on the Indian Meeting at Duck Lake, Sask.,' *Indian Missionary Record Supplement* [Lebret], February 1946.

71 Ibid.

72 Ibid.

73 'Another Indian Pow-wow Called,' *Regina Leader-Post*, 28 January 1946.

74 Saskatchewan Archives Board, T.C. Douglas Papers, Files of the Premier, 'Indians,' R-33.1, file XLV.864 a(49), Douglas to the Reverend W.F. Browne, 18 March 1946.

75 'Another Indian Pow-wow Called,' *Regina Leader-Post*, 28 January 1946.

76 Ibid.

77 Ibid.

78 Saskatchewan Archives Board, T.C. Douglas Papers, Files of the Premier, 'Indians,' R-33.1, file XLV.864 a(49), Shumiatcher's Briefing Notes, entitled 'Indians.' Report of ... Indian Unity, 55-6.

79 Report of ... Indian Unity, 57.

80 Ibid., 61.

81 Ibid.

82 Ibid.

83 Ibid., 62.

84 Ibid., 1.

85 Saskatchewan Archives Board, T.C. Douglas Papers, Files of the Premier, 'Indians,' R-33.1, file XLV.864 a(49), Shumiatcher's Briefing Notes, entitled 'Indians.' Record of ... Indian Unity, 2.

86 Record of ... Indian Unity, 69-70.

87 See, for example, Saskatchewan Archives Board, T.C. Douglas Papers, Files of the Executive Assistant, R-33.2 XXII.401 (24-1-8), Minutes of the Meetings Held by the Oshapawace Band.

88 Within a year of the USI's founding, both these organizations were reported to be inactive, 'their membership having been largely absorbed by the Union.' 'Saskatchewan Indians Are Running Own Show,' *Saskatchewan Commonwealth*, 7 May 1947.

89 Saskatchewan Archives Board, T.C. Douglas Papers, Files of the Premier, 'Indians,' R-33.1, file XLV.864 a(49), League of Nations of North American Indians, Bulletin No. 47, 20 February 1946.

90 Ibid., Norris to Chief Red Eagle, 26 March 1946. It might also be noted that, after moving to Prince Albert, Norris played an active role in the organization of the USI. He became the federation's accredited organizer for the northern part of the province and took an active part in conference deliberations. See Saskatchewan Archives Board, T.C. Douglas Papers, Files of the Executive Assistant, R-33.2, file XXII.396 (24-1-3), Minutes of the Meeting of the Union of Saskatchewan Indians Held at the Board Room of the Grain Building, in the City of Saskatoon, 7-9 January 1948.

91 Pitsula, 131

92 See the criticism of the work of J. Rick Ponting and Roger Gibbons in Kulchyski, 96-7.

93 For a discussion of the Autonomy Movement, see John L. Tobias, 'Canada's Subjugation of the Plains Cree, 1879-1885,' *Canadian Historical Review* 64 (1983): 519-48.

94 Sluman and Goodwill, 191.

95 Cited in ibid., 192.

96 See the discussion of the pass system in chapter 1.

97 Kulchyski, 97-8.
98 Sluman and Goodwill, 138. The same authors also note (p.133) that Indian Affairs seriously considered 'enfranchising' Loft to silence him. In the 1920s and again in the 1930s through to 1951, the Indian Act provided that Indians who could survive in general society could be forcibly enfranchised, a process through which an Indian ceased to be an Indian in a legal sense. Such a person would no longer have Indian status, band membership, or the right to live on a reserve.
99 Saskatchewan Archives Board, T.C. Douglas Papers, Files of the Premier, 'Indians,' R-33.1, file XLV.864 a(49), Boden to Douglas, 24 June 1946.
100 Ibid., Paull to Douglas, 2 October 1946.
101 Ibid.
102 Ibid., Douglas to Paull, 3 October 1946.
103 Ibid.
104 Ibid., Douglas to H.A. Bryson, M.P., 22 November 1957.
105 Ibid., file XLV.864 c(49), Sturdy to Douglas, 5 December 1957.
106 Ibid.
107 1959 Indian Affairs Submission of the Saskatchewan Government, 1029.
108 The mandate of the committee was sanctioned by cabinet in October 1956. Saskatchewan Archives Board, T.C. Douglas Papers, Files of the Premier, 'Indians,' R-33.1, file XLV.864 a(49), Cabinet Memo from Cabinet Secretary to J.H. Sturdy et al., 30 October 1956.
109 Saskatchewan Archives Board, Saskatchewan Social Welfare-Rehabilitation Branch, Provincial Committee on Minority Groups, R-308, 933 file III 24, Report on a Permanent Organization for 'The Provincial Committee on Minority Groups,' 26 January 1960.
110 This membership list was one of the first for the committee and included John Sturdy as chair. Saskatchewan Archives Board, T.C. Douglas Papers, Files of the Premier, 'Indians,' R-33.1 XLV.864 a(49), Dept. Memo from John H. Sturdy to All Cabinet Ministers, 7 December 1959.
111 'Wider Opportunities for Young, Decent Care for Aged, Main Indian Aims,' *Saskatoon Star-Phoenix*, 28 April 1950.
112 Saskatchewan Archives Board, Saskatchewan Social Welfare-Rehabilitation Branch, Provincial Committee on Minority Groups, R85-308, 933 file III 24, Report on a Permanent Organization for the 'Provincial Committee on Minority Groups,' 26 January 1960.
113 1959 Indian Affairs Submission of the Saskatchewan Government, 1029.
114 Saskatchewan Archives Board, Saskatchewan Social Welfare-Rehabilitation Branch, Provincial Committee on Minority Groups, R85-308, 933 file III 24, Report on a Permanent Organization for the 'Provincial Committee on Minority Groups,' 26 January 1960.
115 According to Douglas, provincial involvement was justified not only by practical realities but also by moral right. See Saskatchewan Archives Board, T.C. Douglas Papers, Files of the Premier, 'Indians,' R-33.1, file XLV.864 a(49), Douglas to F.V. Reilly, 26 March 1946.
116 'New Deal for Indians Declared Long Overdue,' *Regina Leader-Post*, 22 March 1946; See also *Regina Leader-Post*, 8 March 1946, Clippings Hansard, vol. 52, Session 1946, 142.
117 *Regina Leader-Post*, 22 March 1946, Clippings Hansard, vol. 52, Session 1946, 174.
118 Ibid.
119 Ibid.
120 Ibid.
121 *Regina Leader-Post*, 8 March 1946, Clippings Hansard, vol. 52, Session 1946, 143.
122 Ibid.
123 'Regina Aids Citizenship for Indians,' *Science Monitor* [Boston], 26 March 1946.
124 *Regina Leader-Post*, 23 March 1946.
125 'Indian Commission Urged by C.C.F. Members,' *Saskatchewan Commonwealth*, 19 June 1946; Dominion of Canada, Official Report of Debates in the House of Commons, 2nd Session – 20th Parliament, vol. 2, 1946 (Ottawa 1946), 1463.
126 Dominion of Canada, *Official Report of Debates in the House of Commons*, 2nd Session – 20th Parliament, vol. 2, 1946 (Ottawa 1946), 1463.

127 Ibid., 1446.
128 Policy, Planning and Research Branch, 'The Historical Development of the Indian Act' (Ottawa: Department of Indian and Northern Affairs Canada 1975), 137.
129 Ibid.
130 Ibid.
131 Special Joint Committee of the Senate and House of Commons Appointed to Examine and Consider the Indian Act, *Minutes of Proceedings and Evidence*, no. 1, Session 1946 (Ottawa 1946), Appendix AX, 879-80.
132 Saskatchewan Archives Board, T.C. Douglas Papers, Files of the Premier, 'Indians,' R-33.1 XLV.864, Balding Eagle (Shumiatcher) to Red Eagle, 31 August 1945.
133 Ibid.
134 Saskatchewan Archives Board, T.C. Douglas Papers, Files of the Executive Assistant, R-33.2, XXII.405 (24-3.1 to 24-3.8), Douglas to Mrs. Jessie Cameron, 1 April 1947.
135 'Indians Explain,' *Regina Leader-Post*, 7 December 1946.
136 Ibid.; and ibid., 9 December 1946.
137 'Saskatchewan Indians Delay Approval of Brief,' *Saskatchewan Commonwealth*, 11 December 1946.
138 Ibid.
139 Affidavit of Harry Bighead, submitted to the Special Joint Committee of the Senate and House of Commons Appointed to Continue and Complete the Examination and Consideration of the Indian Act, *Minutes of the Proceedings and Evidence*, no. 19, 8 May 1947 (Ottawa 1947), 945.
140 Affidavit of John Eyahpaise, ibid., 944.
141 'Indians to Meet Dec. 6 to Ratify Ottawa Brief,' *Regina Leader-Post*, 1 November 1946.
142 Cited in ibid.
143 Ibid.
144 'Saskatchewan Indians Are Running Own Show,' *Saskatchewan Commonwealth*, 7 May 1947.
145 Ibid.
146 Ibid.
147 Ibid.
148 USI Brief, in Special Joint Committee of the Senate and House of Commons Appointed to Continue and Complete the Examination and Consideration of the Indian Act, *Minutes of Proceedings and Evidence*, no. 19, 8 May 1947 (Ottawa 1947), 1000. (Hereafter cited as USI Brief.)
149 Ibid., 974-5, 978-83.
150 'Saskatchewan Indians Are Running Own Show,' *Saskatchewan Commonwealth*, 7 May 1947.
151 USI Brief, 1001.
152 The plagiarism of the IAA brief by the USI undoubtedly reflects the work of Shumiatcher and his association with Laurie. Compare the Alberta brief (21 April 1947) with that of the USI (8 May 1947) in Special Joint Committee of the Senate and House of Commons Appointed to Continue and Complete the Examination and Consideration of the Indian Act, *Minutes of Proceedings and Evidence*, no. 19, 8 May 1947 (Ottawa 1947), Appendix EM, 571-600; and Appendix ES, 969-1002.
153 'Indians to Carry Brief to Ottawa,' *Regina Leader-Post*, 1 May 1947.
154 Ibid.
155 Cited in ibid.
156 Saskatchewan Archives Board, T.C. Douglas Papers, Files of the Premier, 'Indians,' R-33.1, file XLV.864, a(49), Shumiatcher to Castleden, 6 May 1947.
157 Ibid.
158 'Evidence at Ottawa Reveals Opposition to Indian Union,' *Saskatchewan Commonwealth*, 11 June 1947.
159 Ibid.
160 Special Joint Committee of the Senate and House of Commons Appointed to Continue and Complete the Examination and Consideration of the Indian Act, *Minutes of Proceedings and Evidence*, no. 19, 8 May 1947 (Ottawa 1947), 932-42.

161 Ibid., 946.
162 Ostrander was married to A.H. Brass. See 'Speaker Deplores Indians' Low Education Standards,' *Regina Leader-Post*, 1 October 1952.
163 Special Joint Committee of the Senate and House of Commons Appointed to Continue and Complete the Examination and Consideration of the Indian Act, *Minutes of Proceedings and Evidence*, no. 19, 8 May 1947 (Ottawa 1947), 946.
164 Ibid., 956.
165 Dominion of Canada, *Official Report of the Debates of the House of Commons*, 3rd Session – 20th Parliament, vol. 6, 1947 (Ottawa 1947), 5343.
166 Ibid., 5344-5.
167 Ibid., 5344.
168 Ibid.
169 Ibid.
170 See Saskatchewan Archives Board, T.C. Douglas Papers, Files of the Premier, 'Indians,' R-33.1 XLV.864 b(49), Gladys Johnston to Douglas, 18 September 1950.
171 Ibid., Shumiatcher to Albert Eashappie, 14 June 1946.
172 Ibid., John Skeeboss et al. to Chief Red Eagle, 23 July 1953; George Nicotine to Douglas, 3 August 1953.
173 Ibid., Kennedy to Lee, 26 February 1953 and 11 September 1953; Lee to Ochankugahe (Kennedy), 14 September 1953 and 6 October 1953.
174 All details of this incident are taken from 'Indians in Movie Start Off Hungry,' *Regina Leader-Post*, 4 October 1960.
175 The content of the resolutions is found in Saskatchewan Archives Board, T.C. Douglas Papers, Files of the Executive Assistant, R-33.2 XXII.401 (24-1-8), Ochapawace Band, 28 July 1947.
176 Ibid., Shumiatcher to Peter Watson, 4 August 1947.
177 Ibid., Douglas to Glen, 23 October 1947.
178 Ibid., Glen to Douglas, 23 October 1947.
179 Ibid., Douglas to Glen, 31 October 1947.
180 Ibid., Shumiatcher to Peter Watson, 31 October 1947.
181 The title 'Indian agency superintendent' officially replaced the term 'Indian agent' in 1947, but the latter term continued in general usage.
182 Ibid., Peter Watson to Shumiatcher, 11 December 1947.
183 Ibid., Shumiatcher to Keenleyside, 22 June 1948.
184 Ibid., 17 August 1948.
185 Ibid., Shumiatcher to Keenleyside, 8 March 1948, 22 March 1948, 3 May 1948, 8 February 1948, 6 April 1949; Shumiatcher to J.P. Ostrander, 1 December 1948.
186 Ibid., MacKinnon to Douglas, 19 July 1948.
187 Ibid.
188 Ibid., Douglas to MacKinnon, 28 July 1948.

Chapter 4: Citizenship Issues
1 Joint Committee of the Senate and House of Commons, Session 1948, Appointed to Continue and Complete the Examination and Consideration of the Indian Act, *Minutes of Proceedings and Evidence*, no. 5, Tuesday, June 22nd (Ottawa 1948), 187. Acting on the recommendations of the 1947 committee, the JCSHC was reconstituted with the same orders of reference that had been true of the 1946 and 1947 committees. Unlike its predecessors, however, the new committee was more interested in examining the suggestions and recommendations of the two previous committees than in conducting a new investigation. As a consequence, it held fewer meetings and called fewer witnesses, its meetings were held in camera, and its discussions were not printed in the minutes.
2 For a complete list of the recommendations, see ibid., 187-90.
3 'Junior Red Cross Profits from Its Indian Members,' *Regina Leader-Post*, 11 March 1957.
4 For a discussion of the way in which the Indian Act prescribed an inferior status for Indians, see Chief Joseph Dreaver, 'Far Short of Expectations,' ibid., 30 November 1950.
5 The details of the trial are taken from 'Indians on Jury Question Raised,' ibid., 13 January 1959.

6 Cited in ibid.
7 Ibid.
8 Saskatchewan Archives Board, T.C. Douglas Papers, Files of the Premier, 'Indians,' R-33.1, file XLV.864 a(49), Kennedy to Douglas, 17 February 1956.
9 Dan Kennedy, 'Firewater or a Vote,' *Regina Leader-Post*, 27 May 1949.
10 Saskatchewan Archives Board, T.C. Douglas Papers, Files of the Premier, 'Indians,' R-33.1, file XLV.864 a(49), Douglas to Kennedy, 23 February 1956.
11 Ibid., news release citing portions of Douglas's speech delivered to the 1959 annual meeting of FSI, 22 October 1959.
12 Joint Committee of the Senate and House of Commons on Indian Affairs, *Minutes of the Proceedings and Evidence,* no. 12, 16 and 17 June 1960, 1032.
13 Ibid., 1033.
14 Ibid.
15 Ibid., 1048.
16 Ibid., 1034.
17 Ibid.
18 Ibid., 1043-4.
19 Ibid., 1044.
20 Ibid., 1051.
21 Ibid., 1071.
22 Ibid.
23 Victor Mackie, 'The Indian's Right to Vote,' *Saskatoon Star-Phoenix,* 6 March 1947.
24 V.J. Mackie, 'Vote Right for Indians Not Hindered Federally,' *Regina Leader-Post*, 3 March 1947.
25 Ibid.
26 Ibid.
27 'Indians to Vote?' *Regina Leader-Post*, 25 February 1947.
28 Saskatchewan Archives Board, T.C. Douglas Papers, Files of the Premier, 'Indians,' R-33.1, file XLV.864 a(49), Douglas to Ian B. Wilson, 26 January 1948.
29 The entire account of the Sintaluta protest is taken from 'Franchise Proposition is Opposed by Indians,' *Regina Leader-Post*, 12 March 1947.
30 Ibid.
31 Ibid.
32 For a discussion of the confusion over the two terms, consult Joint Committee of the Senate and House of Commons on Indian Affairs, *Minutes of the Proceedings and Evidence,* no. 12, 16 and 17 June 1960, 1041.
33 Saskatchewan Archives Board, T.C. Douglas Papers, Files of the Premier, 'Indians,' R-33.1, file XLV.864 d(49), News Release: Douglas Speaks to Conference of Sask. Indian Chiefs, 22 October 1959.
34 Saskatchewan Archives Board, T.C. Douglas Papers, Files of the Executive Assistant, R-33.2, XX11.396 (24-1-3), Shumiatcher to Dr. H.L. Keenleyside, 10 February 1948.
35 Ibid., News Release: Saskatchewan Indians Object to Vote, 7 May 1948.
36 Mrs. A.N. Wetton, 'Indians Oppose Treaty Changes,' *Saskatoon Star-Phoenix,* 9 April 1949.
37 Ibid.
38 Ibid.
39 Interview of Leona Tootoosis by author, University of Saskatchewan, 9 January 1995.
40 'Wider Opportunity for Young; Decent Care for Aged,' *Saskatoon Star-Phoenix*, 28 April 1950.
41 Ibid.
42 Ibid.
43 Ibid.
44 Ibid.
45 Cited in Policy, Planning and Research Branch, 'The Historical Development of the Indian Act' (Ottawa: Department of Indian and Northern Affairs Canada 1975), 160.
46 Ibid., 159.
47 *Dominion of Canada, Official Reports of the Debates in House of Commons*, 2nd Session, 21st Parliament, vol. 4, 1950, Indian Act – Consolidation and Clarification – Band Funds and Expenditures etc. (Ottawa 1950), 3946.

48 Cited in ibid.
49 Chief Joseph Dreaver, 'Far Short of Expectations,' *Regina Leader-Post,* 30 November 1950.
50 Saskatchewan Archives Board, T.C. Douglas Papers, Files of the Premier, 'Indians,' R-33.1, file XLV.864 b(49), John Laurie to Douglas, 9 September 1950.
51 'Indians Raps Short Confab,' *Saskatoon Star-Phoenix,* 1 November 1950.
52 Policy, Planning and Research Branch, 'The Historical Development of the Indian Act' (Ottawa: Department of Indian and Northern Affairs Canada 1975), 162.
53 Dominion of Canada, *Official Report of the Debates in the House of Commons,* 4th Session, 21st Parliament, vol. 4, 1950, Summary of the Proceedings of a Conference with Representative Indians Held in Ottawa, Feb. 28–Mar. 3, 1951 (Ottawa 1950), Appendix B, 1364.
54 Ibid.
55 Policy, Planning and Research Branch, 'Historical Development of the Indian Act' (Ottawa: Department of Indian and Northern Development, 1975), 164.
56 *The Indian Act, Statutes of Canada,* chapter 29, vol. 1, 1950-51, 3rd Session, 21st Parliament (Ottawa 1951), 156-73.
57 Hon. F.G. Bradley (Secretary of State), Dominion Elections Act, *Official Report of Debates in the House of Commons,* Second Session – Twenty First Parliament, vol. 4, 1950 (Ottawa 1950), 3811.
58 Mr. Gibson, Indian Act, *House of Commons Debates Official Report,* Fourth Session – Twenty-First Parliament, vol. 4, 1951 (Ottawa 1951), 3069.
59 M.J. Coldwell, Dominion Elections Act, *Official Report of Debates in the House of Commons,* Second Session – Twenty First Parliament, vol. 4, 1950 (Ottawa 1950), 3810.
60 *The Indian Act, Statutes of Canada,* chapter 29, vol. 1, 1950-51, 3rd Session, 21st Parliament (Ottawa 1951), sect. 95 (1), 164.
61 'I Wish Liquor Could Be Abolished, ... ' *Regina Leader-Post,* 30 November 1951.
62 'Equal Privileges Proposed,' *Regina Leader-Post,* 7 April 1959.
63 Saskatchewan Archives Board, T.C. Douglas Papers, Files of the Premier, 'Indians,' R-33.1, file XLV.864 b(49), Andrew Paull to Douglas, 25 August 1951.
64 See ibid., Robert Lightle to Douglas, 25 March 1952.
65 'I Wish Liquor Could Be Abolished, ... ' *Regina Leader-Post,* 30 November 1951.
66 Ibid.
67 Saskatchewan Archives Board, T.C. Douglas Papers, Files of the Premier, 'Indians,' R-33.1, file XLV.864 b(49), President of the Hotel Association to J.W. Corman, 23 September 1951.
68 The new Indian Act was designed to encourage integrated schools on a cost-sharing basis. See ibid.
69 Saskatchewan Archives Board, T.C. Douglas Papers, Files of the Premier, 'Indians,' R-33.1, file XLV.864 a(49), Douglas to Jessie Cameron, 6 June 1946.
70 Department of Indian Affairs and Northern Resources, *Indians of the Prairie Provinces (an Historical Overview)* (Ottawa: Indian Affairs Branch 1967), 21.
71 'Govt. Silent about Implementing Indian Affairs Committee Report,' *Saskatoon Star-Phoenix,* 23 March 1949.
72 Ibid.
73 *The Indian Act, Statutes of Canada,* chapter 29, vol. 1, 1950-51, 3rd Session, 21st Parliament (Ottawa 1951), sect. 113 a, b, 169. See also 'Joint Education Progress Possible,' *Regina Leader-Post,* 14 June 1950.
74 *The Indian Act, Statutes of Canada,* chapter 29, vol. 1, 1950-51, 3rd Session, 21st Parliament (Ottawa 1951), sect. 120 (1) and (2), 172.
75 'Adventure in Schooling ... ' *Regina Leader-Post,* 10 January 1948.
76 Saskatchewan Archives Board, Saskatchewan Social Welfare – Rehabilitation Branch, Willow Bunch Project Reports, R.85-308 933, file III 41, Sturdy to Walter Harris, 16 May 1952.
77 'Superintendent Hits Indian Segregation,' *Regina Leader-Post,* 6 November 1956.
78 Ibid.
79 Dominion of Canada, *Report of the Department of Citizenship and Immigration, 1949-1950* (Ottawa 1951), 86, 88; ibid., *1954-55* (Ottawa 1956), 76, 78; and ibid., *1960-61* (Ottawa

1962), 108. In 1950, there were 1,542 Indian students in provincial and private schools out of a national Indian student population of 24,951; in 1955, 3,743 out of 28,448 students; and in 1961, 10,822 out of 43,115 Indian students.

80 Ibid. In Ontario, Indian students in provincial and private schools, in grades one to twelve, constituted 8.4 percent of the total provincial Indian enrollment in 1950, 11.6 percent in 1955, and 23.5 percent in 1961; in BC, they represented 10.2 percent in 1950, 22.4 percent in 1955, and 37.7 percent in 1961.

81 Ibid. Levels of Indian student integration in the other Prairie provinces were similar. In 1961, for example, Manitoba had 12.3 percent of its Indian students in provincial and private schools, while the figure in Alberta was 17.5 percent.

82 Saskatchewan Archives Board, Saskatchewan Welfare-Rehabilitation Branch, Willow Bunch Project Reports, A-85-308 933, file III 41, Paul Martin to John Sturdy, 18 April 1952.

83 Ibid.

84 Ibid.

85 Ibid., Sturdy to Martin, 5 April 1952.

86 Ibid.

87 Ibid., Martin to Sturdy, 18 April 1952.

88 Ibid.

89 Ibid., Sturdy to Walter Harris, 16 May 1952.

90 Saskatchewan Archives Board, T.C. Douglas Papers, Files of the Premier, 'Indians,' R-33.1, file XLV.864 b(49), Douglas to Aylmer Liesemer, 19 June 1952.

91 Saskatchewan Archives Board, Saskatchewan Social Welfare-Rehabilitation Branch, Willow Bunch Project Reports, R-85-308 933, file III 41, George Davidson to J.S. White, 23 June 1952.

92 Ibid., Harris to Sturdy, 4 July 1952.

93 Ibid.

94 Ibid.

95 Ibid.

96 Ibid., J.S. White to George Davidson, 17 July 1952.

97 Ibid., J.S. White to George Davidson, 6 August 1952.

98 Ibid., Record of Meetings between Representatives of the Indian Affairs Branch and the Department of Social Welfare and Rehabilitation Held in Regina, 23 and 24 October 1952.

99 Ibid.

100 Ibid., White to Jones, 6 November 1953.

101 Ibid.

102 Ibid.; also, White to Jones, 26 March 1953.

103 Saskatchewan Archives Board, T.C. Douglas Papers, Files of the Premier, 'Indians,' R-33.1, file XLV.864 b(49), Douglas to L.E. Bruce, 14 April 1952.

104 Ibid., file XLV.864 c(49), E.D. Fulton to W.P. Thompson, 3 December 1957. See Jean H. Lagasse et al., *The People of Indian Ancestry in Manitoba*, 3 vols. (Winnipeg: Manitoba Department of Agriculture and Immigration 1958).

105 Ibid., Diefenbaker to Douglas, 26 February 1959.

106 Ibid.

107 Ibid., 1063-4.

108 Ibid., 1064.

109 Ibid.

110 Ibid., 1066.

111 Ibid.

112 Ibid., 1064.

113 Ibid., 1066.

114 'Native Canadians without Franchise,' *Saskatchewan Commonwealth*, 12 February 1958.

115 'Frank Calder M.L.A. Winnipeg Visitor,' *Saskatchewan Commonwealth*, 9 December 1953.

116 'Officials Will Not Face Problems of Indians, Frank Calder Declares,' *Saskatchewan Commonwealth*, 2 December 1953.

117 Ibid.

118 Legislative Assembly of Saskatchewan, *Debates and Proceedings,* vol. 11, 12th Legislature, 4th Session, 23 February 1956 (Regina 1956) 34. 'MLA Seeks Votes for Treaty Indians,' *Regina Leader-Post,* 15 February 1956.
119 'Sask. Moves for Better Deal for Indians,' *Saskatchewan Commonwealth,* 14 March 1956.
120 'Indians Will Discuss Questions on Liquor,' *Regina Leader-Post,* 13 August 1956.
121 *Act to Amend the Indian Act, Statutes of Canada,* vol. 1, 4-5 Eliz. II, 1956, chapter 40 (Ottawa 1956), sect. 95 (1, 2, 3), 292. See also 'Changes in Indian Affairs,' *Saskatoon Star-Phoenix,* 16 August 1956.
122 Ibid.
123 'Gov't to Confer on Liquor Rights,' *Regina Leader-Post,* 5 July 1956.
124 See a letter from William Van Vliet to the premier. Mr. Vliet claimed to have been a member of the CCF from the beginning of the party and, before that, a member of the Progressives. He nevertheless 'almost came to the conclusion of resigning [from the party] on account of the stance taken by the C.C.F. in regard to giving our Indian friends the right to attend beer parlors ... ' Saskatchewan Archives Board, T.C. Douglas Papers, Files of the Premier, 'Indians,' R-33.1, file XLV.864 e(49), 29 September 1960.
125 Ibid., file XLV.864 c(49), Mirasty to Douglas, 26 April 1956.
126 Ibid.
127 Ibid.
128 'Indians Will Discuss Questions of Liquor,' *Regina Leader-Post,* 13 August 1956.
129 Saskatchewan Archives Board, T.C. Douglas Papers, Files of the Premier, 'Indians,' R-33.1, file XLV.864 c(49), Minutes of the Meeting of the Indian Affairs Committee, 13 December 1957.
130 Ibid., Terms of Reference, Committee on Indian Affairs.
131 Ibid., Cabinet Memorandum, Minute No. 7246, 30 October 1956.
132 The entire discussion of legislative changes to give Indians the vote is taken from ibid., appendix 2: Legislation for Voting at Provincial Elections, 1, 2.
133 All comments pertaining to the liquor issue are taken from ibid., appendix 3: Action re. Purchase of Liquor, 1, 2.
134 The discussion of potential Indian voting patterns is taken from ibid., appendix 4: Projected Effect of Indian Votes, 1-3.
135 Ibid., First Report – November 19, 1956 (Confidential), 2.
136 Ibid., Cabinet Memorandum, Cabinet Minute No. 7440, 22 January 1957.
137 Ibid., Douglas to Hon. F.C. Colborne, 11 March 1957.
138 Ibid., Cabinet Memorandum, Minute No. 7440, 22 January 1957; Cabinet Memorandum Minute No. 8157, 31 December 1957.
139 The entire text of the letter may be found in ibid., file XLV.864 d(49), Sturdy to All Indian Chiefs and Councils in Saskatchewan, 22 September 1958.
140 Ibid., Sturdy to Douglas, 9 July 1958.
141 Ibid., Wuttunee to Sturdy, 6 July 1958.
142 Ibid.
143 Ibid.
144 Ibid.
145 The entire discussion of the conference is taken from ibid., Minutes of the Provincial Conference of Saskatchewan Indian Chiefs and Councilors, Valley Center, Fort Qu'Appelle, 30 and 31 October 1958.
146 Based on interviews of John Tootoosis decades later, James Pitsula has argued that it was Tootoosis who had the idea to defer the decision in order to save Douglas. While it is true that Tootoosis introduced the motion to defer decision, the idea to do so in fact came from Sturdy as chair of the conference. See James M. Pitsula, 'The Saskatchewan CCF Government and Treaty Indians, 1944-64,' *Canadian Historical Review* 75, no. 1 (1989), 34, fn. 56, 58. Compare this account with Saskatchewan Archives Board, T.C. Douglas Papers, Files of the Premier, 'Indians,' R-33.1, file XLV.864 c(49), Minutes of the Provincial Conference of Saskatchewan Indian Chiefs and Councilors, Valley Centre, Fort Qu'Appelle, 30 and 31 October 1958.
147 Saskatchewan Archives Board, T.C. Douglas Papers, Files of the Premier, 'Indians,' R-33.1,

file XLV c(49), Minutes of the Provincial Conference of Saskatchewan Indian Chiefs and Councilors, Valley Centre, Fort Qu'Appelle, 30 and 31 October 1958.

148 Interview of Stan Cuthand by author, University of Saskatchewan, 30 January 1995.

149 Saskatchewan Archives Board, T.C. Douglas Papers, Files of the Premier, 'Indians,' R-33.1, file XLV.864 d(49), Cabinet Memorandum, Minute No. 8997, 9 January 1959.

150 Ibid., Sturdy to All Ministers, 29 June 1959, questions 4, 6, 13, 17.

151 Ibid., question 8.

152 Ibid., file XLV.864 e(49), Woollam to Douglas and Sturdy, 15 January 1960.

153 Ibid.

154 Ibid.

155 'Native Canadians without Franchise,' *Saskatchewan Commonwealth*, 12 February 1958.

156 Saskatchewan Archives Board, T.C. Douglas Papers, Files of the Premier, 'Indians,' R-33.1, file XLV.864 e(49), Woollam to Douglas and Sturdy, 15 January 1960.

157 Ibid.

158 Ibid.

159 Ibid.

160 Ibid.

161 Ibid.

162 Ibid., J.D. Fyffe to Douglas, 8 March 1960; Douglas to Fyffe, 16 March 1960.

163 Ibid., Woollam to Douglas and Sturdy, 4 March 1960.

164 'Group Opposes Vote for Indians,' *Regina Leader-Post,* 10 May 1960.

165 Saskatchewan Archives Board, T.C. Douglas Papers, Files of the Premier, 'Indians,' R-33.1, file XLV.864 e(49), 23 February 1960.

166 As anticipated, the federal franchise was also granted in 1960 and added about 60,000 Indians to the voters lists across Canada. The first opportunity for Indians to vote in a federal election occurred in 1962. 'More Indians Get to Vote,' *Regina Leader-Post*, 18 April 1962.

167 'Law Eased on Liquor for Indians,' *Regina Leader-Post*, 10 June 1960.

168 The entire content of the letter is taken from Saskatchewan Archives Board, T.C. Douglas Papers, Files of the Premier, 'Indians,' R-33.1, file XIV.864 e(49), 22 March 1960.

169 Ibid.

170 'Law Eased on Liquor for Indians,' *Regina Leader-Post*, 10 June 1960.

171 By 1961, referenda were taken on seventeen reserves, twelve of which opted to be 'wet.' 'Fifth Indian Group Votes against Liquor on Reserves,' *Regina Leader-Post,* 24 November 1961.

172 Ibid.

Chapter 5: The Saskatchewan Far North

1 Thomas H. McLeod and Ian McLeod, *Tommy Douglas: The Road to Jerusalem* (Edmonton: Hurtig Publishers 1987), 167.

2 Catherine Littlejohn, 'The Historical Background of the Indian and Northern Education Program,' (Ph.D. diss., University of Calgary 1983), 72.

3 Ibid.

4 Ibid.

5 Helen Buckley, J.E. Kew, and John B. Hawley, 'The Indians and Métis of Northern Saskatchewan: A Report on Economic and Social Development,' Research Division, Center for Community Studies, University of Saskatchewan, Saskatoon, 1963, 5

6 Cited in Murray Dobbin, *One-and-a-Half Men: The Story of Jim Brady and Malcolm Norris* (Vancouver: New Star Books 1981), 169.

7 Ibid.

8 Ibid., and McLeod and McLeod, 167.

9 Brady was first appointed by the CCF in 1947 as a replacement for Norris, a field worker in the remote Métis community of Deschambeault. There he was placed in charge of the government's trading post, a subsidiary of the Saskatchewan Fish Board, and supervised local fishermen. He eventually resigned from that posting for reasons of ill health and later, in 1948, was rehired by the CCF as an assistant conservation officer at

Cumberland House. In addition to his regular duties, he was given the responsibility of organizing cooperatives among the local Métis. Having found his own replacement at Cumberland House, Norris was able to secure a transfer to Prince Albert. He served as a special field officer in the DNR with the responsibility of translating and promoting the government's programs among the Cree-speaking Indians and Métis of more than thirty northern communities. On his own initiative, he also conducted social and economic surveys, many of which were critical of CCF policies, and is credited with organizing the first conferences on trapping and fishing. For details, see Dobbin, 165-9.

10 Littlejohn, 87.
11 The entire discussion of the La Ronge airfield is taken from 'J.L. Phelps Finds Need for Change on Tour of the North,' *Saskatchewan Commonwealth*, 2 August 1944.
12 A 'new deal' for the North was a phrase often used by both Douglas and Phelps. See 'Into Saskatchewan's Northland,' *Saskatchewan Commonwealth*, 31 July 1946.
13 Douglas's message was broadcast over CKCK and CKBI (P.A.) as part of the 1948 election campaign in the North. Public Archives of Canada, T.C. Douglas papers, MG 32C28, vol. 140, file 37, Broadcasts to ... , July 1948.
14 Ibid.
15 Ibid.
16 J.L. Phelps, 'Conserving Resources Developing Industries,' *Saskatchewan Commonwealth*, 13 December 1944.
17 Cited in Littlejohn, 94.
18 J.L. Phelps, 'Conserving Resources Developing Industries,' *Saskatchewan Commonwealth*, 13 December 1944.
19 Littlejohn, 93.
20 See the discussion of the self-help paradigm below in the 'Flaws in Provincial Policy' section of this chapter.
21 Helen Buckley, 'Trapping and Fishing in the Economy of Northern Saskatchewan,' Report No. 3, Economic and Social Survey of Northern Saskatchewan, Research Division, Center for Community Studies, University of Saskatchewan, Saskatoon, 1962, 45. In 1959-60, the trapper population in the northern region consisted of 843 Indians, 1,161 Métis, and 67 whites. The latter made up only 3.2 percent of the total.
22 Ibid., 16.
23 Ibid.
24 Ibid., 17.
25 'Department of Natural Resources,' *Saskatchewan Commonwealth*, 4 February 1948.
26 Ibid.; and Buckley, 19.
27 For a commentary on the discontent over compulsory marketing, see 'Indians Said Irked at CCF Regulations,' *Regina Leader-Post*, 22 February 1947
28 Buckley, 19.
29 Cited in ibid.
30 Cited in 'Fur Conservation Will Assure Trappers' Security,' *Saskatchewan Commonwealth*, 29 May 1946.
31 Details of the of the program are discussed in 'Government Fur Program Gives Impetus to Industry,' *Saskatchewan Commonwealth*, 11 December 1946.
32 Ibid.
33 Ibid.
34 Ibid.
35 'Conservation Brought Back Beaver to Ile-à-la-Crosse,' *Saskatchewan Commonwealth*, 18 February 1953.
36 The connection between the live-trapping program and the declining need for compulsory marketing was explained in 'Publicly Owned Service Brings Good Prices to Trappers as Buyers Come from Far and Wide, *Saskatchewan Commonwealth*, 11 January 1956.
37 Buckley, 57.
38 Ibid.
39 Ibid., 62.
40 Ibid.
41 Ibid., 58.

42 Ibid.
43 Ibid., 59.
44 Ibid.
45 Ibid.
46 Ibid.
47 See 'Solid Basis for Fishing Industry Suggested in Commission Report,' *Saskatchewan Commonwealth*, 2 April 1947.
48 'Criticisms of Fish Board Follow Wheat Trade Pattern,' *Saskatchewan Commonwealth*, 28 January 1948.
49 Buckley, 61.
50 Ibid.
51 Ibid.
52 Ibid.
53 'Department of Natural Resources,' *Saskatchewan Commonwealth*, 4 February 1948.
54 Buckley, 62.
55 Ibid.
56 'Fishermen Receive High Initial Advance,' *Saskatchewan Commonwealth*, 13 February 1946.
57 Buckley, 33.
58 'Criticisms of Fish Board Follow Wheat Trade Pattern,' *Saskatchewan Commonwealth*, 29 January 1948.
59 'Government Purchases Fish Filleting Plant,' *Saskatchewan Commonwealth*, 12 December 1945.
60 Glenbow Archives, Brady Papers, M125 File 68, Saskatchewan Government 1946-49, 'Address by Minister of Natural Resources and Industrial Development at Field Officers' Conference Held in Prince Albert, Sept. 3, 4, and 5th, 1946,' 5.
61 'So-called Monopolism in Fish "Funnelling" Backed by Other Provincial Governments,' *Saskatchewan Commonwealth*, 20 November 1946.
62 Glenbow Museum, Brady Papers, 'Fisheries 1950-60,' M125 File 65, Fisheries Policy as of Oct. 1958, 2. (Hereafter referred to as Fisheries Policy as of October 1958.)
63 Ibid.
64 Cited in ibid., 3.
65 Ibid.
66 Cited in Buckley, 101.
67 Glenbow Museum, Brady Papers, 'Fisheries 1950-60,' M125 File 65, Proposals Submitted by the Fisheries Policy Committee for the Establishment of the Co-operative Fish Marketing Service, 4. (Hereafter referred to as Proposals Submitted by the Fisheries Policy Committee.)
68 Saskatchewan Archives Board, T.C. Douglas Papers, Files of the Premier, 'Indians,' R-33.1, file XLV.864 c(49), Douglas to the Rev. T.A. Hamilton, 2 February 1956.
69 Fisheries Policy as of October 1958, 3.
70 Ibid.
71 Douglas made this claim in November 1958 when announcing the changeover from a crown corporation to a cooperative form of organization. See Douglas's press release in Glenbow Museum, Brady Papers, 'Co-op Pending 1950-62,' M125 File 60, Subject: Northern Crown Corporations to Become Co-operatives. (Hereafter referred to as Douglas Press Release, 1958.)
72 See Proposals Submitted by the Fisheries Policy Committee, 2.
73 Douglas Press Release, 1958, 2.
74 Ibid.
75 Indicative of the Natives' exclusion is the fact that, as late as 1962, Native employment in uranium mining – which was the only large-scale development – was almost nonexistent. The largest uranium company had a payroll of 564 people, of which only 8 were northern Natives. Buckley, Kew, and Hawley, 19.
76 'Review of C.C.F. Legislation,' *Saskatchewan Commonwealth*, 23 May 1949.
77 Buckley, Kew, and Hawley, 16. According to background data compiled in preparation for a national northern development conference in 1958, of the 4,000-odd people

employed in woods operations, saw milling, or in wood-using industries, only about 350 were from the North and, of these, 'only a small part were local indigenous people.' See Glenbow Museum, Brady Papers, 'Miscellaneous 1947-65,' M125 File 47, The Present, the Potential, and the Planned For Northern Saskatchewan, 4. (Hereafter The Present, the Potential, and the Planned for Northern Saskatchewan.)

78 Of 101 men surveyed at Pelican Narrows in 1961, 67 earned money firefighting and, of these, only 4 earned over $100, even though summer conditions made forests prone to fires. See Buckley, 6.

79 See 'Indians of Province Bring Grievances Before Cabinet,' *Regina Leader-Post*, 29 June 1961.

80 Buckley, Kew, and Hawley, 48.

81 Glenbow Museum, Brady Papers, 'Cumberland House Co-op 1948-60,' M125 File 63, Memorandum to CCF Clubs in The Pas and Flin Flon, Man., October 1952. (Hereafter referred to as Memorandum to CCF Clubs.)

82 Buckley, Kew, and Hawley, 48.

83 Ibid.

84 Ibid., 70.

85 Memorandum to CCF Clubs, 3.

86 Buckley, Kew, and Hawley, 16.

87 Ibid., 46.

88 Cited in Littlejohn, 63.

89 Littlejohn, 95, incorrectly implies that the slogan 'humanity first' was not applied to northern policies until after the election of 1948. In fact, Phelps used the concept publicly in his first year in office as minister of the DNR. See Phelps, 'Report to the People,' *Saskatchewan Commonwealth*, 13 December 1944.

90 'Hospitalization for the North,' *Saskatchewan Commonwealth*, 10 December 1947.

91 Buckley, 32.

92 'Hospitalization for North,' *Saskatchewan Commonwealth*, 10 December 1947.

93 See 'Nutrition, Hygiene Program in North,' *Regina Leader-Post*, 10 February 1960.

94 This is not to say that the HBC supported the educational goals of the missionaries. The HBC often opposed the religious teachings of the missionaries, particularly their ban on Sunday business activities, as well as attempts by some missionaries to support Native rights over those of the company. See Littlejohn, 18-19.

95 Ibid., 18.

96 Ibid., 61.

97 Ibid., 64.

98 Cited in ibid.

99 Cited in ibid.

100 Cited in ibid., 65.

101 Cited in ibid.

102 Ibid., 73

103 Ibid.

104 Cited in ibid., 64.

105 Ibid., 70.

106 Littlejohn, 32, argues that there were only five 'new schools' built by 1950, but this seems unlikely because it was reported in the press that by 1951 there was a total of fourteen such schools in the North. See 'New School in Far North,' *Saskatchewan Commonwealth*, 12 December 1951.

107 Littlejohn, 69.

108 Ibid.

109 Ibid., 75.

110 Buckley, Kew, and Hawley, 40.

111 Glenbow Museum, Brady Papers, 'Miscellaneous 1947-65,' M125 File 47, Some Problems and Premises of Policy for the Development of Northern Saskatchewan, by M. Miller, 6 October 1958, 4. (Hereafter Miller Report, 6 October 1958.)

112 Cited in ibid.

113 Littlejohn, 98, 106.

114 Buckley, Kew, and Hawley, 40.
115 Ibid., 39. The downward spiral in fur prices was a result of increased fur ranching, the development of artificial furs, and unprecedented competition from other countries, such as Scandinavia, Japan, Belgium, Germany, and France. See Buckley, 24.
116 Buckley, Kew, and Hawley, 11-12.
117 Ibid., 13.
118 Ibid., 18.
119 Buckley, 7.
120 Ibid.
121 Provincial income is taken from the 1959 Indian Affairs submission of the Saskatchewan government to the Joint Committee of the Senate and House of Commons on Indian Affairs, *Minutes of Proceedings and Evidence No. 12* (Ottawa: Queen's Printer and Controller of Stationery 1966), 1043-4. The national average is cited in Buckley, 12.
122 Ibid., 5.
123 Ibid., 11.
124 Ibid., 12.
125 Buckley, Kew, and Hawley, 15.
126 Ibid., 27.
127 Ibid.
128 Ibid.
129 'North C.C.F. Vote Strong,' *Saskatchewan Commonwealth*, 30 June 1948.
130 Ibid.
131 'Northern Seats Go,' *Saskatchewan Commonwealth*, 28 July 1948.
132 'North C.C.F. Vote Strong,' *Saskatchewan Commonwealth*, 30 June 1948.
133 Ibid.
134 Hon. J.H. Brockelbank, 'Northern Voters Did Not Repudiate Resources Policy,' *Saskatchewan Commonwealth*, 2 May 1949.
135 J.W. Chalmers, cited in Littlejohn, 69.
136 Murray Dobbin, 'Prairie Colonialism and the CCF in Northern Saskatchewan, 1944-1964,' *Studies in Political Economy* 16 (1985): 16.
137 Glenbow Museum, Brady Papers, 'Indian Affairs 1940-60,' M125 File 41, Vic Valentine, The Métis of Northern Saskatchewan, Department of Natural Resources, 25 May 1955.
138 Cited in Littlejohn, 96-7.
139 Cited in ibid., 101.
140 Miller Report, 6 October 1958, 1.
141 Ibid., 6.
142 Ibid.
143 Ibid., 3.
144 The Present, the Potential, and the Planned for Northern Saskatchewan, 3.
145 Cited in Littlejohn, 98.
146 Ibid.
147 Ibid.,102.
148 The emphasis upon training became noticeable in 1959. Training initially was targeted at conservation officers and was conducted under the auspices of the Centre for Community Studies at the University of Saskatchewan. It was later extended to DNR policymakers as well as to administrative and supervisory staff. See ibid., 109.
149 The purpose is taken from a United Nations definition (ESC, 1956), cited in The Present, the Potential, and the Planned for Northern Saskatchewan, 14.
150 Buckley, Kew, and Hawley, 37.
151 Ibid.
152 Ibid.
153 Ibid., 41.
154 Ibid.
155 Ibid., 38.
156 Ibid.
157 'Aim at Co-operative Development in Saskatchewan's North,' *Saskatchewan Commonwealth*, 20 August 1952.

158 'Co-op Development in Northern Sask.,' *Saskatchewan Commonwealth*, 30 September 1953.
159 The presence of reactionary officials in the DNR itself was often the subject of complaint by more left-wing thinkers in the CCF. This was illustrated in a letter from CCF MLA Bill Berezowsky to Jim Brady in 1954: 'As you know I agree with your sentiment indicating prejudice of the petty officials of DNR. I have seen some of these personnel in action at one time or another and realize as you do that they are a stumbling block to integration. I suppose we will just have to continue the fight against reaction until these types of officials are eliminated and men who have the correct attitude and approach to northern problems shall replace them.' Glenbow Museum, Brady Papers, Personal 1952-62, M125 File 8, 22 September 1954.
160 See Buckley, Kew, and Hawley, 34.
161 Saskatchewan Archives Board, T.C. Douglas Papers, Files of the Premier, 'Métis,' R-33.1 XL.859 c(44), Douglas to All Ministers, 6 May 1957.
162 'Native Co-op Sales Good,' *Saskatoon Star-Phoenix*, 24 March 1959; and 'Co-ops Could Help,' *Indian Record*, March 1959.
163 Glenbow Museum, Brady Papers, 'Co-op Pending 1950-62,' M125 File 60, The Role of Saskatchewan Government Trading, 1.
164 'Public Ownership for Northern Trading Post,' *Saskatchewan Commonwealth*, 17 July 1946.
165 'Publicly Owned Northern Stores Help Develop North,' *Saskatchewan Commonwealth*, 4 January 1956.
166 'Co-ops Could Help,' *Indian Record*, March 1959.
167 Buckley, Kew, and Hawley, 34.
168 Ibid.
169 Murray Dobbin, 'Prairie Colonialism: The CCF in Northern Saskatchewan, 1944-1964,' *Studies in Political Economy* 16 (1985): 17.
170 Buckley, Kew, and Hawley, 34.
171 Littlejohn, 75.
172 'Native Co-op Sales Good,' *Saskatoon Star-Phoenix*, 24 March 1959.
173 According to Allan Quandt, Phelps's departure ushered in a more conservative atmosphere in northern administrative affairs, especially among members of the bureaucracy. Increasingly, Quandt and his radical colleagues felt decidedly out of place and became increasingly critical of the lack of meaningful reform. Interview of Allan Quandt by author, La Ronge, Saskatchewan, 17 September 1994.
174 Brady forwarded copies of the document to Douglas, A.G. Kuziak (minister of NRD), R.A. Walker (attorney-general), and A.H. MacDonald (director of Northern Affairs). See Glenbow Museum, Brady Papers, M125 File 2, Personal 1952-62.
175 Saskatchewan Archives Board, Saskatchewan Social Welfare – Rehabilitation Branch, Provincial Committee on Minority Groups, R85-308 933, file III 24, Ray Woollam, 'Some Proposals Concerning Provincial Government Organization and People of Indian Ancestry,' 9 January 1961, 5.
176 Ibid., 1.
177 Ibid., 27.
178 Ibid., 20.
179 Ibid., Minutes – Meeting of Provincial Committee on Minority Groups, Saturday, January 14, 1961, Premier's Office, 3.

Chapter 6: Opposition to Native Reform

1 Murray Dobbin, 'Prairie Colonialism: The CCF in Northern Saskatchewan, 1944-1964,' *Studies in Political Economy* 16 (1985): 11.
2 John Webster Grant, *Moon of Wintertime* (Toronto: University of Toronto Press 1984), 184.
3 Ibid., 186.
4 Henry Somerville, 'Many Catholics Vote CCF?,' *Saskatchewan Commonwealth*, 15 November 1943.
5 Cited in T.C. Douglas, 'Religion and the CCF,' radio broadcast, printed in *Saskatchewan Commonwealth*, 15 November 1943.
6 Ibid.

7 Cited in ibid.
8 According to the 1944 census data, Saskatchewan had 14,158 Indians, of whom 13,441 belonged to some Christian church. Of the total Christian Indian population, 6,934 were Catholic. Cited in Saskatchewan Archives Board, T.C. Douglas Papers, Files of the Executive Assistant, R-33.2 XXII.405 (24-3.1 to 24-3.8), 'Recapitulation – Census of Indians: Arranged Under Provinces, 1944.'
9 Saskatchewan Archives Board, Saskatchewan Welfare – Rehabilitation Branch, Lestock Project, R85-308 933 File III 31b.
10 Ibid.
11 'Premier Investigates Northern Health,' *Saskatchewan Commonwealth*, 1 August 1945.
12 Ibid.
13 Archives Deschâtelets, 'Dr. Shumiatcher Charges,' *Indian Missionary Record* [St. Boniface, Manitoba], December 1946.
14 Ibid.
15 Ibid., February 1951.
16 Cited in ibid.
17 Ibid.
18 Ibid.
19 Ibid.
20 Archives Deschâtelets, 'Integration in Schools Not a Cure-all,' *Indian Missionary Record* [St. Boniface, Manitoba], January-February 1962. See also Government of Canada, *Report of the Department of Citizenship and Immigration, 1960-61* (Ottawa: 1962), 108. In 1961, there were 10,822 Indian students in grades 1 through 12 attending non-Indian schools in Canada; at the same time, there was a total of 43,115 Indian students in grades 1 through 12 in both integrated and non-integrated schools across Canada.
21 Saskatchewan Archives Board, Saskatchewan Social Welfare – Rehabilitation Branch, Lebret Métis Farm, R-85 – 308 933 File III 33e, J.S. White to K. Forster, 27 July 1956.
22 Ibid., K. Forster to J.S. White, 31 July 1956.
23 Saskatchewan Archives Board, T.C. Douglas Papers, Files of the Premier, 'Indians,' R-33.1, file XLV.864 c(49), Sturdy's Speech in the House, 22 March 1957, 1.
24 Ibid., 7.
25 Ibid., Robidoux to Douglas, 2 September 1957.
26 Ibid., Sturdy to Douglas, 5 September 1957.
27 Ibid., Douglas to Robidioux, 4 September 1957.
28 Henry Sommerville, 'Many Catholics Vote CCF?' *Saskatchewan Commonwealth*, 2 August 1943.
29 T.C. Douglas, 'Religion and the CCF,' radio broadcast, printed in the *Saskatchewan Commonwealth*, 15 November 1943.
30 Saskatchewan Archives Board, Saskatchewan Social Welfare – Rehabilitation Branch, Lestock Project, R-85-308 933 File III 31b.
31 Saskatchewan Archives Board, T.C. Douglas Papers, Files of the Premier, 'Indians,' R-33.1, file XLV.864 a(49), Rielly to Douglas, 23 March 1946.
32 Ibid., Douglas to Rielly, 26 March 1946.
33 Saskatchewan Archives Board, Saskatchewan Welfare – Rehabilitation Branch, Willow Bunch Project Report, R-85-308 933 File III 41, J.S. White to J.H. Sturdy, 6 April 1953.
34 Father Blanchard began to doubt the ability of the Willow Bunch Métis to farm cooperatively, favouring instead an earlier work-for-wages approach to farming in the area. He also got caught up in the internal bickering and factionalism of the co-op and seemingly resented the authority of the local Management Board. See Saskatchewan Archives Board, Nicholson Papers, Saskatchewan Social Welfare – Rehabilitation Branch, Rehabilitation, Métis, Willow Bunch, 1952-64, M16 file XIII 295, Willow Bunch Project. Blanchard's firing is discussed in Michelle Heslop, '"Humanity First"?: A Critical Analysis of Métis Policies in Southern Saskatchewan During the CCF Government, 1944-64' (unpublished essay, NATST 404.6, Native Studies Department, University of Saskatchewan 1995), 32-4.
35 Hudson's Bay Company Archives, Canada Committee Office Records, Fur Trade Department-HBC Relations with CCF Government of Saskatchewan, Memo re. Letter of Minister of Natural Resources of 6 February 1945.

36 Ibid.
37 Ibid.
38 Saskatchewan Archives Board, Phelps Papers, M15 Hudson's Bay Company, 1945-6, Phelps to Corporal C.E. Wenzel, 21 February 1945.
39 'Phelps Challenges Charter of 1670,' *Winnipeg Free Press*, 20 March 1945.
40 Cited in ibid.
41 Ibid.
42 Ibid.
43 See Arthur J. Ray, *The Canadian Fur Trade in the Industrial Age* (Toronto: University of Toronto Press 1990), 96-101.
44 Ibid., 171, 222
45 Ibid., 168.
46 Hudson's Bay Company Archives, Canadian Committee Office Records, Fur Trade Department – HBC Relations with the CCF Government of Saskatchewan, 5-3-1, RG2/7/156.
47 Ibid.
48 Hudson's Bay Company Archives, Land Department – Mineral Rights Historical Details, 3 July 1929 – 19 Jan. 1949, RG 2/10/34, CC Minute 1808, 16 Nov. 1944.
49 Hudson's Bay Company Archives, Minutes of the Canadian Committee, 1944, No. 1706, RG 2/1/29, Minute 1706.
50 Ibid.
51 Hudson's Bay Company Archives, Canadian Committee Office Records, Fur Trade Department – HBC Relations with the CCF Government of Saskatchewan 5-3-1, RG 2/9/156, Governor to Canadian Committee, 28 May 1945.
52 Ibid., RG 2/7/156, Chadwick Brooks (for Governor) to Canadian Committee, 24 July 1945.
53 Ibid., RG 2/7/156, Report of Messrs. Chester, Chesshire and Joslyn on Their Visit to Regina, 24 March 1945.
54 Ibid., 1.
55 Ibid.
56 Ibid.
57 Ibid.
58 Ibid.
59 Ibid., 2.
60 Ibid.
61 The community lease was land controlled and managed by the HBC but trapped by local residents; by comparison, the private lease was land over which the HBC had exclusive jurisdiction, both in management and trapping.
62 Ibid., 3.
63 Ibid., 4.
64 Hudson's Bay Company Archives, Canadian Committee Office Records, Fur Trade Department – HBC Relations with the CCF Government of Saskatchewan, RG 2/7/156, Chester to Phelps, 25 March 1945.
65 Hudson's Bay Company Archives, P. Ashley Cooper (Correspondence with Mr. Chester and Mr. Riley), RG 2/11A/7/5/6, Cooper to C.S. Riley, 17 May 1945.
66 Hudson's Bay Company Archives, Canadian Committee Office Records, Fur Trade Department – HBC Relations with the CCF Government of Saskatchewan, RG 2/7/156, Chadwich Brooks (for Governor) to Canadian Committee, 24 July 1945.
67 Ibid.
68 Hudson's Bay Company Archives, Land Department – Mineral Rights – Historical Details, 3 July 1929–19 January 1949, Minute 1808, 16 November 1944.
69 Hudson's Bay Company Archives, Canadian Committee Office Records, Fur Trade Department – HBC Relations with the CCF Government of Saskatchewan, RG 2/7/156, Minute 2115.
70 Hudson's Bay Company Archives, Land Department – Mineral Rights – Historical Details, 3 July 1929–19 January 1949, RG 2/10/34, Minute 1808, 16 November 1944.
71 Saskatchewan Archives Board, Phelps Papers, M15 Mineral Taxation Act 1944–1946, Phelps to Joslyn, 4 January 1946; Joslyn to Phelps, 7 January 1946.

72 Ibid., and Hudson's Bay Company Archives, Minutes of the Canadian Committee, 1946, RG 2/1/31, Minute 2398.

73 'C.P.R. Has Writs Served on Corman and Phelps,' *Saskatchewan Commonwealth*, 28 January 1948.

74 The case was first tried in the Court of King's Bench (1948) where the tax was upheld. In turn, the Saskatchewan Court of Appeal (1950) ruled that the three cent acreage tax was constitutional, but that the fifty cent production tax was *ultra vires*. The ruling of the supreme court confirmed that both taxes were constitutional and within the prerogative of the Saskatchewan government. Following that, the CPR threatened to further appeal to the Privy Council, but later decided not to. *Regina Leader-Post*, 15 June 1959, 29 February 1952, and 26 March 1953.

75 Interview of Allan Quandt by author, La Ronge, Saskatchewan, 27 August 1994.

76 Hudson's Bay Company Archives, Canadian Committee Office Records, Fur Trade Department – HBC Relations with the CCF Government of Saskatchewan, RG 2/7/156, re. Interview with George Cadbury ... , 29 April 1949.

77 Ibid.

78 Ibid., Cadbury to John Payne, 2 May 1949.

79 Ibid., Cadbury to Chester, 7 June 1949.

80 Ibid., Cadbury to Chester, 27 February 1950.

81 Ibid., Chester to Cadbury, 2 March 1950.

82 Helen Buckley, J.E. Kew, and John B. Hawley, 'The Indians and Métis of Northern Saskatchewan: A Report on Economic and Social Development,' Centre for Community Studies, University of Saskatchewan, Saskatoon, 1963, 28

83 Ibid.

84 Ibid., 29.

85 Ibid.

86 Ibid.

87 Saskatchewan Archives Board, T.C. Douglas Papers, Files of the Premier, 'Métis,' R-33.1 XL.859 c(44), The Fort Black Co-operative Store: A Social Experiment Among the Ile-la-Crosse Métis, a Personal Account by Vic Valentine.

88 Ibid.

89 All details concerning the HBC monopoly are taken from ibid., 3.

90 Information on the trucker's monopoly is taken from ibid., 6, 7, 9.

91 Ibid., 5.

92 Ibid., 6.

93 Ibid., 4-5.

94 The reaction to Valentine by the white community is taken from ibid., 9-10.

95 Glenbow Archives, Brady Papers, M125 File 39, Historical Notes 1932-59, W. J. Berezowsky's submission to Members of the Advisory Committee on Northern Development, Provincial Government Building, Prince Albert, Saskatchewan, 30 September 1952, 2. (Hereafter cited as Berezowsky.)

96 Ibid., 3.

97 Ibid.

98 Glenbow Archives, Brady Papers, M125 File 41, Indian Affairs 1940-60, The Métis of Northern Saskatchewan, Confidential Report Submitted to the DNR by V.F. Valentine, 22.

99 Ibid.

100 Ibid., M125 File 39, Historical Notes 1932-59, To the Honorable Woodrow Lloyd, Minister of Education (Rough Draft only), La Ronge, Saskatchewan, December 1959, 1.

101 Ibid.

102 Berezowsky, 3.

103 Cited in ibid.

104 Cited in Saskatchewan Archives Board, T.C. Douglas Papers, Files of the Premier, 'Métis,' R-33.1, file XX 859 b(44), V.F. Valentine, A Social Anthropological Study of the Métis Population of Northwestern Saskatchewan: Preliminary Report, 1953, 11-12.

105 Cited in Ibid., 12.

106 Cited in Ibid.

107 Interview of Allan Quandt by author, La Ronge, Saskatchewan, 27 August 1994.

Chapter 7: Assessment

1 Saskatchewan Archives Board, Oral History Project 21, Tape R-A1185, Interview of T.C. Douglas by Murray Dobbin, 8 November 1976.
2 Ibid.
3 Ibid
4 Saskatchewan Archives Board, J.H. Sturdy Papers, M14 file 198, Metis Conference, 146, 52-3.
5 James M. Pitsula, 'The Saskatchewan CCF Government and Treaty Indians, 1944-64,' *Canadian Historical Review* 75, no. 1 (1994): 21-52.
6 Ibid., 29.
7 Ibid., 22.
8 Ibid.
9 Ibid., 52.
10 Ibid., 23.
11 Morris Shumiatcher, 'Indian Smoke on the Western Sky,' *Canadian Forum* (March 1946): 283.
12 Cited in Pitsula, 24.
13 Cited in ibid., 50.
14 Ibid., 49.
15 Saskatchewan Archives Board, Indians of North America – Societies, R834 file 37, Union of Saskatchewan Indians, Report of the Establishment of Indian Unity in Saskatchewan, Prepared by T.C. Douglas, March 1946, 3.
16 Ibid.
17 Legislative Assembly of Saskatchewan, *Debates and Proceedings*, 4th Session, 12th Parliament, vol. 11, 1956 (Regina, 1956), 34.
18 Cited in Saskatchewan Archives Board, T.C. Douglas Papers, Files of the Premier, 'Indians,' R-33.1 XLV 864d, J.H. Sturdy to All Ministers, 29 June 1959.
19 Ibid., 49-50.
20 For a brief account of the termination policy, see Arrell Morgan Gibson, *The American Indian Prehistory to the Present* (Toronto: D.C. Heath 1980), 546-9.

Index